Gower Rogues

DWDrawsey

An Untrustworthy Brother

Crowned King on 3rd September 1189, Richard was eager to be away on the Third Crusade, but something had to be done about John. So Richard arranged for his brother to marry his second cousin, Isabella, heiress of the Earl of Gloucester, to whom John had been betrothed since the age of ten. The marriage resulted in John becoming Earl of Gloucester and also Lord of Glamorgan which, at the time, was an appendage to the earldom, but Richard's generosity did not rest there. In a bid to appease his brother, Richard also made him Count of Mortain in Normandy, gave him the Honour of Lancaster and the revenue of six counties. There was, however, a catch in that John had to swear that he would leave the country for three years. Then their mother Eleanor persuaded Richard to release John from his oath and, like a dimwit, Richard agreed.

Richard had no sooner left for the Holy Land than John began masquerading as King. His new-found wealth enabled him to have his own court and to ride around the country with an armed escort; he even established contact with his brother's rival, King Philip of France. At Southampton, he was about to leave to do a deal with Philip in person when his mother appeared on the quayside, threatening that, if he left, she would see to it that he was relieved of his estates.

John bided his time until early in 1193, when news arrived that Richard had been taken prisoner by the Emperor of Germany. While Philip prepared to invade Richard's Continental possessions, John raised the flag of revolt in England. Unfortunately, few rallied to him – the Government, the barons, the Scots and his mother all remained loyal to Richard. That left John with no option than to agree to a truce.

When Richard arrived home early in 1194, John fled, taking refuge in Normandy. In May that year Richard went to Normandy himself, intending to relieve the castles to which King Philip had laid siege. On his way to the front Richard made an overnight stop, dining with the Archdeacon of Lisieux. "What's up?" Richard asked. "Is my brother here? You've seen him, haven't you? Then, tell him to come, he has nothing to fear, I'll not hold his foolishness against him."

The Archdeacon went to John, saying, "You can come out, your brother is more merciful to you than you would have been to him."

John threw himself at Richard's feet, begging his forgiveness, but Richard raised him up, saying, "Think no more of it, John, you're only a child who has had the misfortune of bad councellors."

For the next five years John seems to have been a reformed character: loyal to his brother, fighting at his side, excelling in what would, today, be called commando raids. Where he failed in his loyalty was in his relationship with his wife, Isabella. During his ten-year marriage he is known to have had several mistresses and to have fathered at least five illegitimate children.

No one ever painted a portrait of John, but there is an effigy of him at Worcester Cathedral, shaped some 15-20 years after his death. As to his character in later years, the evidence hints that he may have been schizophrenic, always suspicious, believing that

Effigy of King John,
Worcester Cathedral

people he disliked were plotting against him; he had a mania for personal cleanliness. On the positive side he proved to be a genius when it came to raising money – by whatever means – to finance his military ventures. He could be generous, but woe betide anyone who roused his vindictive nature; he showed himself to be ruthless in his pursuit of anyone who upset him. When it came to battle he developed a tendency to hold back, preferring to intimidate by a show of superior strength, which most of his opponents could never match. In a word he became a tyrant.

So much for John; now for his crony, William de Breos, or at least the man's family.

The De Breoses

The name Breos, or Braose, comes from Briouze-Saint-Gervais, a village near Falaise in Normandy. In 1073 a William de Breos (I) attested a grant as the first Lord of Bramber, a rich and extensive lordship in Sussex, which may have been the reward for his (unproven) part in the Battle of Hastings in 1066, a battle whereby William, Duke of Normandy – known also as the 'Bastard' and the 'Conqueror' – became King of England. William de Breos I was certainly favoured by the Conqueror, for in the Domesday Survey of 1086-7 it is apparent that, apart from Bramber, he held 56 other lordships in England.

William de Breos I was succeeded by his son, Philip, who, about 1093, availed himself of land on the border of Wales, namely Radnor, an acquisition which set him apart from the majority of his peers in England and France in that it made him a Marcher lord, meaning that within his Lordship of Radnor he ruled as a petty king, taking the place and privileges of the Welsh prince whom he had ousted, although he still owed allegiance to the king of England. From Radnor he invaded the neighbouring Welsh districts of Builth and Elfael.

In the 1130s, Philip was succeeded by his eldest son, William de Breos II who married Bertha, a daughter of Milo, Earl of Hereford. This marriage proved beneficial to William II because, on the death of his brother-in-law, Bertha and her two sisters became co-heiresses of the huge estate that had once belonged to their father. This windfall resulted in William II becoming Lord of both Brecknock and Abergavenny, and possibly of other lands in England.

As stated above, it was the custom among the nobility to give their sons territory once they were of age. By 1175 William II's eldest son, yet another William (III), who was about 25 at the time, had become Lord of Brecknock, and it is he who concerns us – the William who became King John's crony.

A Murderer

Churchmen praised William III for his piety, mindful no doubt of his donations to the Church, but a darker side to his character was revealed when, in 1175, he summoned Seisyll ap Dyfnwal, the Welsh Lord of Upper Gwent, and Geoffrey, Seisyll's son, along with leading Welshmen of the said territory, to a banquet at his Castle of Abergavenny. While his Welsh guests were seated at table, William III read out a royal ordinance to the effect that no traveller should carry a bow or any other unlawful weapon.

William, of course, knew that no self-respecting Welshman would comply with such an ordinance, and no sooner had his guests expressed disapproval than, at a given signal, men rushed into the hall, brandishing swords. Shouts rang as benches were upturned; within moments Seisyll and his followers lay, writhing in the blood-stained straw. Then armed men were dispatched to Seisyll's court where they rampaged, seizing Seisyll's wife and murdering his seven-year-old son, Cadwaladr.

In his *Itinerary Through Wales* Gerald, Archdeacon of Brecknock, tried to shift responsibility for the massacre away from William by pointing a finger elsewhere, but to accept such a view is to overlook that Gerald was dependant upon William's generosity. Any doubts about William's duplicity can be dispelled by an act of cruelty which took place 22 years later when Trahaearn Fychan, Lord of Llangors, was summoned and seized by William, who gave orders for the Welshman to be bound by his feet to a horse's tail and dragged through the streets of Brecon as far as the gallows; there Trahaearn's head was cut off and his lifeless body swung to and fro, suspended by the feet, for three days.

By the time John had become king at the age of 32, William III was about 50 and had long succeeded his father, enlarged the family estate, and become the most powerful Marcher baron in Wales, at the same time holding numerous estates in England. He was also Sheriff of Hereford. His son, William IV, known as William the Younger, had by then also made a name for himself, for in 1189 at the age of 21 he had secured custody of the castles of Carmarthen, Sweyneshe and Llanwaden, all of which were Crown properties, and in 1194 he was serving with King Richard in France.

The marriage arrangements of William's family were no less impressive, several of his offspring marrying into the most powerful families in the realm, while he himself had married Matilda or Maud (the names are interchangeable) de St. Valery (also known as de Hugh and St. Waldred), her dowry adding to his possessions. Matilda was a formidable woman who repulsed a Welsh assault on Painscastle, bore William at least seven children and whose sharp tongue would one day cost him dearly.

At War with King Philip of France

Within three weeks of his coronation, John left for France with English troops and with William de Breos III in close attendance. What he had to deal with was a combination that was to dog him for years: rebellious Bretons, untrustworthy barons and a belligerent King Philip of France. His nephew, Arthur, who was then barely 12 years old, had been sent to King Philip for safekeeping. Arthur's mother, Constance, had roused her Breton subjects to revolt and had since captured Angers. To the east, Philip had launched an attack on Normandy while further south the barons of Anjou, Maine and Touraine had opted to support Arthur as Richard's chosen heir. In short, northwest France was in turmoil while, to the south, Aquitaine remained loyal to John's mother, Eleanor, and she supported John. For the next few months John held his own until a truce was called before Christmas. By May 1200 John and Philip had agreed to terms – terms that earned John the nickname of 'Softsword.'

Another event that took place in 1200 was that John divorced Isabella on grounds of consanguinity and married, instead, twelve-year-old, Isabella of Angoulême. It was a union that resulted from a mixture of politics and passion, and yet John never forgot his first wife to whom he periodically sent gifts of cloth and wine; he also put her on the marriage market for 20,000 marks – a mark being two-thirds of a pound, in those days 13 shillings and 4 pence. It is behaviour such as this adds weight to the suggestion that John was schizophrenic; that and the fact that he trusted no one.

Mirebeau

John returned to England in the autumn of 1200 to spend many peaceful months touring his English realm. Despite trouble in Poitou during the summer of 1201, his treaty with King Philip held, but by June the following year he was again at war with Philip, due to the upset caused by his second marriage. Confident that a line of castles would hold up Philip's advance into Normandy, he rode south, into Maine where he met a courier with a message from his mother. Eleanor had herself been travelling south when she learned that John's nephew, Arthur, along with his rebellious Bretons, was hard on her heels, determined to take her prisoner. Shouting, "Forward," John led off, setting a fast pace for his men and picking up more en route.

Arthur, meanwhile, had caught up with Eleanor at Mirebeau and his Bretons had not only taken the town, but had broken into the castle, with the result that Eleanor and her supporters were holding out in the keep. Fortunately for her, the approach of darkness brought a halt to the fighting and while the rebels slept, John approached the town cautiously, deploying his men for a surprise attack. As dawn broke so John's men stormed into the town, forcing Arthur's bleary-eyed rebels to beat a hasty retreat into the castle where, hotly pursued, they failed to make a stand. John did not lead the attack himself, but left leadership in the capable hands of one William des Roches, aided no doubt by William de Breos. Nevertheless, John was no less excited because shortly after the event he wrote to his English barons, telling them:

we were on the road to Chinon when we heard that our lady, our mother, was closely assailed at Mirebeau, and we hurried there as fast as we could, arriving there on Tuesday 31st July. And there we captured our nephew, Arthur, whom William de Breos delivered to us and … upwards of 200 knights and none escaped.

Custody of Arthur fell to William de Breos, no small responsibility, for Arthur, through his father Geoffrey (John's older brother who had died in 1186), had a genuine claim to the Angevin Empire; moreover, Arthur was a Breton through his mother, Constance, and his name had a special significance to the Bretons, who spoke a language similar to Welsh and who equated his name with the legendary King Arthur. Arthur was also favoured by the barons of Maine, Anjou and Touraine. From John's point of view it would be expedient to dispose of Arthur.

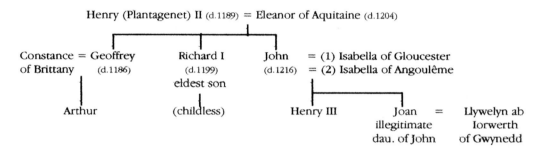

King John's family tree

The Benefits of Favouritism

For his steadfast support, William de Breos could count on John's generosity as, indeed, he had since the coronation. Back in September 1199, John had shown his gratitude by ensuring that William's second son, Giles, was made Bishop of Hereford. As to William's acquisitions, only two need be mentioned here. Firstly, in January 1201, John accepted William's offer of 5,000 marks for the Honour of Limerick in Ireland, a profitable acquisition. As to the 5,000 marks, William put off paying the instalments, believing that John would not press him for money. That suited John because, when a baron owed him money, he had a hold on him: he could call in the debt at any time; if the baron could not pay, then his chattels and his land became Crown property. It was just one of John's nasty, little schemes, and William must have known the debt could be used against him, but for the moment William ranked high in the King's favour.

Secondly, in October 1202 William was awarded custody of Glamorgan, Gwynllwg and Gower, all of which were Crown properties. The advantage of having custody of these properties was that William became the most powerful Marcher lord in Wales, having control of almost the whole of south-east Wales, from Builth to the Bristol Channel, as well as a great deal of land on the English side of the border, from Ludlow to Gloucester. He also held St. Clears in West Wales, which he had taken by force in 1194.

A Gift Under Duress

The capture of his nephew should have been, for John, a favourable turning point in the war. Unfortunately, John managed to upset some of his French barons over what should be done with Arthur; consequently, a number of barons went over to King Philip with the result that Anjou, Touraine and northern Aquitaine were thrown into a state of civil war. In the west the Bretons seized Angers again; in the east, Philip made steady progress, advancing into Normandy.

In January 1203, John received word that his wife, Isabella, had been surrounded at Chinon by rebel forces. John set out to rescue her, just as he had his mother, and was told at one point that another baron had defected to Philip, a baron whose territory John had only just passed through. John lost his nerve, took shelter in a nearby castle and sent his men to save Isabella.

How serious the situation had become can be judged by a charter whereby John gave the Lordship of Gower to William de Breos. Many years later a descendant of William was required to produce his title to Gower and he claimed that the charter had been drawn up in Normandy in the time of war between King John and the King of France on account of de Breos threatening to depart from him and return to England, the King being terrified of the said war. A translation of the Latin used in the charter reads:

> John, by the grace of God, King of England, Lord of Ireland, Duke of Aquitaine and Earl of Anjou, to the Archbishops (etc), greetings. Know ye that we have given and granted, and by this charter confirmed to our beloved and trustworthy William de Breos, all the land of Gower...to have and to hold...by the service of one knight for all service...Given in the hand of Hugh de Wells at Rouen the 23rd day of February in the fourth year of our reign (1203).

So Gower was given to William in return for one fully-armed horseman who would serve in the King's host (at William's expense) for a period of 40 days each year in times of war. Awarding land in return for 'the service of one' (or more) knights was common throughout Europe at that time. It was a means by which kings such as John could raise a formidable force of knights, whose service would not have to be paid for until after the expiry of 40 days. As to the charter, a copy of the original was found in a collection of papers known as the *Breviate of Domesday* (originally kept at Margam Abbey to which de Breos and his descendants were patrons). Attached to the charter, and written many years later in Norman-French, is a description of the boundaries of Gower as they were in c.1300.

Briefly, the bounds were as follows: on the south it was bounded by the sea; on the west by the River Loughor; on the north by the rivers Ammon, Llynfell and Twrch;

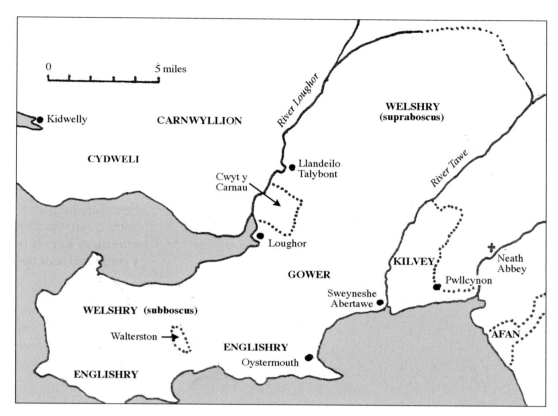

Gower in the time of King John

on the east by the River Tawe as far as the confluence with the River Glais. An appendage known as Kilvey lay on the east bank of the River Tawe; it was bounded on the north by the River Glais as far as the Meinihirion (a standing stone); from there the boundary ran south through the Crymlyn Bog; from there it ran eastwards to the River Neath and the sea.

What the description does not say is that Gower consisted of a fertile peninsula and an inhospitable, mountainous hinterland. For the most part, the lordship was heavily forested, except on the south side of the Peninsula where the fertile soil lent itself to manorial cultivation. Between 1106 and 1116, Anglo-Norman conquisadors had usurped the fertile land on the south side of the Peninsula, creating in the process small estates known as fiefs. These fiefs were held by members of the Anglo-Norman aristocracy, men who served as heavily-armed horsemen in times of war. These aristocrats held their fiefs 'by the service of one knight for all service' to whoever was lord of Gower. They often had their own private castles, and their tenants were, by and large, English *coloni* from across the Bristol Channel. Elsewhere – on the north side of the Peninsula, in the hinterland to the north of Swansea, and in the appendage

11

known as Kilvey – the population was almost entirely Welsh, living according to their ancient customs and laws.

The most important place within the lordship was at Abertawe – the mouth of the River Tawe – where stood an exceptionally large castle known as Sweyneshe (Swansea – Sweyneshe being the spelling used in a charter of 1215), which had a garrison. Outside the castle walls lay a town, or borough, of the same name, the leading citizens of which – the burgesses – profited from farming, artisan, and mercantile activities. A castle and a small borough also existed at Loughor. Records relating to a later period show Gower to have been an extremely profitable piece of real estate, one that could provide several hundred fighting men, which de Breos could call upon whenever the need arose.

The Fate of Arthur

Overwrought and suspicious, John wondered what should be done with Arthur until someone advised that he should pull out his eyes and castrate him; that way he could never rule nor father a child. So two men were sent to Falaise Castle where the custodian, Hubert de Burgh – who, months previously, had relieved de Breos of his charge – refused permission for the order to be carried out. To cover up his leniency, de Burgh let it be known that the mutilation had been performed and that Arthur had died of his wounds. When word spread of Arthur's fate the whole of north-western France was roused to violent indignation, so much so that it fell to de Breos to present Arthur safe in life and limb. Arthur was, then, transferred to the Castle of Rouen where, according to the Margam chronicles, John showed the murderous side of his nature, for

> after dinner on the Thursday before Easter, when he was drunk and possessed by the Devil, he slew him [Arthur] with his own hand, and, tying a heavy stone to the body, cast it into the Seine. It was discovered by a fisherman in his net, and being dragged to the bank and recognized, was taken for secret burial, in fear of the tyrant, to the prior of Bec called Notre Dame des Prés

Strangely enough, Arthur's sister, Eleanor, who had also been taken prisoner at Mirebeau, was treated in a more humane way. Although she remained a prisoner till her death in 1241, John often sent her gifts just as he did his first wife. One wonders whether his conscience bothered him, or whether his generosity was just another example of his schizophrenia.

Siege Warfare

Since the outbreak of hostilities in May 1202, King Philip had been systematically laying siege to the border castles in eastern Normandy. True, he could have bypassed the castles, but that would have left his lines of communication open to attack by the garrisons of the castles he bypassed. More to the point, the territory through which he advanced would never be conquered territory until the garrisons had been battered into submission. Thus for more than a year Philip hammered away at castle walls, using every siege device available – everything from catapults to undermining the walls. John, on other hand, seemed incapable of effectively countering Philip's assault.

One chronicler claimed that John was so bewitched by his young wife that he lay in bed all morning, and when men came to him with stories of doom and gloom he is supposed to have replied, "Let be, let be, whatever Philip takes I will one day recover." It may, however, be more realistic to say that his Norman subjects had had enough, that had it not been for English and mercenary troops the Normans would have yielded to Philip much sooner than they did, that John had to deal with defeatism and treachery on all sides, and the fact that Arthur had vanished did not help his cause. John needed the help of his English subjects, and when he sailed to England in December 1203, taking his wife with him, it was rumoured that he would not be back in time to save Normandy.

If John had cause to regret 1203, then William de Breos could look back over the year with a smirk on his face, for it had been his best yet when it came to enlarging his estate and gaining custody of castles and baronies in England, Ireland and Wales.

The Loss of North-west France

John met his English barons at Oxford in January 1204 and found that many of them were prepared to sail with him when he returned to the Continent, especially those who held land in Normandy as well as in England, but John did not want them as brothers-in-arms, he wanted their money. In times of war a king could call out the feudal host by commanding his tenants-in-chief – earls, barons, bishops and abbots – to provide him with agreed quotas of knights and foot soldiers, all of whom were expected to serve for 40 days at their expense; after 40 days they served at the king's expense

Knight/man-at-arms in 13th-century armour

and knights especially could be expensive; moreover, a feudal host was slow and cumbersome, the knights and barons impatient of control – they were men who fought by a chivalrous set of rules, preferring to restrict the fighting to the campaigning season.

Mercenaries, on the other hand, were less expensive, far more flexible, all-year-round professionals, most of them from the overpopulated Low Countries – from Flanders and Brabant – recruited by enterprising commanders who organized them into companies. John's brother, Richard, had come to depend on them. The *routiers* – the common infantrymen – and the crossbowmen were employed in large numbers, whereas the specialists, those who made and operated huge catapults, who built moveable assault towers and who dug under walls, causing them to collapse, such men were prized craftsmen.

Knights and men-at-arms who held land in return for military service could be released from service on payment of *scutage*, and it was at Oxford that the barons agreed that landed knights and men-at-arms should pay *scutage* at the rate of two and half marks per man; that, along with taxes raised by royal officials, was money for hiring mercenaries.

Welsh longbowman – his bow would have been at least five feet in length

Both John and King Philip employed mercenaries in considerable numbers, but John had the option of hiring mercenaries that were not available to Philip – Welshmen, or better still Welsh longbowmen who could bring down armoured horsemen with ease, who frequently fired their arrows, *en masse*, so that they rained down on enemy formations, and who could pick off garrison troops with a remarkable degree of accuracy; they were feared, they were merciless, they were bred for the use of arms.

Documents called the *Pipe Rolls*, which record royal expenditure, provide examples of how John hired Welsh mercenaries; one dated 28th March 1204 reads: 'To William de Breos ten marks for the service of Leisani Walensis [Leison the Welshman, Lord of Afon] son of Morgan who was proceeding upon the King's service with 200 Welshmen to join the King's forces.' Afon was part of Glamorgan – Crown property – custody of which was in the hands of William.

End of an Era

Preparations for John's return to the Continent were well under way when, on 6th March 1204, after a six-month siege, Château Gaillard fell to Philip's assault troops. An attempt was made on John's behalf to arrange a truce, but Philip quashed the move with the words, "First show me Arthur."

While John mourned his mother, Eleanor, who had died in her 80s, Philip made a surprise move, advancing through southern Normandy as though he were in command of a panzer division; then turning north to Caen, which surrendered without a fight, he linked up with his Breton allies. Soon barons and townspeople were everywhere bending a knee before him, and when, on 24th June, Rouen opened its gates to let him in it was all over: Normandy was lost save for the Channel Islands.

In following up his success Philip sent troops to link up with rebel barons in Anjou and overrun Poitou, the northern province of Aquitaine, so that, with the exception of La Rochelle and a few inland castles in Poitou and Touraine, John lost the whole of north-west France. Yet there was something positive to emerge from this catastrophic event. Preparations for a return to Normandy, coupled with the threat of invasion by Philip, resulted in John having at his disposal some 50 galleys – fighting ships similar to the dragon boats of the Vikings. He also made provisions for an administrative set-up that would one day become known as the Admiralty.

All for Nothing

The winter of 1204-5 was so cold the Thames froze to the extent that people could cross on foot. The ground became so hard that winter crops were ruined. By the spring of 1205 the word 'famine' was upon everyone's lips and the price of food soared, but John would not be deterred from winning back his lost possessions. In March he met his barons and over the next few months they made ready. The *Praestita Rolls* record that William received 20 marks for his Welshmen, but William would have had more to offer than Welsh mercenaries. By 1205 he held in fief or in custody some 350 fiefs, each of which could provided him with a fully-armed knight or man-at-arms; he also held 16 major castles which, collectively, could provide a considerable number of crossbowmen.

When the armada was ready to sail in June 1205, it became apparent that while the barons were willing to return to Normandy, they were not prepared to do what John wanted, which was to sail to Poitou and advance on Normandy from there. What William's position had been in all this is not known. What is known is that, initially, only one baron had the courage to stand up to John and, in doing so, encouraged others to say no to the proposed expedition to Poitou. That baron was William Marshal, a man who had started out as a landless servant, but who had earned a reputation for his invincibility in tournaments, making a living by selling captured horses and ransoming the men he defeated. Through his marriage to an heiress he became Earl of Pembroke and Lord of both Leinster and Strigoil

(Chepstow and Usk). By 1205 he was in his 60s, a great landowner in both England and Normandy. He also appears to have been a good friend of William de Breos.

It seems likely, then, that de Breos also refused to accompany John to Poitou, a view supported by the fact that, from 1206 onwards, both these men were out of favour with John. Whatever the truth, the refusal of his barons to embark for Poitou caused John to board the royal galley in a huff and sail up and down the Channel till he calmed down. On his return to *terra firma* he stomped down the gang-planks to call off the expedition; from then on he harboured a grudge against his barons.

Dependable Captains

Had the armada sailed it would have been too late to relieve the garrison at Chinon. Under its custodian, Hubert de Burgh, the man who spared Arthur from mutilation, the garrison had held out until it was forced to come out fighting, only to be over-powered and disarmed. It was fortunate that John had need of men such as de Burgh, for he helped to pay the man's ransom and eventually made him Justiciar in England. In John's eyes it was better to show favour to his mercenary captains than to elevate his untrustworthy barons.

Poitou

John was to have his way over an expedition to Poitou, albeit with limited objec-tives. When he disembarked at La Rochelle on 7th June 1206 he did so in the company of many barons, though whether William de Breos was among them is not known. During the next few months John demonstrated what he was good at: he marched about Poitou and Anjou, showing the flag, intimidating barons and towns-people who had gone over to King Philip to reconsider their position. Oddly enough, Philip, despite raising an army, did not intervene and, on 26th October, both kings agreed to a two-year truce, one that left John in control of most of Poitou.

Out of Favour

Something odd took place during the closing months of 1206 which supports the view that William de Breos and his friend, Marshal, did not take part in the expedi-tion to Poitou. It appears that John encouraged his Justiciar in Ireland – who was responsible for upholding his interests there – to carry out attacks on William's Honour of Limerick and Marshal's Lordship of Leinster. Both barons protested to John who tried to make out that it was all a mistake, saying that he 'found no fault' in de Breos and ordered his Justiciar to make amends. A further example of John's malice took place early the following year when he relieved William of the custody of Glamorgan and Gwynllwg. Marshal also suffered the loss of royal offices and from then on spent most of his time in Ireland where he considered himself safe.

An Heir for a Lustful King

In one respect 1207 was a good year for John in that his wife, Isabella, gave birth to a son on 1st October, whom they named Henry. John may have been pleased with Isabella, but that would not have stopped him lusting after other women, some of whom where low born, while others, it was rumoured, were the wives and daughters of barons.

At Odds with the Pope

Hubert Walter, Archbishop of Canterbury, died in November 1205, initiating a lengthy controversy between John, his bishops and the monks of Canterbury Cathedral over who should be Hubert's successor. The Pope came up with a solution, nominating Stephen Langton, an English Cardinal who had made a name for himself teaching at the University of Paris. Langton proved totally unacceptable to John who refused to allow him into the country. The Pope, however, was quite prepared to sit it out, hoping that with a little pressure John would relent. Eventually, the Pope came to realize that he would have to adopt a more positive approach. On 17th June 1207 he consecrated Langton Archbishop of Canterbury and later warned that, if John did not 'bow to the divine ordinance', then an interdict would be proclaimed in England and Wales. Yet John refused to budge.

According to the Margam chronicles, all the laity, most of the clergy and many monks were on the King's side, believing the King to be wronged by a high and mighty Pope, which is understandable because John took pains to appear 'Mr. Nice Guy', always ready to enter into negotiations when his intention was to play for time. Life went on, papal threats or not, and John did what his predecessors rarely did, he toured his realm, dispensing justice, seeing to business and proving himself to be an extremely able administrator. People flocked to him with requests for justice, for special privileges and for charters.

Early in 1208 he was approached by a group of Cistercian monks from Neath Abbey, requesting a charter which would confirm the dispersed parcels of land in their possession – gifts from generous benefactors – so that in the event of a dispute they could refer to the charter as proof of ownership. John obliged, putting his name to a confirmatory charter, dated 6th January 1208, which listed the outlying possessions and privileges of the monks; those which relate to Gower including:

(1) the gift of Henry de Vilers of the Chapel of St. Michael (the remains of which stand in what is now marshland) with the land that belonged to it; that is, the grange of Cwrt y Carnau (a grange being an estate worked by monks), and
(2) the thirty acres given by William de Barry from his fief of Walterston, and
(3) the fishery rights of Pwllcynon which Ranulf the Hermit formally held, and which a former lord of Gower, Henry de Warwick, gave to the monks; that is, the liberty of fishing between Pwllcynon and the Tawe River with nets and other engines, and leave to raise a weir across the Tawe from the land of the monks at Glyntawe, called Enysumwen, to the firm and dry ground of Gower, etc.

The monks were happy with their confirmatory charter, John was happy with the money that had crossed his palm; the Pope's patience ran out. On Sunday 23rd March 1208 the interdict was proclaimed in churches throughout the land and came into effect the following day when the clergy went on strike. Everywhere churches were closed and clergymen were not allowed to conduct any service other than the baptism of infants and to hear the confessions of the dying. There could be no mass, no marriage ceremonies, no burying the dead in consecrated ground.

John's reaction was to seize Church property and then allow the clergy to administer their own property for him – at a price – which is what the clergy did rather than see their property pass from their control. Then John had another idea. A large number of clergymen were either married or kept mistresses. So John had the women rounded up, declaring that they would be released at a price. John was pleased: he was making money out of the Church and the interdict lasted six years. For William de Breos, however, the interdict placed him on the receiving end of John's wrath, which in turn would lead to civil war and ultimately to John's downfall.

CHAPTER II
King John and the de Breoses (2)

Hostages

John, someone said, 'neither feared God, nor regarded men' – an overstatement in that John trusted no one. His biggest worry was that the interdict might encourage disaffected barons to renounce their allegiance to him. So, at the beginning of March when the interdict was about to be pronounced, he decided that suspect barons were to hand over a son, or near relative, as a hostage. William Marshal complied within days of the interdict being pronounced, but when John's agents turned up at a castle belonging to William de Breos and requested a son, William's wife, Matilda, retorted, "I'll not deliver up any son of mine to your lord, King John, not when I know he murdered his own nephew, Arthur."

William must have been alarmed by his wife's outburst. He is reputed to have said, "You have spoke like a stupid woman against our lord, the King," but his language may have been a little stronger than that. He, then, addressed the King's agents, saying, "If I have offended our lord, the King, in any way, I am ready to make amends."

When John heard of Matilda's outburst he undoubtedly flew into a rage, the stamp of all Plantagenets. One chronicler recorded what John had been like when he flew into a rage over a man named Longchamp:

> His whole being became changed to the point where he was barely recognizable. Rage contorted his brow, his burning eyes glittering, his pink cheeks discoloured by bluish spots; God knows what he would have done to Longchamp had the man fallen into his hands as they sawed the air,

which is probably what he did before killing Arthur.

Years later, when he felt obliged to explain his action against William de Breos, John claimed the cause to have been William's failure to keep up the instalments on the 5,000 marks promised for the Honour of Limerick, and that William had resisted all attempts by the Chancellor to distrain upon his chattels. John also claimed that William had removed all chattels from his English estates and transferred them to

Wales – an impossible feat, for William could never have moved his entire household goods, his herds and flocks without someone reporting the movement to the King.

When John summoned William to appear before him, William excused himself on the grounds that he was sick – a likely story – whereas the *Patent Rolls* state that, on 19th March, William gave a son – probably Reginald – to one Walter de Lacy as a hostage. It is also known that, on 18th April 1208, one Gerard d'Athies, Sheriff of the shires of Gloucester and Hereford, took steps to distrain (seize) upon William's chattels in Wales. D'Athies was a Frenchman, a native of Touraine, a mercenary captain whose origin, it was rumoured, was that of a serf. In 1204-5 he had, with fierce bravery, defended the Castle of Loches until forced to surrender. John valued the man so much that he paid 2,000 marks for his release. When he came to England, d'Athies brought with him a number of like-minded kinsmen, all of whom were given positions in John's administration. This clan of disreputables was hated so much that a clause had to be inserted in the Magna Carta of 1215 to the effect that all the relations of d'Athies were to be removed from office.

In company with the Sheriff of Shropshire, d'Athies entered William's domain at the head of 25 mounted serjeants and 500 foot soldiers. William must have known that John was harassing him with the intention of provoking armed conflict; he did not respond. Then, as if to add insult to injury, on 29th April, William was ordered to pay 1,000 marks within four days to cover the cost of the expedition that had been sent against him.

The course of events from here on is fragmentary and confused, but it appears that it fell to Matilda to approach John, taking the precaution of having at least two other barons with her as witnesses. The outcome was that William met John at Hereford and agreed to hand over certain castles and provide hostages, three of whom may have been grandsons, the offspring of his third son, Reginald. That should have defused the situation, but in later years John claimed that, when d'Athies had summoned the royal custodians of the above castle to collect garrison pay, two of William's sons attacked the castles, though to what purpose is unclear. All things considered it is unlikely that William would have allowed his sons to provoke armed conflict with the King. What is likely is that John kept up the pressure until such time as William had had enough and fled with his family so that, on 21st September, John was able to confirm an agreement between d'Athies and William's tenants, one in which the tenants vowed never to return to William's allegiance.

Aggrieved Tenants
Before the close of the year John began granting away parts of the de Breos estate – the baronies of Barnstaple and Totnes, both in Devon, being the most noteworthy. Other baronies John kept for himself – border baronies such as Builth, for example, were placed in the custody of Engelard de Cigogne, a mercenary captain related to d'Athies. Engelard was also responsible for the detention of all those Breoses to end

up in John's clutches. Gower, John retained for himself, a fact confirmed by two charters, dated 11th November 1208, one of which reads:

> The King, to all (etc). Know ye that we have released the Welshmen of Gower from the custom which our servants of the Castle of Sweyneshe have had of taking their food with the aforesaid Welshmen, and we will that thereafter they be neither molested nor aggrieved.

The charter probably refers to a custom which serjeants of the peace had of being fed and billeted whilst doing their rounds – arresting criminals, distraining debtors and carrying out the decisions of the lord's court at Sweyneshe. The practice had become a grievance due to the serjeants molesting their hosts, English as well as Welsh, for an almost identical charter was addressed to them. The *Pipe Rolls* for 1208 suggests the charter had cost the Welshmen 50 marks (£33.33) and horses for the chase; they suggest, too, that the Welshmen may have been slow in parting with their money.

Under John, Gower became the responsibility of Faulkes de Brêautê, a mercenary captain with a reputation for plundering churches. Early in 1207 de Brêautê had replaced William de Breos as custodian of Glamorgan and Gwynllwg and the *Pipe Rolls* for 1208 record a payment to him of 100 marks (£66.66) for keeping the Castle of Sweyneshe.

On the Run

Sometime between 27th April and 21st September 1208, William fled his Welsh domain, taking with him his wife, Matilda, his eldest son, William the Younger, William's wife, Matilda de Clare, and their children. William's third son, Reginald, may have already been in Ireland as a hostage in the custody of Walter de Lacy. The family landed at Wicklow after a stormy crossing to be met by William Marshal, who refused to hand them over to John's Justiciar in Ireland. Three weeks later the family settled with William de Breos's son-in-law, Walter de Lacy, Lord of Meath.

If John could not get at them, then he could at least vent his spleen on other members of the family. William's second son, Giles, Bishop of Hereford, had his ecclesiastical estates confiscated twice by d'Athies before fleeing to France. Giles's sister, Loretta, who had married the Earl of Leicester, had also to flee to France, whereas William's brother-in-law, Thomas de St. Valery, had to pay 1,000 marks for obtaining the King's 'good will.'

No matter how much John would have wished to sail to Ireland there were other matters that required his attention. In January 1209 the Pope threatened to have him excommunicated, and there were rumours of a conspiracy, one known to historians through a letter from King Philip to a nobleman who had already informed Philip that the barons of northern England and Ireland were prepared to rebel against John the moment Philip invaded southern England; it was a conspiracy that involved the King of Scotland. Although de Breos was not mentioned in the letter it can be assumed that he was one of the main conspirators.

In August, John pre-empted the opposition by marching north with a mighty host, intimidating the King of Scotland into agreeing to humiliating terms, which also served as a warning to the northern barons. That same year he decided to have a go at the Jews, demanding huge amounts of money, then hanging some and mutilating others. Finally, in November, he was excommunicated, which meant that, should he die, his soul would go straight to hell. The only people to be affected by this were a few high-ranking clergymen who felt obliged to leave for France.

The Move to Pembroke

Early in 1210, John decided to settle with William de Breos and teach the Irish barons who shielded him a lesson they would never forget. Detachments of a huge host made up of Englishmen and Flemish mercenaries were soon heading westwards for Pembroke. John himself was at Sweyneshe on 28th, 29th and 30th May as chancery rolls verify. One account records that Faulkes de Brêautê, custodian of Gower, was paid 50 marks (£33.33) for strengthening the Castle of Sweyneshe, undoubtedly in connection with John's stopover; he was also paid, according to an account dated 27th May, £8 6s.9d. (£8.34 in today's currency) to provide entertainment for the King while he stayed within the castle bailey. Another account, dated 28th May, records a payment to de Brêautê of £5 to cover the cost of four ships, which were to proceed to Pembroke. Obviously, these ships were privately-owned merchantmen, commandeered to convey troops across the Irish Sea. Ships such as these were probably square-sailed with no provisions for oarsmen; some would have been fitted with wooden 'castles' on the bows and sterns which, in later times, became known as fore-castles and poops respectively.

Before John sailed, William appeared off the Pembrokeshire coast and through intermediaries – one of them a nephew serving in the feudal host – he managed to propose terms, offering an incredible 40,000 marks for the King's 'good will', but John spurned the offer, declaring there could be no terms while Matilda remained free. So William laid waste the country, hoping to divert John from his purpose – to no avail. After John set sail, William remained in Wales, stirring up trouble, regaining territory, and may even have persuaded the Prince of Gwynedd to take up arms.

Ireland

John, meanwhile, disembarked at Crook, not far from Waterford, early in June and led his host northwards, through Leinster where the astute William Marshal placed himself at John's disposal, as did a number of Irish chieftains. Walter de Lacy, Lord of Meath and William de Breos's son-in-law, offered to submit without a fight only to be dispossessed of his lands. His brother, Hugh de Lacy, Lord of Ulster, conducted a fighting withdrawal until he decided he had an urgent appointment in Scotland. Matilda, who had been staying with Hugh, sailed with him as did her sons, Reginald and William the Younger,

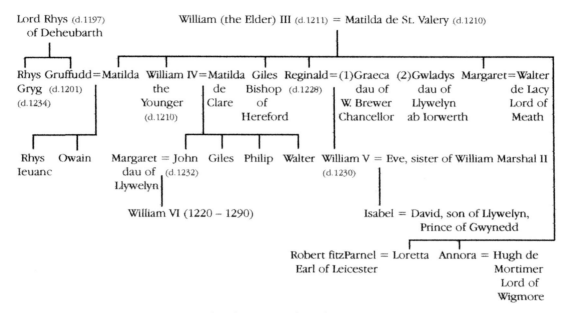

The de Breose family tree

and William the Younger's family. When they came ashore, Hugh and Reginald made good their escape, but the rest of the Breoses were taken prisoner by a Scottish lord; he handed them over to John's agents who shipped them off to Bristol.

Flushed with success, John arrived back in Wales at the end of August. When Matilda stood before him at Bristol she offered to ransom herself for 40,000 marks. To his credit, William (who had remained in Wales) did not abandon her, but turned himself in to confirm the offer, although he must have known that he had no hope of raising such a vast sum of money. John also knew how impossible William's position was and probably delighted in the man's distress; as if to give one final twist to the blade he had Matilda and William the Younger transferred to Windsor Castle where they starved to death while he waited for William to return with 40,000 marks.

In despair, William fled for France where he died in his early 60s at Corbeil, just outside Paris, on 9th September 1211. There were many exiles at his funeral – his offspring, Giles and Loretta, among them and possibly his son, Reginald. The funeral was conducted by the exiled Archbishop of Canterbury, Stephen Langton.

No explanation is needed as to why John wanted Matilda to suffer such a horrible death, but it is difficult to determine why he vent his spleen on William the Younger, even though two Welsh chroniclers claimed that John's determination to destroy the family was due to the enmity and envy he had towards William the Younger as well as William the Elder. What is known for sure is that John's treatment of William the Elder caused disgruntled barons to ponder their position until self-preservation forced them to become William's avengers.

Llywelyn ab Iorwerth

John focused his attention in 1211 on yet another pretentious underling, Llywelyn ab Iorwerth, Prince of Gwynedd in North Wales. Llywelyn had been born in 1173 when Gwynedd had for several years been fragmented between several members of the ruling dynasty. At 14 he had set out to remove, one by one, those relatives whom he saw as rivals until, 14 years later, he was master of Gwynedd, a fearful threat to his fellow princes. So impressive had his rise to power been that John singled him out for special consideration, giving him the hand in marriage of his illegitimate daughter, Joan.

John had cause to be ever watchful of his up-and-coming son-in-law who, by expanding beyond his borders seemed destined to become pre-eminent among the princes of Wales. Then, in 1210, Llywelyn overstepped the mark in support, perhaps, of William de Breos. John was not a man to overlook treachery, and early in 1211 he was ready to descend on Llywelyn with a mighty host, aided by the lesser princes of Wales, who felt threatened by Llywelyn's rise to power. When John advanced into North Wales, Llywelyn had the people of Perfeddwlad (east of the Conway) and the Island of Anglesey move, with all their chattels, to the Mountains of Snowdonia. John advanced as far as Degannwy and there his host suffered from a shortage of food, so much so that an egg was sold for one and half old pennies (about a day's wages for a serf), and the flesh of horses became their finest dishes; having lost many men, John returned home in shame.

Llywelyn may have outwitted his father-in-law, but that only made John all the more determined to get back at him, and early in July he left Oswestry with a more numerous host, supported by thousands of workmen to widen forest trackways and build castles. This time John had the provisions so there was nothing to hold up his advance. After crossing the River Conway he sent men to torch Bangor, at which point Llywelyn decided enough was enough; he sent his wife, Joan, to seek whatever terms she could – and they were harsh. Llywelyn lost all his lands east of the Conway, he had to pay a heavy tribute and provide 30 hostages.

John, of course, could never be gracious and, with typical insensitivity, he gave orders for castles to be built that were threatening to his Welsh allies; in doing so he achieved the almost impossible, causing the Welsh princes to unite. At first, everything seemed peaceful enough when, at Easter 1212, Llywelyn spent time at Cambridge with his father-in-law. Then, at the end of June, Maelgwn and Rhys Gryg, sons of the illustrious Lord Rhys (d. 1197), attacked and burnt the new castle at Aberystwyth. The attack was followed by Cadwallon ab Ifor Bach of Senghenydd ravaging the lowlands of Glamorgan. In July, Llywelyn joined his former enemies and, to his surprise, the Pope sided with him, with Gwenwynwyn of Powys, with Maelgwn of Ceredigion and with anyone else who opposed John, by releasing them from their allegiance to the King and lifting the interdict from their lands.

John responded to the occasion, determined to finish his son-in-law off. Troops mustering for a return to France were redirected to Chester; that same month John

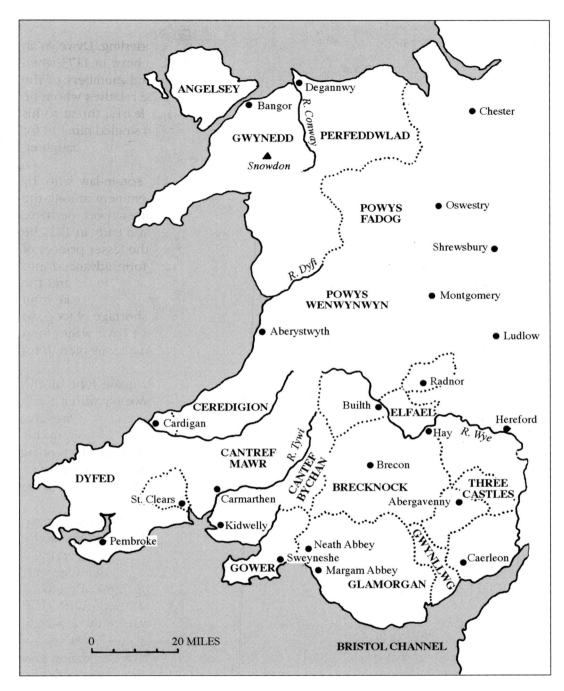

Wales in the time of King John

gave orders for 28 hostages, the sons of Welsh princes, to be hanged for their fathers' treachery. After watching the hostages hang, John sat down for dinner, when messengers arrived, one from the King of Scotland, the other from his daughter, Joan, both warning that, if he entered Wales, his barons would kill him in the midst of battle. John lost his nerve and called off his invasion of Wales. Historians have pondered on whether this story is true, and whether the rumours had their origin in Llywelyn's court. Whatever the truth, Llywelyn felt free to reconquer his lost lands while, further south, Rhys Gryg burnt Sweyneshe, meaning the town not the castle, and Rhys Ieuanc made considerable gains in the Lordship of Brecknock.

A Change of Heart

John, meanwhile, rampaged, rooting out suspect barons. When he calmed down he decided that perhaps he had gone too far with his barons, so he implemented measures that would once more make him out to be 'Mr. Nice Guy'. In November he initiated moves to end his dispute with the Pope. The Pope, however, remained distrustful of John.

While negotiating with the Pope, John countered the threat of invasion by sending his navy on commando-style raids against Philip's fleet. The most successful raid involved some 500 ships entering the harbour of Bruges, where 400 French vessels were either cut adrift or set ablaze. John had temporarily crippled Philip at a stroke; the Pope was in for a shock too. On 15th May 1213, John not only agreed to the Pope's demands, he went one step further, proposing to make England and Ireland fiefs of the Apostolic See. In theory England and Ireland would belong to the Pope. It was a brilliant move: the Pope loved the idea; John was pleased too, for it meant that if Philip made any further attempt to invade, he would be declaring war on the Pope. It also put his barons in a difficult position, for if they rebelled, they did so against the Pope. The big drawback, however, was that Stephen Langton, the exiled Archbishop, had to be allowed into the country to assess Church losses, for which John would have to make recompense before the interdict could be lifted, but here again John proved to be slippery. Despite Langton's complaints to the Pope about the way John was wriggling out of his obligations, John got off lightly, paying little in the way of recompense.

While all this Church business was going on, John made plans for another expedition to Poitou, but his barons, especially his northern barons, made excuses for not supporting him until, finally, he set off with his mercenaries, intending to teach these northern barons a lesson. Langton caught up with him at Northampton to remonstrate and remind him that, when absolved from excommunication in July, he had promised to act only on the judgement of his barons; he also threatened excommunication on all who marched with him. John had no option other than to refrain from armed conflict, although he still marched about the north in a manner that warned his barons to beware.

A Return to Poitou

John gave orders for his troops to muster on 6th February 1214. To his dismay many barons failed to turn up, so that when he sailed for Poitou he did so with a host composed mainly of hired foot soldiers. The details of his expedition are beyond the scope of this book; suffice to say that John returned to England in October, having achieved nought, to find many barons on the verge of revolt, provoked by the heavy-handedness of his Justiciar in England, the man responsible for governing the country in his absence.

The Return of an Exile

Among the many exiles to return with Stephen Langton in June 1213 was William de Breos's second son, Giles, Bishop of Hereford, a man who, given the chance, intended to restore the family estate – but for a while Giles had to tread carefully: John was now the Pope's man and many members of the Breos family were in the custody of John's henchman, Engelard de Cigogne. Giles may have had something to do with the release, in July, of his late brother's wife, Matilda de Clare, and the eldest son of his brother, Reginald. He certainly had a hand in the release of his sister, Annora, in October 1214.

Giles obviously kept in touch with former exiles and with those barons conspiring to kerb John's excesses. He probably knew about the charter of liberties they had compiled during the winter of 1213-14, a blueprint for what would eventually become known as Magna Carta. Throughout 1214 the opposition gathered momentum; in January 1215, Giles was present when a group of barons presented John with their charter and were told that he would need time to consider it when, really, all John wanted was time to inform the Pope and recruit mercenaries. John produced his trump card on 4th March when he vowed to go on crusade, which meant that, according to the rules of chivalry, he had put himself and his kingdom under the protection of the Church for three years, safe from King Philip and from his barons. John gave his barons something else to consider when, the following day, he confirmed Giles's offer of 9,000 marks for what remained of the family estate; thus Giles became a Marcher Lord.

John may have been angling for Giles's support: he obviously knew about Giles's connection with dissident barons and may also have reasoned that Giles was the link between those barons and the troublesome Welsh princes. With the return of Langton in June 1213 the princes had been relatively quiet, but they were likely to take up arms if Giles committed himself to a baronial revolt.

If John had been angling for Giles's support, he was in for a disappointment. On 26th April the dissident barons, impatient for a reply to their proposed charter, mustered at Stamford in Cambridgeshire and Giles was there with them. John's response was to order loyal barons and his mercenaries to muster at Cirencester. On the face of it John was in a strong position. Apart from his mercenaries, he eventually had the support of around 40 barons, many of them from the west Midlands, the southern counties, the

The British Isles in the time of King John

Welsh March and Ireland. Chroniclers often referred to the opposition as the 'Northerners', and while it is true that some dissident barons were from the North of England, they also came from the eastern counties and from around London. At best they numbered a little over 40. John could have dealt with them, but he had to keep an eye on the 100 or so barons who sat on the fence. For the sake of winning the support of waverers he once again adopted the roll of 'Mr. Nice Guy', always ready to negotiate, aware that the opposition were also trying to draw support from the same quarter.

At the end of April the barons sent their demands to John who, at the time, had cause to be pleased with himself, for his delaying tactics had paid off. At the beginning of March he had written to the Pope, knowing that it would take a month or so for his letter to reach Rome, and another month for the Pope's reply to reach him. That reply he received at the end of April and it proved exactly what he had expected, for not only did the Pope appeal to the barons to desist from conspiracies and threats, but the Pope reproached Stephen Langton for taking sides with the dissidents and ordered him to excommunicate any baron who would not submit to the King; that surely was something for the uncommitted barons to ponder. The dissident barons responded on 3rd May by renouncing their oaths of allegiance and marching on Northampton. Giles, by then, had already taken the initiative, for about 1st May he sent Reginald

> his brother, to Brecknock where the Welsh of that land received him honourably. And … he [Reginald] took the castles of Pencelli, Abergavenny, Whitecastle, Grossmont and Skenfrith before the end of three days.

Presumably the garrisons surrendered without a fight, they were, after all, Giles's men. Giles himself may have gone to Devonshire to stir up trouble in his father's former baronies of Barnstaple and Totnes, for it is known that John sent mercenaries to the West Country to put down an uprising there, but the mercenaries turned back because the rebels proved too strong for them. At an unspecified date, Giles joined his brother and the castles of Radnor, Hay, Brecon and Blaenllynfni were surrendered to him without any resistance. The action taken by the brothers must have made John pause for thought, for he now had to consider campaigning on three fronts. The prospect, however, may not have become apparent until the end of May.

In the meantime, John kept the negotiations going for almost two weeks, trying to win over dissident barons, Giles in particular and for good reason. In a letter written by the sheriff of Herefordshire it was stated that in his county all the people, including the barons and their men, were with the Bishop and were prepared to send men to wherever they were needed. Furthermore, there were a number of Marcher barons who were also prepared to align themselves with Giles.

In Gower the situation proved to be different, for it had been in the hands of Faulkes de Brêautê until a writ, dated 29th January 1214, instructed him to hand it over (along with the castles of Carmarthen and Cardigan) to William Marshal whose loyalty lay with John. It would appear that the foreign settlers in Gower were also prepared to support the King. Indeed, the burgesses (privilege citizens) of Sweyneshe were confident that John would prevail, so much so that, about the beginning of May, they sent a deputation to him to obtain a charter that would allow them to trade in other towns without paying tolls. The charter they received reads:

> John, by the Grace of God [etc] … Know ye that we have granted and by this charter confirmed, to our burgesses of Sweyneshe, that they may go … through all our land

with their merchandise, to buy and sell and do business … freely and quietly and honourably; and that they be quit of tolls, passage, pontage, stallage and lasage and all other customs; saving in all things the liberties of our City of London … Witnesses … William Marshal, Earl of Pembroke … at Reading 6th May 1215.

What the charter meant to the burgesses of Sweyneshe was that, on producing a certificate, they were free to trade in any town, save London, without having to pay tolls such as *passage* (a toll for using a ferry-boat in or near a town, similar to the one over the Tawe Estuary), *pontage* (a toll for crossing a bridge in or near a town), *stallage* (the right to erect a stall within a town without having to pay for the privilege) and *lasage* (the right to peddle within a town without paying for the privilege). In later times, in a seafaring town such as Bristol, the citizens there had a list of non-resident burgesses who were free of all tolls and it included the burgesses of boroughs such as Swanzey, Neeth, Cowbridge, Carmardin, Kidwelley and Laugharne.

The Road to Civil War
It is likely that the King's advisors became impatient and, pressed to do something, John ordered his troops to advance on London. Unfortunately, the now rebellious barons beat him to it, arriving there on Sunday morning, 17th May; the citizens of London welcomed them with open arms. About this time, Llywelyn made for Shrewsbury where the town and castle were surrendered to him without a fight. As always, John flew into a rage and then did nothing, dithering this time at Windsor, while Stephen Langton and a number of uncommitted barons moved to and fro between the parties, trying to find a way to avert civil war.

Meanwhile, in West Wales, Rhys Ieuanc, Lord of Cantref Mawr and Cantref Bychan, made peace with his uncle Maelgwn, Lord of Ceredigion, and together they descended on Dyfed and ran amok. Then

> Rhys Ieuanc gathered a host … and gained possession of [the districts of] Cydweli and Carnwyllion, and burned the castle [of Kidwelly].

The people of Gower were, then, to pay a price for their loyalty to John, and it is obvious that, where Gower was concerned, Rhys Ieuanc was acting in the interest of Giles who was in fact his uncle, as Rhys's father, Gruffudd, had married Giles's sister, Matilda (d. 1210). Rhys advanced on Gower from the west

> and set fire to the Castle of Loughor … And he made for the Castle of Hugh de Meules at [Llandeilo] Tal-y-bont, and the garrison sought to hold it against him. But he took it by force and burned some of the garrison and slew others. And on the following day he made … towards Seinhenydd [the Welsh word for Sweyneshe] and for fear of him the garrison burned their town. But he, not desisting from his plan, made for the Castle of Oystermouth, and on the first day he took the castle, and there he encamped that night. And on the following day he burned the castle and the town [meaning the

village]. And he took all the castles of Gower before the end of three days and … returned home joyful with victory.

Magna Carta

On 10th June, John made his way down the Thames to a meadow called Runnymede – between Windsor and Staines – to enter into dialogue with the rebel barons. On 15th June he allowed his great seal to be affixed to a draft document that developed into what is now known as Magna Carta – the Great Charter. The document was a charter of liberties, formulated primarily to protect the privileges of the barons against the excesses of King John. For their support, there were clauses in the charter to uphold the interests of churchmen, knights, freemen and burgesses, especially those of London. The majority of the population, the unfree peasants, were only mentioned in so far as they were not to be fined beyond their means. Three clauses applied to Welsh princes in respect to land and the release of hostages. One clause applied to the King of Scotland. Most important of all was the establishment of a committee of 25 barons to ensure that the terms of the charter were upheld – the first step on the long road to a democratically elected government.

Hostilities Renewed

The rebel barons renewed their oaths of allegiance on the 19th June, and the following day John sent a letter to the Pope. While he awaited a reply he set about putting wrongs to right and disbanded his mercenary host, but despite the appearance of a return to normality, both sides were soon preparing for war. Langton tried to mediate until a letter from the Pope put him in an impossible position. The letter had come in response to John's whinging about the situation as it had been some two weeks before Runnymede, and called for the excommunication of all rebels and for an interdict to be placed on their lands. Langton refused to carry out the Pope's instructions, claiming the letter to be irrelevant since the King had come to terms with the opposition; for his trouble Langton was suspended from office by clergymen loyal to John. At the end of September, Langton set out for Rome, little realizing that another letter from the Pope was on its way, declaring Magna Carta to be null and void.

By then, John was in Kent, awaiting the arrival of mercenaries, when the rebel barons took Rochester without a fight. John responded by directing his mercenaries to lay siege to Rochester Castle, sparing no effort to reduce the walls to a pile of rubble. At the same time he must have been angling to win over certain barons, for it is recorded that Giles came to terms 'for fear of the Pope', although it is more likely that what bothered Giles was that he had been excommunicated. Writs dated 21st October gave instructions for Giles to be restored to most of his father's estates – the baronies of Barnstaple, Totnes and Bramber being specifically mentioned; in November, William Marshal was ordered to hand over Gower. As a gesture of goodwill, Reginald's two youngest sons, Giles and Philip, were to all intents and purposes released, being placed in the custody of men who were well-disposed towards the family – good news for Reginald because it meant that all his sons had been removed from the custody of John's henchman, Engelard de Cigogne.

Disappointing it may be that Giles changed sides, but there is a possibility that he knew his days were numbered. Indeed, on his way home from John's court he was taken seriously ill at Gloucester and died on 17th November. John responded with typical lack of tact, issuing orders for the de Breos estate to revert to the Crown, forcing brother Reginald to rebel and align himself with Llywelyn, Prince of Gwynedd. Thus Reginald placed himself and his Welsh lands under the Prince's protection, and to seal the arrangement he married the Prince's daughter, Gwladus. Neither of these men, nor any Welsh prince had anything to fear from John, for Reginald had his sons and the princes had theirs – Magna Carta had seen to that.

Castles Fall

After a seven-week siege, the garrison of Rochester surrendered on 30th November when part of the keep fell to the ground as a result of mining activity beneath the walls. Nothing much happened in the east during the weeks that followed, mainly because John lacked the will to enter London and go for a straight fight, whereas in Wales the situation deteriorated to all-out war. During the first week in December, Llywelyn marched on Carmarthen, the acknowledged leader of up to a dozen princes, and, following a five-day siege, Carmarthen surrendered to him on 8th December; from there, Llywelyn led the confederation of princes through Dyfed and Ceredigion, taking castles one after the other, the garrisons too fearful to hold out for long. The *Chronicle of the Princes* lists ten castles captured or destroyed before the end of the year, Sweyneshe and Kidwelly among them – a mistake surely as Gower belonged to Reginald and he was Llywelyn's vassal. It is far more likely that Sweyneshe and Kidwelly were added to the list because Rhys Ieuanc had attacked them earlier that same year.

It was unusual to campaign during winter and yet the *Chronicle of the Princes* records that, on this occasion, 'so great was the mildness of the air and the weather that a winter as mild as that had never been heard of before'. Even more unusual was an event which took place early the following year. At Aberdyfi the princes actually assembled to decide what should be done with their conquests. Llywelyn wisely took nothing for himself, the conquered lands being divided by council among the brotherly princes, Maelgwn and Rhys Gryg, and their nephews, Rhys Ieuanc and Owain. What Llywelyn wanted was to maintain his position as the accepted leader of all the Welsh princes, and one way of preventing John from disrupting the arrangement was to ensure that the princes were happy with the division of conquered lands.

Fickle Barons

John came to a decision on 20th December: instead of closing for a kill on London, he took advantage of the mild weather and led his mercenaries northwards, bent on laying waste the lands of rebel barons. At one point the King of Scotland, who had been heading south in support of the rebels, about-turned and made for the hills. The appalling devastation that John inflicted on the North was repeated in the eastern counties. By the end of March 1216, John was back where he started – on the outskirts of London – only to find that the rebels had been reinforced by French troops; worse, King Philip's son, Louis, was expected to arrive soon. When the French prince disembarked on the Isle of Thanet on 22nd May, with numerous horse and foot, John did no more than watch, fearful that his own mercenaries would desert him if he offered battle. During the next few months the fortunes of war fluctuated with the movement of fickle barons. At first, large numbers flocked to support Louis, but when those barons realized that Louis and his French nobles had come to conquer and usurp they renewed their allegiance to John.

One baron who remained steadfastly loyal to the rebel cause was Reginald. The man had proved himself to be a real thorn in John's flesh and, on 26th May, John initiated desperate moves to persuade Reginald to change sides. When the moves failed, John advanced on Hay and Radnor, burning the towns and demolishing the castles, after which he headed north, intending to intimidate Llywelyn by burning Oswestry. Confident that he had made his point, John made another attempt at reconcilliation on 7th August, hoping that by then Reginald and Llywelyn would have learned their lesson. Both rebels were unimpressed; John gave up.

A Disastrous Meal

By mid-September, John had enough barons on his side to go on the offensive, advancing eastwards down the Thames Valley, then heading north-eastwards for Lincoln. On 10th October he did something strange, granting permission for Margaret de Breos, wife of Walter de Lacy, to clear land in the royal forest of Acornbury, the purpose of which was to establish a place where monks could pray for the souls of her father, her mother and her brother, William the Younger. Here again we have an example of John's generosity towards a woman, a loved one of those he had effectively put to death. Perhaps he had come to realize that the biggest mistake of his life was the way he had dealt with his former associate, William the Elder.

At King's Lynn the burgesses gave John a conqueror's welcome, feasting him to the extent that he contracted dysentery. He rode out of King's Lynn on 11th October, wincing as he bobbed in the saddle. The following day, whilst fording the Wellstream, a number of packhorses were sucked into quicksand because John would not wait till the tide had receded. Many servants drowned in the estuary and a certain amount of household baggage was lost, although later writers exaggerated the incident to the point where it became a disaster in which no one survived.

Finding it increasingly difficult to ride, John rested at Sleaford, then pressed on to Newark Castle, near Nottingham, where he could go no further. So alarming had his condition become that the Abbot of Croxton was sent for in the hope that his herbal remedies might alleviate the King's frightful condition. So enfeebled had John become that during the early hours of 18th October the Abbot listened hard while

John whispered a confession. John died on 19th October 1216. In his will he stated that he wished to be buried before the Altar of St. Wulfstan in Worcester Cathedral. Before his body was taken away his intestines were removed and interred at Croxton Abbey. In death John was as he had lived – gutless.

Epilogue

That should have been the end of the story, but the civil war continued, even though, on 28th October, John's nine-year-old son, Henry, was crowned King at Gloucester and the well-thought-of William Marshal became regent. In a bid to appease rebellious barons the new government declared, on 11th November, that it would honour a slightly modified version of Magna Carta. Nothing much happened during the winter months, but in February 1217, Marshal took the offensive against Louis, forcing him to retreat towards Kent. A more significant event took place on 20th May when Faulkes de Brêautê led his mercenaries into Lincoln Castle 'by an unfamiliar door and inflicted terrible slaughter on the rebels' who were thrown into even greater confusion when royal troops forced their way in through the city gates. This success alone caused many barons to go over to the young King, leaving Louis to fight on with dwindling support; his position became even more precarious in August when ships bringing reinforcements from the Continent were intercepted off Sandwich by the royal fleet under Hubert de Burgh, Justiciar of England since the previous year. That left Louis with no option other than to come to terms and return to France. On 12th September the war ended.

A significant factor in the outcome of the war had been Marshal's ability to win barons over to the royalist cause. Out of respect for William de Breos he made several attempts to win over Reginald, but did not succeed in doing so until after the assault on Lincoln when it became obvious that the rebels were fighting a lost cause. Reginald responded early in June, taking advantage of the safe passage he had been offered to declare his allegiance to the young King. His action led to a number of lesser Marcher barons following his lead, one of them Fulk fitzWarin, John's former playmate.

A writ dated 23rd June gave instructions for the Breos estates in Herefordshire to be handed over to Reginald. On 24th he was granted possession of the baronies of Barnstaple and Totnes, at the same time, instructions were sent to the Justiciar in Ireland for the restoration of Limerick and other Munster estates. The recovery of Bramber came later. Reginald may have come to terms with the King, but in doing so he incurred the wroth of his overlord, Llywelyn; this was to cost Reginald dearly and cause a feud between himself and the eldest son of his departed brother, William the Younger. Gower was to suffer from devastation and the evils of ethnic cleansing, so much so that a poet asked the question: 'are not the women of Sweyneshe altogether widows?'

But all that is another story.

Chapter III
Rhys Gryg and John de Breos

Hotheaded and stubborn, the baron, Reginald de Breos, had steadfastly opposed King John until his death in October 1216. He then continued to support the baronial party until 23rd June 1217 when he finally made his submission to John's nine-year-old son and heir, Henry III. All things considered, Reginald seemed to have made the right move; the previous month his fellow barons had suffered a serious setback at Lincoln, enough to convince many that the time had come to change sides.

As a rebel, Reginald had held sway over a considerable number of lordships in south-east Wales; now, as one reconciled to the Crown, he had every reason to believe that he would recover the lost family estates in England and Ireland, but there was a problem. When he rebelled in 1215, Reginald had covered his rear by swearing allegiance to Llywelyn ab Iorwerth, Prince of Gwynedd; to seal the alliance he had married the Prince's daughter, Gwladus. Llywelyn may not have had the resources that were available to the Crown, but he was still a man to be reckoned with, one who would not take kindly to Reginald's defection.

The first sign of a backlash came when Reginald's Welsh nephews, Rhys Ieuanc and Owain, overran the Lordship of Builth and took possession of it, save for the Castle of Builth itself. Then Llywelyn marched out of his mountain fastness of Gwynedd, bent on laying waste Reginald's possessions in Wales. In an earlier offensive (in December 1216), Llywelyn had led a host against English settlers in West Wales, with the result that the garrisons of eight major castles had either surrendered or been overwhelmed, all in the space of three weeks; now it was the turn of settlers and soldiers in south-east Wales to take refuge behind stout walls, and none more so than the burgesses of Brecon, for that was where Llywelyn was heading. According to *The Chronicle of the Princes* the burgesses of Brecon,

> unable to resist him, came to him; and with the help of Rhys Ieuanc ... they made peace with him, and gave him five hostages from amongst the most influential of their number against ... paying him 100 marks to spare the town. And thence he turned ... towards Gower over the Black Mountain; and there many of his packhorses were lost. And he encamped at Llangwig. And when Reginald saw what destruction he ... [he had

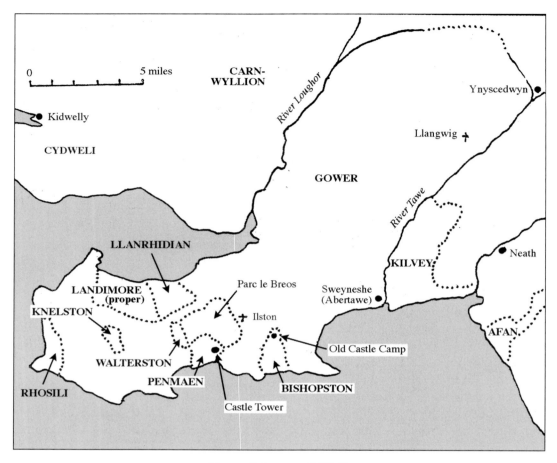

Map of Gower 1217-32

inflicted on Brecknock] he came ... [with] six knights ... and surrendered to Llywelyn. And on the following day he gave the Castle of Sweyneshe to Llywelyn, who entrusted ... [its] keeping of Rhys Gryg. And there Llywelyn stayed for a few days [before marching on Dyfed to fight the Flemings].

It is likely that, during his stay at Sweyneshe, Llywelyn held council with several prominent Welshmen over what should be done with Gower. It was not his policy to take possession of captured territories in South Wales, but to grant them to princes and men of worth in return for their allegiance, which was his way of winning the Welsh aristocracy of South Wales over to his side, at the same time making it difficult for the Crown to bribe them into changing sides. It was a wise policy and it worked well. With regard to Sweyneshe, by granting it and indeed the greater part of Gower to Rhys Gryg, he effectively made the man his vassal and could, therefore, have claimed to have reined in one of the most bellicose princes in South Wales.

Rhys Gryg

It is not known when Rhys Gryg – formerly known as Rhys Fychan – was born, only that he was one of at least 18 children fathered by the illustrious Lord Rhys (d. 1197), a prince whose forefathers had held sway over west Wales for centuries. During his father's lifetime, Rhys Gryg had been an unruly son, frequently taking sides with his older brother, Gruffudd, against his younger brothers, Maelgwn and Hywel Sais, but no sooner had his father died than he united with Maelgwn to dispossess Gruffudd, his father's chosen heir.

Over the next 18 years or so the fortunes of Rhys Gryg fluctuated until, early in 1216, when the princes of Wales met at Aberdyfi to decided on the division of captured territory, he did exceedingly well, becoming Lord of Cydweli, Carnwyllion, most of Cantref Mawr and Cantref Bychan; now, with the greater part of Gower added to his possessions, he was Lord of almost all that had been the old Welsh kingdom of Ystrad Tywi.

With regard to his character, Rhys Gryg was both aggressive and stubborn; as his name Gryg – the Hoarse – suggests he was probably rasping in his speech. A chronicler at Margam Abbey referred to him as 'Resus Bahhan' – Rhys the Fierce – when recording that he burnt Sweyneshe in 1212, and the burgesses must surely have hated him for this act of vandalism. Indeed, there is reason to believe that the Anglo-Norman and English settlers of Gower would have regarded him as an usurper and a tyrant. This ill will towards Rhys Gryg appear to have got out of hand, following Llywelyn's departure, for the *Brut* records that

> Rhys Gryg destroyed the Castle of Sweyneshe and all its [subsidiary] castles of Gower…and he expelled all the English … that were in the land without hope of their ever returning, taking as much as he pleased of their chattels and placing Welshmen to dwell in their land.

To this passage may be added the words of a poet, Llywelyn ap Iorwerth, otherwise known as Prydydd y Moch, who extolled the actions of Rhys Gryg as follows:

> And Abertawe, town of calm
> Broken towers, and today is there not peace?
> And St. Clears, and the bright happy lands
> Not Saxon, the people who possess them
> In Abertawe, strong key of England
> Are not the women altogether widows?

At first hand it appears that Rhys Gryg resorted to ethnic cleansing, but historians have played down the extent of his actions. There is, however, evidence to support the claim that 'Rhys Gryg destroyed the Castle of Sweyneshe and all its [subsidiary] castles' in that Sweyneshe Castle, Castle Tower, Penmaen, and Old Castle Camp, Bishopston, were all destroyed about this time. It can, therefore, be assumed that all other castles were likewise rendered useless, their destruction a pre-emptive move on the part of Rhys Gryg to prevent his English vassals from using them should they rebel. The question, then, is what exactly did the chronicler and the poet mean when they made use of the word 'English'?

Many of the Anglo-Normans at this time could claim their forefathers had settled in England 150 years previously and could, therefore, rightly regard themselves as Englishmen, even though they still spoke Norman-French. This development towards national awareness had been transmitted to Welsh chroniclers and poets who, from the late 12th century onwards, no longer distinguished between French and English, but had reverted to using one word to describe the intruders from the east – 'Saesneg', meaning English.

As to the statement that Rhys 'expelled all the English', this may well be an exaggeration. The English *coloni*, the customary tenants whose existence may be equated with serfs, were not a threat to Rhys Gryg – on the contrary, their labour obligations were indispensable if the rhythm of the land was to continue uninterrupted. The fief-holders, on the other hand, those who held their estates in return for military service, they were a threat and it is likely that they were the men who were expelled from Gower. Evidence in support of this hypothesis is slight, the best example being that, in 1241, Henry III gave instructions for Philip Hareng to be restored to the fief of Penmaen from which his father, or grandfather, had been ousted during the war.

The poem makes it clear that the castle at Abertawe (the Welsh word for Sweyneshe) was in ruins. The poem also suggests that blood had been spilled in the town, the result perhaps of an uprising – 'Are not the women altogether widows?' – It is unfortunate that the truth of what happened in Sweyneshe and Gower during the closing years of 1217 may never be known.

Morgan Gam

Another Welshman to benefit from becoming Llywelyn's vassal was Morgan Gam, Lord of Afan, in that he was granted, in Gower, the dispersed manor of Landimore (which included the fiefs of Landimore proper, Llanrhidian and Rhosili) and the land of Kilvey in return for the service of one knight – evidence that, by 1217, the Welsh were using heavily-armed horsemen to complement their longbowmen. The circumstances surrounding Morgan Gam's acquisition are unknown. In the late 12th century the dispersed manor of Landimore had been in the possession of one William de Turberville, and it is possible that a descendant of this William was dispossessed of his fiefs to become one of the Englishmen expelled from Gower. What is certain is that, many years later, Morgan Gam (d. 1241) gave the dispersed manor of Landimore to his eldest daughter, Maud, as a dowry on her marriage to Sir Gilbert de Turberville, Lord of Coety, thereby ridding himself of what had by then become a much-disputed piece of real estate.

Gruffudd Gwyr

Another Welshman to benefit from Llywelyn's policy of rewarding would-be allies was Gruffudd ap Cadifor of Yniscedwyn, otherwise known of Gruffudd Gwyr (Gower). In his march on Gower, Llywelyn must have passed through, or close by Yniscedwyn, at which point Gruffudd may have offered his services. Many centuries later it was recorded that Gruffudd 'came in the company of [Llywelyn?] … who conquered that country [Gower] and had part of it given him who was, therefore, called Gruffudd Gwyr of ye sundry conquests.' The extent of Gruffudd's acquisitions is unknown, but his son, Thomas, certainly held the fief of Knelston until his death in the 1270s.

Contenders for the de Breos Estate

With the civil war in England at an end, Llywelyn deemed it wise to reconsider his position, and on 25th May 1218 he did homage to the ten-year-old King Henry III. The lesser princes of Wales followed Llywelyn's example. Only Rhys Gryg remained obdurate, adamant that he would neither pay homage nor return conquered territories, such as Gower, to their former owners. The uneasy peace may have been a welcome respite for Reginald, but he now had to fight several legal battles with contenders who laid claim to part or all of his lands, one of them Hubert de Burgh, Justiciar of England. In 1201 Hubert had been granted custody of the Three Castles of Grosmont, Skenfrith and White Castle on the Welsh border, which he held until his capture at Chinon in 1205, after which the Three Castles became part of the de Breos estate. A more serious contender was Reginald's nephew, John de Breos, the first-born son of his elder brother, William the Younger, whom King John had starved to death in 1210.

John de Breos

Born on 6th October 1197, John de Breos is said to have been nicknamed 'Tadey' or 'Tadody' and to have been fostered in Gower – by a Welshman according to one source, by a Welshwoman according to another. At the age of 13, when his father had been imprisoned at Windsor Castle, John was placed in the custody of one of King John's henchmen, Engelard de Cigogne, and later transferred to the custody of Hubert de Burgh. His release came in January 1218 when, on 24th of that month, a number of earls and barons stood before the King's Council and declared themselves guarantors for the loyalty of John de Breos and his three younger brothers. Soon after his release John began proceedings before the King's justices at Westminster for the recovery of what would have been his father's inheritance had he lived.

In his plea John laid claim to the following lordships: Brecknock, Elfael, Builth, Radnor, Kingsland, Gwent Uwch-coed, Abergavenny, Skenfrith, Grosmont, Llantilio and also the Castle of Bramber in Sussex with all its appurtenances. John's mother, Matilda de Clare, who was also due to appear before the same justices, claimed as her dower, Shoreham, Bramber, Lower Breeding, Steyning, Findon, Knapp, Horsham, Warnham and Washington, all within the County of Sussex, and also the manors of Hampnett and Tetbury in Gloucestershire. No claim was made for Gower as it was in the hands of Rhys Gryg.

The suit, however, was postponed due to Reginald's participation in a campaign on the King's behalf. Then, in March 1219, several knights were sent to Reginald – who at the time claimed to be sick – to enquire of him who would plead his cause at Westminster. The litigants were, then, summoned to appear before the justices on 15th July that year. John had reason to be confident as he had several noteworthy supporters, among them his mother's brother, Gilbert de Clare, Lord of Glamorgan, and Prince Llywelyn who was keen to have Reginald, the most powerful Marcher lord in Wales, replaced by someone more acceptable to him – namely John de Breos. Unfortunately, John's involvement with a troublesome Welsh prince did not go down too well with the Crown, the more so when, at an unspecified date that year (1219), he married Llywelyn's daughter, Margaret. Equally suspicious to the Crown was the marriage of John's mother, Matilda, that same year, to Rhys Gryg, and the fact that Matilda's brother, Gilbert de Clare, a Marcher lord of considerable standing, was somehow involved in the arrangement only added to the Crown's suspicions.

The Crown's distrust of John is borne out by the papal legate, Pandulf, who wrote, in a letter to the Justiciar of England, Hubert de Burgh, that Reginald was 'necessary' for carrying out the King's business in Wales, and requested that the July hearing be postponed. The word 'necessary' sums up the situation nicely: as a Marcher lord, Reginald was 'necessary' to counter any threat posed by Llywelyn, whereas John was neither 'necessary', nor could he be trusted. As a result of Pandulf's letter the case was adjourned until later that year.

John could see which way the wind blew, and when he appeared at Westminster on 29th September 1219 he changed his plea, claiming only the Castle of Bramber with its appurtenances. Unfortunately, even when faced with a much reduced claim to the family estate, Reginald proved himself adept at keeping the proceedings going for a further six and half years, a task made easy, perhaps, because the Crown considered him 'necessary'.

An Unexpected Gain

John's circumstances improved twice over in 1220. At an unspecified date his wife, Margaret, gave birth to a son whom they called William (VI – William V is yet to be considered). His second gain proved to be territory from an unexpected quarter, for in July the Crown ordered Rhys Gryg to pay homage to the young King and to surrender to Llywelyn all the castles and lands in his keeping that had been captured since 1215. Rhys stubbornly refused to obey. So Llywelyn entered Ystrad Tywi in September and met Rhys at Carmarthen bridge, forcing him to yield, with the result that Rhys agreed to pay homage and to hand over the territories of Cydweli, Carnwyllion, Widigada and Gower.

According to the Treaty of Worcester (March 1218), Llywelyn had been empowered to hand back captured castles and lands to the Marcher lords to whom they 'rightfully' belonged, and this he did by returning Gower to its 'rightful' owner, John de Breos, and not Reginald as the Crown would have wished. Yet despite the fact that he was now a Marcher baron, John must have been frustrated by the successive post-ponements at Westminster, so much so that, early in December 1221, he prepared for action by obtaining the leave and council of Llywelyn to repair the Castle of Sweyneshe. He then made an incursion into the Lordship of Brecknock, causing damage to the extent that, when Reginald stood before the justices in January-February 1222, he complained that John had, in person, carried out an attack on his lands, burning townships and killing his men, so that he had to fortify castles against him, with the result that he suffered damages and costs to the value of £600. John, of course, denied the accusation and, with no further reference to the event, it can be assumed that the justices did not pursue the matter; that must surely have left John satisfied that he had, at last, scored against his uncle. He could be confident, too, that if his uncle retaliated, then he had the means to defend himself.

The Old Castle of Sweyneshe

Sweyneshe is believed to have had three successive castles, the first a primitive construction in wood, and the entry in the *Brut*, stating that John repaired the Castle of Sweyneshe (or Seinhenydd as it appears in the text) after its destruction by Rhys Gryg, has led many historians to accept 1221 as the year in which the castle was completely rebuilt in stone, although the *Brut* specifically states that it was repaired.

Gateway and drum towers, Carmarthen Castle. Similar defences may have been used to protect the town and castle of Sweyneshe

The only earlier references to work on the castle are to be found in the *Close Rolls*, which record that, in 1187, the sum of 20 marks was paid for repair work and, in 1210, the sum of 50 marks was spent on strengthening the castle. Neither of these entries provide clues as to whether the castle walls were in wood or stone, and there is no further record of renovation until 1401 when repair work was carried out on a much later castle (the third) called the New Castle (built *c.*1300) which is the only castle still visible today.

It is possible that John rebuilt the castle in stone over a period of several years, which would coincide with when Carmarthen Castle was rebuilt in more durable material than wood. Alternatively, the work may have been carried out in the late 12th century, a hypothesis supported by the somewhat dubious statement of John Leyland (1543) that 'the Old Castle of Sweyneshe was built or repaired by the Normans, and destroyed by Llywelyn'. It is unfortunate that the foundations and surviving walls of Sweyneshe's first stone castle – known in later centuries as the 'Old Castle' – are buried under the buildings and open ground on either side of Worcester Place, but they were partially uncovered in 1913 as a result of excavation for town improvements, thereby providing a glimpse of the 'Old [stone] Castle'.

Changing Fortunes

An opportunist and a Marcher baron of little import, John appears to have sat out the next few years while, around him, powerful men strove to improve upon their wealth and influence. The fortunes of even John's younger brother, Walter, seemed destined to improve when, in July 1223, he was granted the hand in marriage of Hawys de Londres, heiress to the lordships of Ogwr, Cydweli and Carnwyllion, but Walter's claim to her inheritance was not realized until 1225 when Hawys became of age. In March 1223, William Marshal the Younger landed in Pembrokeshire with 'a multitude of knights and foot soldiers from Ireland' and, despite stiff opposition from men such as Rhys Gryg, soon took control of the greater part of West Wales. Llywelyn, meanwhile, was active on the Welsh border, skirmishing with Reginald who was falsely reported dead in June. Then, early in September, Llywelyn laid siege to Builth, forcing Reginald to appeal to the Crown for aid. On the 24th September the bailiffs at Carmarthen were ordered to seize Sweyneshe Castle and hand it over to Reginald, presumably because John's loyalty to the Crown was suspect. The order does not appear to have been carried out, presumably because, on 8th October, Llywelyn came to terms rather than take on a huge English army led by Hubert de Burgh.

The events of 1223 may have brought relative peace to Wales, but the following year a power struggle took place in England between men who were once King John's cronies. Among those who objected to the growing power and influence of Hubert de Burgh, Earl of Kent and Justiciar of England, were Peter, Bishop of Winchester, Engelard de Cigogne and Faulkes de Bréauté. Faulkes was ordered to quit the realm after his Castle of Bedford had capitulated to forces loyal to the Crown. On 26th October 1224, Faulkes was presented with a safe passage to the coast where a ship would take him to France. Among those who were detailed to ensure he quit the realm was Reginald de Breos's eldest son, William V, who, as a young man, had been a hostage in the custody of Engelard de Cigogne.

That same year (1224), William Marshal the Younger, Earl of Pembroke, had been sent to Ireland to deal with a rebellion, but his opposition to what Hubert de Burgh had ordered should be done there put him on the wrong side of Hubert. William's action in West Wales two years previously had certainly curtailed Llywelyn's influence in the region, and this may have prompted John to seek a more cordial relationship with Hubert, who had been his custodian for two years prior to his release in 1218. This would account for a progressive change in John's circumstances in that not only did he acquire additional territory, but he was several times placed in a position of trust. He may even have become 'necessary' to Hubert if his relationship with Llywelyn had lapsed.

The first sign of change came early in 1226 when Reginald de Breos finally agreed to settle his long-standing dispute with John, whose right to Gower he agreed to recognize, added to which, John would receive the Honour, or Barony of Bramber in Sussex for the sum of £252, and also the manor of Tetbury in Gloucestershire – all on the condition that John made no further claim to the de Breos estate. The next change came soon after 13th August 1226 when William Marshal was ordered to hand over Carmarthen and Cardigan castles to one Henry Audley. On 25th October, Audley was, then, ordered to hand over custody of both castles to John, who held them until April 1228. Why John should be favoured – even trusted – with these castles is unclear, but it appears that Hubert de Burgh had designs on becoming a Marcher lord himself, and that at the expense of both Marshal and Reginald.

A number of surviving documents provide a glimpse of John's custodianship of the castles. It is known, for example, that John maintained a garrison at Carmarthen consisting of 30 men-at-arms (or serjeants as they were otherwise known) and 10 crossbowmen. There is evidence to show that John was responsible for supplying both castles with bacon, corn and other victuals. More important still, there are documents to show that John had custody of Carmarthen at a time when the castle was being rebuilt in stone. The *Brut* records that, when William Marshal recaptured Carmarthen from the Welsh in 1223, he repaired the Castle of Carmarthen. In subsequent years it appears that William undertook to rebuild the castle in stone, a task that was to continue under the direction of John. Repairs to the castle drawbridge, for example, were the responsibility of two master carpenters, Burnell and Hugh. It is possible that at a later date John employed the gangs of workmen at Carmarthen to rebuild Sweyneshe Castle in stone – or at least initiate work that may have been completed after his demise.

In June 1228 John was relieved of the custody of Carmarthen and Cardigan castles, but the following month he was granted custody of the Three Castles which, since 1225, had been in the keeping of Hubert. Although custody of the Three Castles proved only a temporary arrangement it, nevertheless, supports the view that something was afoot between John and Hubert, whose bid to become a powerful Marcher lord became a reality on 8th October 1229 when the King granted him the Castles and Honours of Carmarthen and Cardigan as Marcher lordships. Then, on 21st November 1230, Hubert received the homage of John, which effectively made John one of Hubert's vassals.

In the meantime – in June 1228 – Reginald died to be succeeded by his eldest son, William V. While it is true that William's uncle, Giles, had lost Limerick, Elfael and Gower, and that his father had to forgo Barnstaple, Totnes, Three Castles, Bramber and several smaller holdings, William V still inherited several important lordships along the English-Welsh border, as well as the Lordship of St. Clears in West Wales, which made him a powerful Marcher lord, one whom a Welsh chronicler described as 'a man eminent in arms, young though he was'.

William de Breos V

For several years Llywelyn had been relatively quiet, but by the summer of 1228 he appears to have been alarmed by Hubert's acquisition of the Castle of Montgomery. According to one source, men from the Montgomery garrison were engaged in clearing woodland when they were suddenly attacked by the Welsh and driven back to the castle where they were besieged by their attackers. The garrison managed to send word to Shrewsbury, with the result that the King and Hubert de Burgh hastened to raise the siege. Then, on 3rd September, the King issued orders for the Marcher lords to muster at Montgomery, among them William de Breos V. The following day orders were dispatched for the English barons to muster at Shrewsbury.

When the English army moved on 25th September its sheer size caused the Welsh princes to unite under Llywelyn, who skillfully deployed his troops in woods from which they harried the advancing columns relentlessly, inflicting substantial losses on enemy troops. In one encounter William V was wounded and captured, apparently whilst foraging. By October, continued resistance and mounting casualties forced the King to come to terms. It was agreed, on 11th February 1229, that William V would be ransomed for an incredible £2,000, that he would never again bear arms against Llywelyn, that his daughter, Isabel, would marry Llywelyn's son, David, that Builth would be her dowry and that Llywelyn would hold Builth on her behalf. On the 22nd February William V was set free; Llywelyn razed the Castle of Builth to the ground, thereby denying its recapture in the event of further hostilities.

The relationship between Llywelyn and William V appears to have been cordial from thereon, but Llywelyn had reason to suspect that William V was having an affair with his wife, Joan, and this came to a head when William paid him a visit in April 1230. In the dead of night Llywelyn burst into the chamber to catch William V and Joan in the act. The lovers were both imprisoned, as were the knights in William's train. What happened to Joan is unrecorded, but William's fate is well documented, for Nicholas, Abbot of Vaudey, sent an eye-witness account to the Chancellor, which stated:

> As for William de Breos, he was undoubtedly hanged from a tree in a certain manor called Crokein on the 2nd May in the presence of more than 800 persons, called together for the lamentable spectacle, especially those who were enemies of William de Breos senior and his sons.

At the time the King and Hubert de Burgh were in France. They did not respond, presumably because, unlike his father, William V was not considered 'necessary', not when the terms of his ransom stipulated that he would never again bear arms against Llywelyn. All things considered, Llywelyn may have gambled on the lack of response, but he, nevertheless, took the precaution of writing to William Marshal the Younger to explain that the hanging was unavoidable 'so great was the outrage and fury of his nobles'. Llywelyn, then, changed the subject by enquiring of Marshal his opinion on the proposed marriage between his (Llywelyn's) son and Isabel de Breos, who was in fact Marshal's niece. Llywelyn also wrote a similar letter to William V's widow, Eve – Marshal's sister. It can be assumed that neither Marshal nor Eve raised any objection as David and Isabel were married later that year.

William V's death marked the end of the de Breos dynasty in south-east Wales, for he left no heir, only four co-heiresses, with the result that the estate was eventually divided between the heiresses. Initially, however, the estate was placed in the custody of Marshal and remained in his care until his death on 5th April 1231. Six days after Marshal's death the King placed the de Breos estate in the custody of his brother, Richard of Cornwall, though it is doubtful whether Richard was in position to counter any threat posed by Llywelyn.

The sudden death of Marshal left a power vacuum in the March: William V had been hanged in 1230; that same year Gilbert de Clare, Lord of Glamorgan, had died, leaving an heir who was only a child. That left Hubert de Burgh as the only Marcher lord capable of keeping Llywelyn in check, and Llywelyn was not slow to take advantage of the situation. Before the end of April Llywelyn advanced into Radnor, but once he heard that the King's army had reached Hereford he withdrew and negotiations followed. At first hand Llywelyn's action seems pointless – unless, as has been suggested by one historian, his advance into Radnor had been to test the King's response. Whether or not this was so, on 20th May the King relieved his brother of the custodianship of the de Breos estate and placed it in the hands of Hubert de Burgh.

At the time, Hubert already held sway over the Three Castles, Archenfield (southern Herefordshire), the lordships of Carmarthen, Cardigan and Gower; after the death of Gilbert de Clare, he had custody of the Lordship of Glamorgan as well; now, with the de Breos estate in his grasp he had become the most powerful Marcher lord in Wales – and Llywelyn was not going to tolerate that. Once the King's army had retired in early June, Llywelyn fell upon Montgomery, destroying the town, but failed to take the castle. He, then, struck southwards, burning the towns of Radnor, Hay, Brecon and Caerleon. After destroying both the castle and town of Neath, he passed through Gower, leaving the lordship unmolested, and continued his relentless advance with his southern allies to destroy the town and castle of Kidwelly and then batter the garrison at Cardigan Castle into submission.

The King's response proved sluggish; by the time he entered Wales, Llywelyn was in a position to meet him in Elfael, but no serious fighting took place as both sides settled for a truce. The negotiations dragged on throughout 1232, during which time two noteworthy events took place. In July, Hubert fell from power to be succeeded by Peter, Bishop of Winchester, a rival and former crony of King John. Hubert's downfall may be attributed to both pressure from rivals and to the fact that he had failed to prevent Llywelyn from devastating the Marcher lordships in his care, but there was yet another reason. According to the English chronicler, Wendover, he was accused of providing information to Llywelyn about the affair between Llywelyn's wife, Joan, and William de Breos V, which led to the latter's execution. The final twist to the tale is that on 16th July 1232 John de Breos, at the age of 34, lost his life in a riding accident near Bramber. The *Brut* records that he was

> drawn at his own horse's tail and so died a cruel death.

Epilogue

Nothing is known of Reginald's 14-month tenure of Gower, though it has to be said that he surrendered the lordship in the hope of sparing it from depredation at the hand of Llywelyn. Rhys Gryg, on the other hand, was harsh in his dealings with English vassals. After surrendering Gower to Llywelyn in 1220, Rhys continued to be actively hostile towards all foreigners, involving himself in several noteworthy campaigns (in 1223, 1228 and 1233) and in 1227 he was 'seized by Rhys Fychan, his son, at Llanarthnau, but was released in return for the Castle of Llandovery'. Rhys Gryg died in 1234; he was buried at St. Davids 'near the grave of the Lord Rhys, his father'.

In contrast to the above two men, John de Breos ruled Gower for twelve years and, apart from his incursion into Brecknock in 1221, there is nothing in the records to suggest that he was either bellicose or a man 'eminent in arms'. Indeed, at first hand, John appears to have been a young man who, in his determination to take possession of at least part of what should have been his inheritance, was prepared to enlist the support of first Llywelyn and then Hubert de Burgh. In short, there is nothing to warrant labelling him a tyrant or even a rogue.

There is no evidence to suggest that he ousted Welshmen from lands granted to them by Llywelyn. Morgan Gam, for example, continued to hold Landimore and Kilvey, and although, prior to his death in 1241, Morgan Gam found it expedient to give Landimore to his daughter, Maud, as her dowry, it is likely that this took place after John's death because:

(1) during his lordship of Gower John granted Morgan Gam the towns (or manors) of Leissaneston (Leason) and Kutehulle (Kittle) and

(2) in 1231, Morgan Gam assisted Llywelyn in razing Neath Castle to the ground – it would, therefore, have been unwise for John to take action against a man who had remained one of Llywelyn's staunchest allies.

John also proved to be a generous benefactor of several ecclesiastical institutions. He gave two parcels of land to Talley Abbey. Prior to 1230, he gifted the Church of St. Iltinti (Ilston) and all the land called Mallewood (Millwood – the area around modern-day Hafod) and Borlakesland (Cwmbwrla) to the Order of Knights Hospitallers. To Neath Abbey he granted fishery rights at two locations on the Tawe River, one of them close to Sweyneshe Castle, and also gave plots of land near the same fisheries on which the monks might build houses. It should be noted that these fisheries were valuable assets as salmon was still to be found in the Tawe as late as the 15th century.

On the death of Bishop Goldcliff of Llandaff in January 1229, John appropriated the manor of Bishopston and pocketed the revenue for a period of almost 20 months. John could claim that, during the vacancy of the See, he had every right to pocket revenue that would ordinarily have gone to a bishop. However, when Elias, treasurer of Hereford, was confirmed in the vacant See on 30th August 1230, John surrendered not only his claim to all revenue from the manor, but by a charter he relinquished all rights to the manor and bound his heirs and successors to honour the arrangement. The charter would appear to have been a generous gesture, but it has to be said that John probably granted it under pressure from the Crown.

Assuming that John was responsible for rebuilding Sweyneshe Castle in stone, it follows that he would have required a considerable sum of money to pay for the work. Unfortunately, there is nothing in the records relating to his fiscal affairs other than his seizure of the manor of Bishopston and his grant – or rather his alienation – of two manors to Morgan Gam. Nearly 90 years after John's death an inquisition (inquiry) was made into the number of alienations that had been effected in Gower by the de Breos family. An alienation was an illegal sale or transfer of demesne; that is, land which formed part of the lord's personal estate. With regard to Gower, the lordship was held of the king; to dispose of any part of the demesne it was, therefore, necessary to obtain the king's permission. The grant to Morgan Gam is the only alienation that is known to have been effected by John, but both John's son and grandson were involved in numerous alienations and it is likely that the one connected with John was only one of many.

The hunting preserve known as Parc le Breos was in existence by 1230 because, in a confirmatory charter of Bishop Gervase (1215-30) to Neath Abbey it was referred to as 'Silva de Bruiz' (Woods of Breos). It is possible that John's grandfather, William de Breos III, was responsible for the park's creation, but John is the more likely creator because, for six years (1220-26), Gower was his only residence and it would, therefore, seem probable that he created the deer park for his own pleasurable pursuit. The park covered some 2,000 acres and appears to have been carved out of the parishes of Penmaen, Llanrhidian and Ilston. The Church and, therefore, the manor of Ilston was evidently in John's hands prior to 1230 because, in Bishop Anselm's confirmatory charter to the Hospitaller, dated 1230, it was recorded that John had granted the church to the said order. The manor of Llanrhidian at that time belonged to Morgan Gam, and it is possible that a portion of the manor was absorbed into the park in exchange for the manors of Leason and Kittle.

As to Penmaen, the bounds of this parish were once the bounds of the fief bearing the same name. In 1166 the fief had belonged to the Hareng family, and they continued to hold it until a member of the family was ousted during the war with Llywelyn. It was not until long after John's death that one Philip Hareng was restored to the fief on the orders of the King; by then, a large part of the fief had been absorbed into Parc le Breos; moreover, Philip had to suffer the ignominy of sharing what remained of the fief with a member of the Blancagnel family and they remained entrenched in Penmaen for more than a century.

There remains to be considered what relates to William de Barry, Lord of the fief of Walterston, which adjoined Parc le Breos on the west. At an unknown date during John's lordship, de Barry came to an arrangement with Neath Abbey, exchanging his fief for 100 acres of the Abbey's land in Somerset. Why de Barry should have done this is a mystery. Perhaps, like free tenants some 60 years later, he preferred not to live under the lordship of a de Breos.

When John died in 1232 his son and heir, William, was still a minor, aged about twelve and, for nine years thereafter, Bramber, Gower and Tetbury were in the hands of custodians for the Crown, the first of whom, Philip de Bret, took charge of Gower in July that year. It is not known exactly when, in 1241, William de Breos (VI) succeeded to the patrimony, but in the space of 50 years he proved himself to be a rogue and a spendthrift, and John's great-granddaughter, Alina (1226-31), proved equally unscrupulous, but the biggest rogue of all was John's grandson, yet another William, whose tyranny became legendary and whose shady dealings plunged the realm into civil war.

But all that is another story.[1]

---

* For a brief outline of John's descendants read *A History of Gower* by Derek Draisey. For a more detailed account of John's grandson, William, read *The People of Gower* by the same author.

CHAPTER IV
Matthew Cradock and George Herbert

Lawlessness and corruption in high places were so rife in early 16th-century Wales that the Ludlow-based law-enforcement agency, known as the Council in the Marches, could do little to alleviate the situation. Part of the problem was that there were too many Marcher lordships, which made it easy for felons to evade capture in one lordship simply by taking refuge in another; moreover, corrupt law-enforcement officers within these lordships exacerbated the situation. In 1533-4 a member of the Council, Thomas Holte, stated that murder and cattle-stealing often went unpunished because, if any gentleman or mischievous person committed murder, or was arrested for theft, they obtained a pardon by paying a fine to the officer in charge of the lordship. The felons then recovered their money by levying a *commortha* on the king's poorer subjects; that this state of affairs existed in Gower is borne out by a Sweyneshe man, Sir Matthew Cradock, who affirmed in 1524 that men 'of small substance' often demand *commortha* from their tenants to offset the cost of gifting their daughters in marriage, or for carrying out repairs to their houses, and the tenants, fearing to displease these gentlemen and their relatives and friends, gave an animal, corn or money to their own impoverishment.

Lawlessness and corruption were at their worst in territories in the possession of Henry Somerset, Earl of Worcester, who held in Wales the lordships of Raglan, Chepstow and Gower, and also had custody of Abergavenny, Brecon, Elfael, Ewias Lacy, Kerry, Magor, Montgomery, Monmouth, Ruthin, Glamorgan (the Vale of Glamorgan) and Morgannwg (the uplands of Glamorgan). The situation in Gower was so bad that, on the King's instructions, Earl Henry travelled there to apprehend certain murderers and felons, the outcome of which he summed up in a letter written in 1527.

> I have to my great cost ... endeavoured myself by the best means ... that I could to attache [apprehend] the said misdoers ... insomuch that at my last being at Gower I made pursuit after such of the said murderers as were then in the country, so nigh that they fled in their shirts from their beds to sanctuary. And the said offenders be so friended, related and favoured that ... no number of men be raised in the country where they be, but that they shall have knowledge ... to avoid. And therefore it is hard for me ... to take them.

The Earl also stated that he had charged his officers in the lordship to 'endeavour themselves' as he had and bring the felons to justice. It is, however, unlikely that the officers would have troubled themselves further once the Earl had departed. Indeed, the man responsible for law and order in Gower, George Herbert, would appear to have been more concerned in feathering his nest than enforcing the law; this is borne out by the king's attorney, Thomas Holte, who stated in 1532-3 that:

> George Herbert … steward of Gower … did take a young man … of the age of 16 years … a rich man's son dwelling thereby, and laid to his charge that [he] had stolen certain shipe [sheep?] from his own father, which his father utterly denied, and yet by means [threats or torture] the young man was caused to confess the felony. Upon which confession the said steward sent unto his father to bring him a great sum of money or else his son would be hanged. Whereupon his father complained to the Council in the Marches and … thereupon the Council awarded the King's letter to the said George Herbert, commanding him to respite the execution till the matter were examined before them. Upon which letter the said George would not appear before the Council, but … caused the young man to be hanged. And as the father informed the Council he [threatened] to hang him [as well] if he may take him.

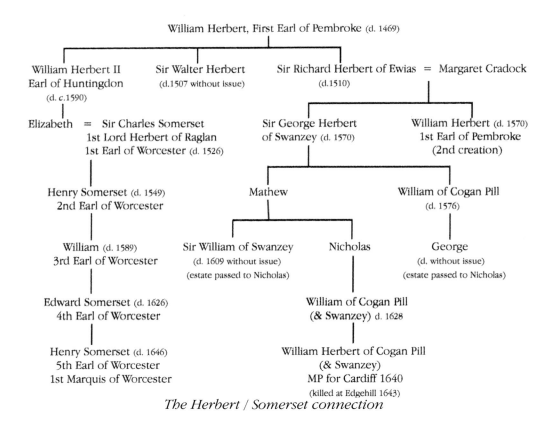

The Herbert / Somerset connection

It is generally accepted that George Herbert was born in *c.*1500, possibly two or three years earlier. He was the eldest son of Sir Richard Herbert of Ewias and Margaret Cradock of Sweyneshe. Sir Richard was an illegitimate son of William Herbert of Raglan (d. 1469). Illegitimacy, however, did not prevent Richard from making good, for he became a gentleman usher of King Henry VII, was knighted, appointed Constable and Porter of Abergavenny Castle in 1497, and Approver and Receiver of the Lordship of Abergavenny in 1507. Richard undoubtedly held land, which apparently passed to his son, George, because a document dated 1545 shows that George held property valued in total at £14 in the lordships of Llanfair, Ewias and Crickhowell, as well as in the town and surrounding area of Abergavenny. Sir Richard died 12th September 1510 and his tomb in Abergavenny Church carries an effigy of him, his wife, Margaret, and their four children – three boys and a girl. Sir Richard may have been a middling sort of gentleman, content to live out his life on the Welsh border with Herefordshire, but the rest of George's paternal relatives – bar one – were an exceptional breed.

The Herberts of Raglan

George's paternal grandfather, William Herbert of Raglan, had been pre-eminent among the Welsh gentry for his part in the War of the Roses (the red rose represented the house of York; the white rose that of the house of Lancaster). In March 1461, William had fought at the Battle of Towton, which resulted in the deposition of the insane Lancastrian king, Henry VI, and the crowning of the Yorkist, Edward IV. As a reward for his services William was appointed Justiciar and Chamberlain of South Wales; as such it fell to him to subdue Lancastrian supporters in West Wales, which he effected within a matter of months, except for Harlech Castle, the garrison of which held out for more than seven years until forced to surrender through starvation, a feat immortalized by the song 'Men of Harlech'. Shortly after Harlech fell in August 1468, William reached the peak of his career – custodian of up to 20 lordships, Lord of Chepstow and Gower, Earl of Pembroke, Justiciar and Chamberlain of both North and South Wales.

When the Earl of Warwick (the 'King-maker') led a rebellion against Edward IV in 1469, William raised a force of at least 6,000 Welshmen – possibly 13,000 – in support of the Yorkist King. At the Battle of Edgecote (Banbury) in July, William led his men into a fight that lasted several hours. When the fighting came to an end, about 5,000 Welshmen lay dead; others had been captured, including William who was beheaded two days later.

William's eldest son, William Herbert II, did not attain majority until 1475 and, due to his inadequacy, was soon forced to accept a degrading change in circumstances, being relieved of the earldom of Pembroke and all the lands that his father had acquired. He was compensated with a dozen manors and the meaningless title of Earl of Huntingdon. In short, William II was not a chip off the old block – but his younger brother, Walter, was.

When the Lancastrian claimant to the throne, Henry Tudor, landed in Milford Haven in 1485, his 2,000 French, Breton and Welsh troops were alarmed by a rumour that Sir Walter Herbert, Steward of Gower, was laying in wait for them at Carmarthen with a large army. The alarm of his troops may have been the reason why Henry Tudor took a circuitous route up through Cardiganshire and across mid-Wales to Shrewsbury before moving on to Market Bosworth where, with an army enlarged by Welsh and English supporters, he defeated the Yorkist, King Richard III. Henry – who became King Henry VII – married Elizabeth of York, daughter of Edward IV (d. 1483) and so the houses of York and Lancaster were united, bringing the War of the Roses to an end.

Although the Herbert 'clan' had become surprisingly numerous by 1510, both as a result of legitimate and illegitimate offspring, only one other Herbert need be considered here – Elizabeth, daughter and heiress of William II. After William II's death in c.1490, Elizabeth tried to claim the lordships in Wales that her father had managed to recover before his demise, lands which for the most part her uncle, Sir Walter Herbert, had since taken as his own. As a result of her marriage to Sir Charles Somerset, a relative of Henry Tudor, a settlement was reached with Sir Walter Herbert that resulted, in time, in all the Herbert lands passing to Sir Charles Somerset. In 1514, Sir Charles was created First Earl of Worcester, and when he died in 1526 he was succeeded by his son and heir, Henry, whom he had by Elizabeth. George Herbert, therefore, not only descended from a family of renown on his father's side, but he was also related to the earls of Worcester through his first cousin, Elizabeth. There were no peers on his mother's side of the family, but it was, nevertheless, a family of wealth and influence.

The Cradocks of Sweyneshe

George's mother, Margaret, daughter of Matthew Cradock of Sweyneshe, had no children by her first husband John Malefant of St. George's Castle, who apparently died young and childless between July 1493 and December 1495. Sometime after the death of her second husband, Sir Richard Herbert, in 1510, she married Sir William Bawdripp of Penmark. Margaret was still alive in 1531; the year of her death is unknown. It was from his mother's side of the family that George acquired most of his wealth and influence. Virtually nothing is known of George's early years, but the fact that he succeeded his grandfather, Matthew Cradock, in numerous offices and in the ownership of certain property makes it worthwhile to consider their commonality. Where the two men differed was in their temperament. Matthew Cradock appears to have been an astute businessman and an able administrator, whereas George Herbert was a corrupt, hot-tempered blackguard.

Matthew Cradock was a well-to-do Sweyneshe burgess who, in his will, claimed descent from Einion ap Collwyn, a somewhat legendary figure who is said to have aided the Normans in their conquest of Glamorgan in the 1190s. Matthew could certainly claim descent from Jevan ap Cradock Vreichfras, a Sweyneshe burgess who, in 1400, was recorded as the holder of one whole and two half burgages and who was

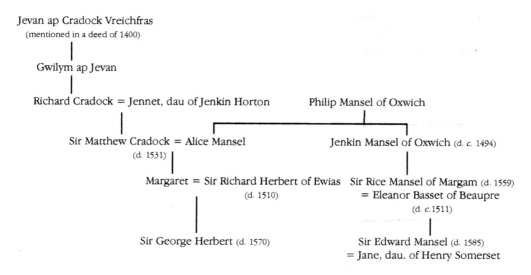

The Cradock / Mansel connection

reputed to have earned a reputation for killing a huge, wild boar in the forests of Clyne. Jevan had four sons, one of whom, Gwilym, had two sons, Rhys and Richard, both of whom adopted Cradock as their surname.

Richard Cradock married Jennet, daughter and heiress of Jenkin Horton of Candleston Castle near Ogmore, who also held Llandough and Horton (in Gower), and it was through this marriage that a compact group of burgages in Sweyneshe (which later became known as The Plas) passed to the Cradock family. Richard and Jennet had at least two sons and three daughters, the eldest son being Matthew, born in *c*.1468 according to most authorities, although there is evidence to suggest that he may have been born at least six years earlier. As a boy Matthew would have known his surroundings well.

The Castle Overlooking the Town

In Matthew's time Sweyneshe was quite small, consisting of less than 180 house-holders (*familiae*), most of them living in homes that radiated from the high ground centred on modern-day Castle Street where, to the east, stood the ruins of the 'Old [stone] Castle' and the 'New Castle' that was built *c*.1300 (the ruins of which can be seen today). One of the most prominent features of the 'New Castle', then as now, is the half-round tower that overlooks what is today called Castle Square. The tower contains at least two garderobes (dry toilet chutes) and a stairway to the wall walk. To the east, overlooking Castle Lane, is the south block, the ground floor occupied by stone-vaulted service rooms. Access to the first-floor hall from the courtyard was orig-inally by way of an external stone stairway, which no longer exists (the present stair turret is a later addition). A cross-passage separated the hall from two service rooms

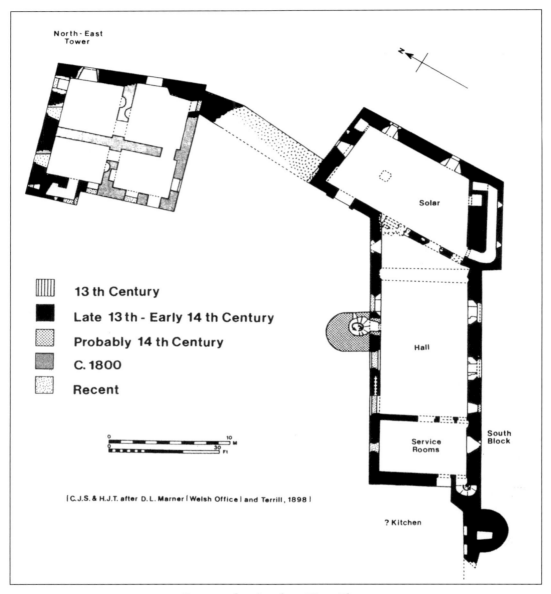

North-East
Tower

||||| 13 th Century

Late 13 th - Early 14 th Century

Probably 14 th Century

C. 1800

Recent

Solar

Hall

Service
Rooms

South
Block

? Kitchen

[C.J.S. & H.J.T. after D.L. Marner (Welsh Office) and Terrill, 1898]

Sweyneshe Castle – First Floor

(one above the other) and the kitchen, which no longer exists. When the lord was in residence, the hall (open to the rafters) was where he and his entourage dined, where he conducted his business and where his entourage slept.

The east wing of the south block, which overlooks the Strand, contained a first-floor solar (private quarters for the lord) and a passageway in one wall led to the lord's personal garderobe. The east curtain wall (little of which is now original) extends

The New Sweyneshe Castle as seen from the south

northwards from the east wing to a large, square tower that is often referred to as the 'North-East Tower'. The lower part of this tower is original, whereas much of the first floor was rebuilt in the 18th century to serve as a debtors' prison. The north curtain wall (which no longer exists) extended westwards from the square tower. This wall was 2m. thick and 6m. high, with a parapet above it. A passageway was incorporated in the thickness of the wall at 'the level of the first floor of the adjoining [North-East] tower'. Lean-tos extended into the courtyard from the inner face of the north curtain wall. Flanked by D-shaped towers, the gateway may have occupied a position at the north-west corner of the 'New Castle', a view supported by the fact that, in later documents, a location known as the 'New Postern' (entrance) can be identified as that part of Worcester Place that leads from Castle Street to what was once the Castle Cinema. A well occupied a position in the courtyard that now lies a metre below the grassy area that can be seen today.

No description of the 'New Castle' would be complete without at least a brief mention of the arcaded parapet that can be seen high up on the outside walls of the south block and the two gun-loops in the half-round tower. The arcades served no military function, but were intended to impress. They were a later addition to the 'New Castle', the work being carried out in the second quarter of the 14th century by masons who had already installed arcaded parapets at the bishop's palaces at St. David's and Lamphey. The two gun-loops that appear as circular holes high up on the half-round tower have been dated to around 1440-80, and may be attributable to the first William Herbert, who held Gower between 1462 and 1469, and whose castle at Raglan has similar gun-loops. Those at Sweyneshe were positioned to enable men to align their muskets on Wind Street and on what is now Caer Street.

The 'New Castle', which may have become somewhat dilapidated in Matthew's day, still functioned as such, though fief-holders no longer did castle guard, for it had become customary for such men to make yearly payments (*scutage*) to be excused such an onerous duty. If a guard was deemed necessary, then men were hired for the task, as happened in 1526 when, on the orders of the Earl of Worcester, Matthew paid 20s. to 24 men for guarding the castles of Sweyneshe and Oystermouth for 14 days. The 'New Castle' was also used as a prison in the days of George Herbert, as evidenced by borough accounts relating to 1534, which state:

> The porter of the Castle of Sweyneshe request allowance for the table [that is, the feeding] of Ieuan ap Johann ap Ieuan Gwynn for 26 days, who was hanged on the 22nd of April 1534.

Accounts for the same year refer to payments for cleaning the castle stables 'against my lord's coming', meaning in preparation for a visit by Henry, Earl of Worcester. There is also a reference in the accounts for 1537 to repairs to the castle, which includes making windows.

The Cradock's Tenement

Both castles originally stood within a fortified enclosure known as the Outer Bailey. The stone walls of the Outer Bailey (and no doubt the surrounding ditch) were certainly in existence by the mid-13th century, as were the north and south gates with their adjoining D-shaped towers, and also the wall towers known as 'Donelstour' and the one 'which formerly was Thomas de Singleton's', as they are all mentioned in a document relating to the 13th and early 14th centuries. By 1324 the Outer Bailey had ceased to have a military function, for in that year a John Pistor of Penmaen disposed of a piece of land within the said bailey. Several property deals relating to 1383-4 resulted in a John de Horton acquiring a compact group of 'place burgages' (plots of land) in what is now Castle Gardens, but which in 1383-4 formed the south-western corner of the Outer Bailey. These 'place burgages' passed to Richard Cradock as a result of his marriage to Jennet Horton, and it was probably here that their son Matthew Cradock lived during his formative years.

The Cradock's house – or tenement – may have been a timber-framed, hall house; that is, a hall open to the rafters with additional rooms at either end. The hall in this kind of house doubled as the family dining room and the place where male servants slept. An open hearth usually occupied a central position in the hall, the smoke finding its way out through a louvre in the roof. Alternatively, a fire might be sited centrally in one wall, in which case there would have been a stone chimney on that side of the house; directly opposite the chimney a doorway led out through a porch.

A partition at the upper end of the hall created a separate room that served as both a parlour and a master bedroom. Above the parlour there might be one or more chambers for storage or for children to sleep, being reached by way of a ladder. At the opposite end of the hall, and separated by a cross-passage, there was usually a service area comprising of either a kitchen, or two or more service rooms, one of them a buttery; the kitchen was often a separate building due to the risk of fire. Above the service rooms there might be one or more chambers for female servants.

Surviving wills give the impression that timber-framed hall houses still existed in Sweyneshe a century or so after Matthew's day, as evidenced by the will of John Moris, a wealthy burgess, which recorded that in 1608 his house comprised of a hall, parlour, seven chambers, a shop, buttery, kitchen and one cellar. One such building certainly survived into the 19th century as the Carmarthen Arms, which stood on the western side of the junction between Castle Street and College Street. A photograph taken in 1845 shows that, apart from the later additions of a dormer and a massive chimney, the Carmarthen Arms had retained its appearance as a hall-house. Alternatively, the Cradock's house – and, indeed, other houses of the well-to-do – may have been similar to one that is known to have stood close by, and is described in a document dated 1400 as:

> two cellars near the bridge of the [outer] bailey; four shops above the aforesaid cellars; two chambers above the aforesaid shops.

In 1425 the same house was described as:

> one cellar next to the bridge of the fortress, which is worth by the year [in rent] 3s. 4d., and four shops above the said cellar, which is worth by the year 4s., and two galleries above the said shops, which are worth by the year 6s.

The exact location of this house was just inside the south gate of the Outer Bailey. It was obviously owned by the burgesses, who rented out the rooms, and this was still the case in 1583 when Richard Sadler, merchant, took out a lease on

> one cellar room set and laying by the market place of Sweyneshe under the town house there adjoining on the one side onto the garden of Sir William Herbert, knight, and the street called the Market Place on the other side.

Sir William Herbert was Matthew's great-great-grandson, who inherited the compact group of 'place burgages', including the garden mentioned above. As to the 'Market Place', its location was at the top of what is now Wind Street, and it is significant that no mention was made of the 'bridge of the bailey or fortress', presumably because, by 1583, the bridge no longer existed, the ditch on that side of the Outer Bailey having been filled in. It is believed – though the records do not actually say so – that the chambers/galleries in the 'town house' were where the burgesses met to administer the borough. In Matthew's day it is possible that this 'town house' consisted of a half-timbered first floor over a stone-walled ground floor, the roof either of thatch or shingles (wooden tiles).

The Cradock tenement would not have stood alone. A 12th-century charter states that every burgess should have 'on their burgages an oven [and a] brewhouse'. There would also have been stables, possibly a barn, a granary and a dairy for fresh milk. The Cradocks would almost certainly have had a garden and possibly an orchard as well. Gardens are frequently mentioned in leases; one as early as 1383-4. An area called the Orchard is referred to in a document dated 1400; it belonged to the lords of Gower and its name has been preserved in today's Orchard Street.

A Town within Stout Walls

The Episcopal returns of 1563 record that there were 180 householders in the Sweyneshe Parish, most of them residing within the town walls, which were in existence as early as the 14th century, if not earlier. To some extent nature lent itself to the defence of the town. On the east, where the wall lined the top of an escarpment, the steep slope to the Strand provided additional protection on that side. To the south the walls were fronted by a stream known as the Cadle or Pill, which originated in the St. Helen's area. A smaller stream known as the Town Ditch afforded a degree of protection on the west, to the south of College Street, until it joined the Pill. Elsewhere man-made ditches fronted the walls, as revealed by excavations in King's Street and Whitewalls. Four town gates are known to have existed – the North Gate (at the junction of High Street and King's Street), the West Gate (at the Kingsway roundabout), the Wassail Gate (near the statue of Henry Hussey Vivian, not far from the south-west corner of St. Mary's churchyard) and the South Gate (at the bottom of Wind Street). There may also have been a gate known as the Postern, at the junction of Welcome Lane and Worcester Place, which gave access to the Strand, as well as towers at various points along the town walls.

The names of several streets within the town walls appear in documents dating to the 14th and 15th centuries – High Street, West Street (College Street), Goat Street (a little to the east of Princess Way), Market Place (at the top of Wind Street), St. Mary Street, Streetend (believed to have been the southern half of St. Mary's Square, but it could have been the northern half of the Square, one 'end' of which terminated at the town walls) and Fisher Street (extending from the western end of St. Mary Street, continuing round to the bottom of Wind Street), which was also referred to as the 'street of fishermen' in 1460. The names of other streets would have been known to Matthew, but they do not appear in documents earlier than the 17th century.

The Strand, meaning the shore of the river, refers to an area rather than a street; that is, the strip of land between the foot of the escarpment (east of the castle) and the River Tawe, where there were a number of tenements. There also appears to have been two other districts in the town, and historians have deliberated over exactly where they were. The earliest reference to one of these districts is in a document dated 1432, which records the purchase of half a burgage

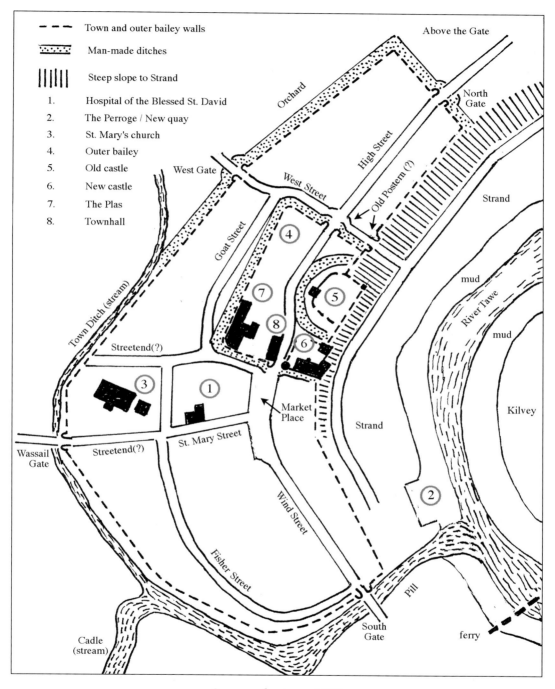

Sweyneshe in c. *1500*

lying in le denton [possibly a clerical error, which should have been 'le donton', meaning the down town, and] extending from the High Street on the southern part, up to Le Stronde [the Strand] on the northern part.

The next reference, dated 1478-9, concerns rent for land 'in the Bouteyn', often interpreted as 'Boveton', meaning 'the above town'. A bylaw of 1553 mentions 'the bove town within the north [High Street] gate', which points to 'the bove town' being centred on that part of High Street within the town walls. However, the poor-law assessment of 1663 records that in High Street there were tenements 'above the gate' and 'within the gate', which places 'Boveton' outside the town walls. It may be that 'le denton' lay outside the North Gate and that 'the Bouteyn' was originally confined to that part of High Street within the town walls until such time as 'the above town' became applicable to the whole length of High Street, both 'above the gate' and 'within the gate'.

St. Mary's Church and the Cross Keys Inn

Within the town walls there were two buildings that Matthew would have known well. The more important of the two was St. Mary's Church, which was certainly in existence in 1291, as it is mentioned in the Pope Nicholas Taxation of that year. It is possible that the appearance of St. Mary's in Matthew's day differed little from what was sketched by Thomas Dineley in 1684. Viewed from the south, Dineley's sketch shows that the tower stood separate from the main body of the church, although there are many who argue that it was not detached. Inside the main body there were at least two chapels, one of them, St. Anne's (on the north side of the chancel where the altar stood) had originally been the creation of 'John Horton the elder, one of

St. Mary's Church as sketched by Dineley in 1684

[Matthew's] ancestors [who] builded the said chapel'. In time it became known as Sir Matthew Cradock's Chapel, which Matthew 'caused to be newly builded and edified' before his death in 1531. That Matthew continued to have strong links with St. Mary's in later life is borne out by a document, dated 1549, which records that the church had four bells, one of them bearing an inscription that said Matthew had been the donator.

East of St. Mary's, on the opposite side of what in 1650 had been called Cross Street, stood the Hospital of the Blessed St. David, founded in 1332 by Henry de Gower, Bishop of St. David's. The hospital, a part of which has survived as the Cross Keys Inn, was originally intended to be an almshouse for 'priests, blind, decrepit or infirm and other religious men in the bishopric'. Six chaplains were to attend to the inmates, and to cover expenses the Bishop endowed the hospital with 13 whole or half burgages and numerous properties in Gower that amounted to 330 acres of land.

Bishop de Gower also endowed the hospital with two-thirds of the income of St. Mary's Church. This is interesting in that documentation relating to the endowment records that one of the de Breoses – William III most likely – had granted St. Mary's to the monastery of St. Taurin at Evreux in Normandy. St. Taurin already held property in Gower at that time, the most notable being the priory at Llangenydd (formerly a Welsh monastery dedicated to St. Cenydd). The prior of Llangenydd managed all the Gower properties held by St. Taurin, including St. Mary's Church. Thus St. Mary's connection with Llangenydd may be the reason why, in the early 13th century, Welsh monks referred to Sweyneshe as Seinhenydd, presumably meaning St. Cenydd. The upshot of all this was that the monastery of St. Taurin granted St. Mary's Church to Bishop Gower, and he awarded two-thirds of its income to the Hospital of the Blessed St. David.

Surviving 14th century windows in the Cross Keys Inn

The L-shaped building that now forms the southern half of the Cross Keys Inn may originally have been part of a complex built around an open courtyard. With regard to the main block, 17th-century alterations to the frontage that aligns with St. Mary Street make it impossible to visualize what the original façade looked like. Inside the main block the first floor consisted of a hall, open to the rafters, with a fireplace in the east wall, whereas the ground floor consisted of service rooms. The arrangement of having a hall on the first floor appears to have been common in town houses of 14th-century date, and signs of this arrangement can be detected in the north wing of the main block where 14th-century windows have survived in the north wall.

An Unwholesome Town

The town was far from idyllic. In 1554 it was said of Sweyneshe that:

> in times past … many beautiful houses … have been within the walls …[that are now] fallen down and decayed, lying as desolate and void grounds, and many of them adjoining right unto high streets, replenished with much odour, filth and uncleanness, with pits, cellars and vaults lying open and uncovered.

The streets were as much an eyesore as derelict houses. Despite efforts to pave or cobble thoroughfares in the 14th century, there were many streets that were little more than rutted, dirt tracks, muddy in winter, dusty in summer. Even thoroughfares that were paved were constantly in need of repair, the stones dislodged by hooves and heavily-laden carts. To make matters worse, rotting garbage, even human excrement, littered the streets, attracting rats and flies. One of the earliest bylaws on record, dated 1553, laid down:

> that no man or woman nor their servants shall [throw] no dung nor filth of their houses or streets in any place [on] the Strand side, except they cast it [outside] the marks that shall be limited to them by the Portreeve and aldermen and that no person [shall] cast any filth in the gardens in Fisher Street except [they] cast it over the bank to the …

Some streets were worse than others. In his *Itinerary* (1534-43) John Leland defined Sweyneshe as a market town – market day being Saturday – and in later borough accounts there are references to payments made to persons, mostly women, such as 'Anes Lovid for making clean the market and lane to Wind Street'.

Dung must have been everywhere, for not only did those who could afford to own horses ride through the streets, but almost everyone kept livestock. Even a labourer might own a cow, a mare and poultry, as it made sense to be self-sufficient rather than pay for eggs, milk, butter, cheese and meat (which could be preserved with the aid of smoke or salt). The storage of corn was cause for further concern, as it had to be winnowed before it could be ground, and the chaff blew everywhere; hence the by law of 1553, which laid down:

that no man or woman, nor their servants shall winnow any corn or malt in the streets; that is to say Wind Street, Fisher Street, St. Mary Street, the Market Place, the bove town within the North Gate, on pain of [a fine].

It was safer to drink ale or wine than to drink water, for another bylaw of 1553 stated:

that no woman nor servant shall wash any manner of clothes, skins, innards of beasts, or any other filth near to any winch or well in this town.

The Waterfront

By far the busiest place – and for a boy the most interesting – was the Strand. Until it was diverted to the New Cut in the 1840s, the River Tawe curved westwards from just below High Street Station to flow through what is now the Parc Tawe shops and leisure complex. At a point near Sainsbury's Store the river, then, emptied into what (in the 17th century) was called Fabian's Bay. At this point, too, a ferry boat (first mentioned in 1306) took passengers across the river (the approach to this ferry has been preserved in the street named Ferryside, near the Dylan Thomas Centre). A little further southward (near the recently constructed barrage) a ford cut across Fabian's Bay and, 'when the tide was at its lowest', carts and livestock were taken through the shallow waters.

Apart from tenements, possibly a quay called the Perroge (its location was near the building known today as Quay West) and a limited amount of shipbuilding activity, the Strand was a place where, close up, numerous vessels could be seen either afloat or lying in the mud at ebb tide. These ships, which were rarely more than 40 tons, arrived daily to pick up coal from 'coal places' on the Strand, each 'coal place' bearing the name of the coal supplier. Most ships using the harbour were not Sweyneshe-based, but came from Somerset, Devon, Cornwall and, in smaller numbers, from Jersey, Guernsey, Normandy, Brittany and south-western France; occasionally they came from Southampton, London and Ireland. Some came laden – as did the *Vincent* of Guernsey in 1499 – with wine, cards, white paper, Guernsey cloth, canvas and chamlet (a fine cloth), but the vast majority of them arrived carrying ballast only, which, from 1583 onwards, they were not allowed to dump in either the river or Fabian's Bay, as that would have eventually rendered the harbour unnavigable. Although the ordinance of 1583 was enacted long after Matthew's day, it nevertheless provides a glimpse of riverside activity, stating that:

any ... vessel arriving at the said town shall, before they go up to the Coal or Landing Place, discharge and cast upon the Perroge by the Pill ... now called the New Quay Place ... all ballast, as sand, gravel or stones ... saving so much as shall be needful for them to bear their masts. And after such [vessels] come to the Coal or Loading Place, either [they] bring so much ballast as ... be within them to the Quay, or [they] cast the same ashore ... in such safe and convenient place out of the river.

Ships owned by the Sweyneshe burgesses were less numerous, and although they participated in the coal trade, they invariably sailed with mixed cargoes, which might include lead, locally-made friezes (woollen cloth), bridgewaters (a woollen cloth originating in Bridgewater), barley, butter and calf-skins. These ships might return from ports such as la Rochelle – as did the 30-ton *Jonas of Swansey* in 1587 – with a cargo of salt, wine, tar, pitch, iron, cloth and oakum. Salt was undoubtedly the most common import from la Rochelle, but cargoes from elsewhere might include tobacco, prunes, apples, pears and brass. It is possible that Matthew's father was a merchant, for in later years Matthew had strong connections with the sea, on one occasion having overall command of several ships, the *Mathue Cradocke*, the *Anthony Cradock* and the *Mary Cradock* among them.

The Burgesses

Using calculations based on the chantry returns of 1545-6, it has been estimated that 900-1,000 souls were in the care of the vicar of St. Mary's Church at that time. The figure in Matthew's childhood days may have been somewhat smaller, and it has to be said that not all those in the vicar's care resided in the town. Furthermore, only a small percentage of the total were actually burgesses. It has been estimated that, in 1583, there were only 79 burgesses – all of them men – and that at a time when the number of souls in the vicar's care would certainly have been at least 1,000.

In the 12th century, when Welsh attacks were a frequent occurrence, it was necessary for the Anglo-Norman lords of Gower to offer an inducement to traders and artisans to settle outside the castle walls, initially to service the garrison's needs. One lord, William de Newburgh, Earl of Warwick, found it necessary to issue a charter to the burgesses, confirming their existing privileges and possibly granting new ones as well. In this charter, dated *c.* 1170, Earl William confirmed 'to every burgess' the right to 'a burgage' on which to build a tenement, 'an oven, brewhouse' and other outbuildings – providing they paid him 'each year, a rent of twelve pence'. The ownership of a burgage freed the burgesses from manorial obligations such as tilling the lord's land (serfdom) and castle guard (the obligation of fief-holders). Thus they were free to practise a craft, open a shop or engage in mercantile activity.

By Matthew's day the burgesses still paid the 'burgage shilling', or a portion thereof as many burgages had been reduced to half or quarter burgages, possibly as a result of division among heirs; moreover, a wealthy burgess, such as Matthew's father, might own several whole or part burgages. It also becomes clear that in Matthew's day there were four avenues to the freedom of the borough: by birth (which applied to Matthew as he was the son of a burgess), by marriage (which applied to George Herbert as he married Matthew's daughter), by apprenticeship (that is, if a son of a non-burgess agreed to learn a trade from a burgess, he would become one of the elite after completing a lengthy apprenticeship) and finally by gift (that is, a non-burgess might be admitted to the freedom as a special favour).

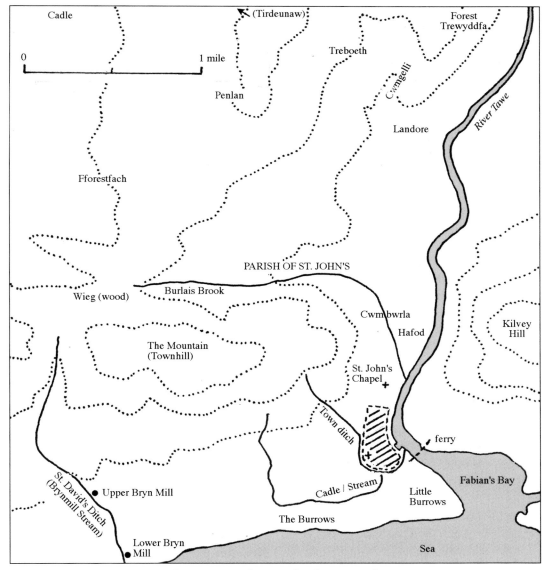

The manor / borough of Sweyneshe

With burgesship went privileges, such as the right to 'farm' (take out a lease on) anything that belonged to the lord, or formed part of the collective property of the burgesses, such as a weir, a room for storage in the 'town house', the ferryboat and passage, or one of the two corn and malt mills that were sited adjacent to the Brynmill Stream. These two mills were referred to in a document of 1423 as the 'two water mills called Brynmylles', which prior to their demise in the 19th century were known as the Upper and Lower Bryn Mills. For properties such as these the burgesses paid a fixed rent and then endeavoured to make a profit on their investment. In 1478-9 Matthew's uncle, Rhys ap Gwilym, in partnership with two other burgesses, farmed 'the Pole and the Ford'.

Another important privilege was the right to pasture animals on land within the borough, which extended far beyond the town walls. The bounds of the borough had been established in the 12th century. The River Tawe formed the boundary on the east as far inland as the confluence of the Burlais Brook, after which it ran in a north-westerly direction, following the Burlais Brook (now culverted) along the Upper Strand and Cwm Road to Cwmbwrla, and continuing roughly in line with Heol y Gors until it reached the 'Weig' (wood) at Cockett; from there the boundary ran south, following 'St. David's Ditch' (now the Brynmill Stream) which flowed down the valley below Hill House Hospital, through Sketty and Singleton Park until it reached the sea near the bottom of Brynmill Lane.

Borough land consisted of:

(1) the sandy lowlands known as the 'Burrows' (now the Sandfields), extending from the Tawe to the Brynmill Stream and
(2) the upland grazing area that was often referred to as 'the mountain', which extended from 'Pantygwidr' in the south to the 'Weig' near Cockett, and from there over Townhill to what was then 'St. John's Church' (now St. Matthews, opposite the Tax Office in High Street). 'The mountain', also known as 'Craig Lwyd' and 'Kevin Coed,' was in Matthew's day covered in brush and gorse, with denser woodland near brooks and streams.

Undoubtedly, the best privileges were to do with trading. Burgesses were exempt from paying tolls for quayage, wharfage and market dues; nor did they pay tolls on any goods which they brought into the town, either by land or sea. Tolls were levied on non-burgesses; moreover, a bylaw of 1553 stipulated that foreign merchants were not permitted to sell their wares to anyone other than burgesses for a period of 15 days, after which the merchants were free to sell to non-burgesses. Two years later (1555), a new bylaw stipulated that all merchandise brought in by sea – with the exception of perishables – should be conveyed immediately to the town house, there to remain until a third part had been disposed of among the burgesses.

Occupations

While some burgesses sold coal, or engaged in miscellaneous shipping ventures, the majority were involved in other forms of business activities. A considerable number were occupied in the clothing industry, some running fulling mills outside the town, others making a living as dyers, tuckers, hatters and felt-makers. Smaller numbers were engaged in the leather industry as tanners, shoemakers, glovers and the like, all of whom appear to have had more apprentices than other traders. The glovers were well established, having their own chapel in St. Mary's Church. Other burgesses traded as butchers, bakers, fishmongers, innkeepers, shopkeepers and joiners – the list of occupations is too lengthy to enumerate in full.

It would appear that in Matthew's day the burgesses and their families constituted almost half the population of the town. Of the other half a varying number were 'chensers' – men who for a fee were permitted to trade in the town, but were excluded from the privileges of the burgesses. There were 46 chensers in a document of 1400, their occupations unstated, but the 10 chensers recorded in 1642 included a weaver, a tanner, a cooper, a glover and a tailor. As to the remaining population there were an unrecorded number of apprentices, many of them former orphans or the sons of poor parents. There were also a great many servants who, like the apprentices, were incorporated into the households of the well-to-do. There must also have been a considerable number of mariners – some of whom had families residing in the town – as well as a few labourers, colliers, iron-workers and yeomen.

The Welsh in Sweyneshe

In the 12th century the population of Sweyneshe would have consisted of Anglo-Normans, Danes, Saxons and possibly Flemings. By the early 13th century the descendants of these people would have regarded themselves as English, even though some of them still spoke Norman-French. The people who were excluded from the town were the Welsh: they were not to be trusted; they were the ones who periodically attacked the town, sometimes burning it to the ground. The rules of exclusion may have become somewhat relaxed during the time of John de Breos (1220-32). This was certainly the case after John's death, for in 1233 two Sweyneshe bailiffs with apparently Welsh names were pardoned for their part in a revolt against King Henry III.

During the time of John's son, William de Breos VI (1241-90), a William ab Ithel was permitted to purchase the south gate of the Outer Bailey for 6d. Then, in the time of John's grandson, William de Breos VII, a man bearing a Welsh name, John Iweyn (Owain), was granted:

> all the lands and tenements which formerly belonged to Thomas de Singleton in the [outer] bailey ... to be held ... as an entire burgage with customs and rights belonging to the burgesses of the town.

In short, John Iweyn became a burgess by gift. Both William ab Ithel and John Iweyn may have been just two of a small minority of Welshmen who were favoured by the de Breoses, but their numbers were to grow in the 14th and 15th centuries for several reasons.

For a start, Welsh independence had finally been extinguished in 1283, although there were several serious revolts over the next 30 years. The last of these revolts took place at a time when the population of both England and Wales suffered as a result of a severe famine. Then the Black Death made its first appearance in

Wales in the spring of 1349, to return with diminishing severity on no less than nine occasions over the next 70 years. On each of these occasions the population of rat-infested ports such as Sweyneshe must have suffered an appalling loss of life. The dearth may have, to some extent, been rectified by occasional entries into the town of English immigrants, but there was also an influx of Welsh as well, so much so that a document dated 1400 records the names of 63 men who held burgages in certain streets, eight of whom had unmistakable Welsh names such as Jevan ap Cradock, and several more bore names that had a Welsh connection such as Thomas Maredith. There must also have been many Welsh non-burgesses – sailors, servants and the like. By Matthew's day it is likely that half the population were Welsh, the Cradocks being a particularly numerous 'clan'.

The Corporation

To some extent Sweyneshe was administered by an oligarchy – a privileged body consisting of a portreeve, 12 aldermen and the burgess body, which collectively became known at a later date as the Corporation. Several times a year the Corporation met (in Common Hall) in the 'town house' to consider aspects of borough administration. On two occasions – on 1st May and 29th September – the Corporation came together at court leets to admit new burgesses to the freedom and to choose the borough officers from amongst the burgess body. In George Herbert's day the number of borough officers was considerable, their duties ranging from guardians of the market to common attorneys (borough treasurers). Once selected, any burgess who refused to take the oath of office, or who failed to carry out the duties imposed upon him, was immediately disfranchised – removed from the freedom of the borough.

To avoid the disruption caused by having too many Common Hall meetings, the affairs of the borough were, for the most part, placed in the hands of 12 aldermen, who were chosen from among the burgess body by 'most of voice' at Common Hall. Aldermen were usually wealthy and influential burgesses, and unless they failed in what was expected of them, they held office for life. Exactly when the aldermanic council originated is unknown, but a bylaw of 1569 states that 'the custom and usage' of having a council to make 'laws and ordinances for the well government' of the town existed 'long before time of memory' and must, therefore, have existed in Matthew's day; moreover, the fact that Matthew's father was a wealthy burgess is reason to assume that he had been an alderman.

The earliest reference to the chief officer of the borough is in a deed dated *c.* 1200, his title then being *preposito ville de Sweynes*. By 1306 his title had changed to that of portreeve. In Matthew's lifetime the portreeve held office from Michaelmas (29th September) to the same day the following year. During his year in office it was the portreeve's responsibility to preside over the Common Hall and the aldermanic council, and to impose fines on anyone in breach of borough ordinances. The names of only six portreeves are known from documents relevant to Matthew's lifetime, one of them a relative, John Cradock.

It was the portreeve's responsibility to collect all money in the form of burgage shillings, rents from leases, fines and tallages (taxes) that were due to the lord of Gower. It was also the portreeve's responsibility, at the end of his year in office, to compile an account of all money collected and, with the said money, hand it over to the lord's receiver. Few of these early accounts have survived, that of John Cradock, Portreeve 1478-9, being one of them. Had it not been for the chance survival of this particular account, then John Cradock's term in office would have been lost to historians. It is, therefore, likely that Matthew's father, Richard, may also have been elected Portreeve, perhaps more than once, because the office was usually occupied by men who were regarded as either gentry or prosperous merchants, and Matthew's father appears to have qualified on both counts.

Under the Lord's Control

It may appear that governance of the town – at least as far as the burgesses were concerned – was surprisingly democratic, but the reality was that the borough was synonymous with the Manor of Sweyneshe; it was the lord's demesne; it was his personal property. Any privileges the burgesses had were dependent on the lord's good will; in return the lord had every reason to expect what was due to him – the burgage shillings, rents on leased property, tolls on market and fairs, assizes of ale and fines levied in his courts. In short, the Manor of Sweyneshe was a valuable source of income to the lord. It was, therefore, imperative that a non-resident lord appointed a steward (*seneschal*) to safeguard his interests in Sweyneshe and in the Lordship of Gower as a whole.

With regard to Sweyneshe, the steward presided over the lord's court leet, which enabled him to have the final word on all issues relevant to the borough. Until 1569, for example, it was necessary to obtain the steward's permission before any bylaw could be put into effect. When it came to selecting a new portreeve 'the whole burgess body … assembled together and chose by most of voice two of the 12 aldermen … to be portreeve' and the steward chose one. In short, it was the steward's decision that prevailed, and this form of selection probably applied to who should be admitted to the freedom, who should be appointed aldermen, and who would be sworn in as borough officials. It was, therefore, not a wise move to get on the wrong side of the steward.

Apart from upholding the lord's interests, the steward was responsible for administering justice in the lord's manorial courts (as at Oystermouth and Pennard), in the hundred or borough court at Sweyneshe (which was reserved for the burgesses) and in the three county courts of the lordship (which dealt with serious offences such as murder). The county courts – which, presumably, were all held in the Shirehall in Sweyneshe – differed in that one dealt with offences committed in the Englishry, another with offences committed in the Welshry, and the third dealt with offences committed in the Lordship of Kilvey. In the mid-13th century, possession of

Kilvey had passed from the descendants of Morgan Gam to the lords of Gower, and they continued to regard the acquisition as a separate entity; hence the designation 'Lordship of Gower and Kilvey'.

As a result of his many administrative duties the steward – not the lord – was the man who actually held sway over Sweyneshe and the Lordship of Gower and Kilvey, and this was to be the destiny of both Matthew Cradock and his grandson, George Herbert.

Men of Harlech

Men of Harlech, march to glory,
Victory is hovering o'er ye,
Bright-eyed freedon stands before ye,
Hear ye not her call?
At your sloth she seems to wonder,
Rend the sluggish bonds asunder,
Let the war-cry's deafening thunder,
Ev'ry foe apal.

Echoes loudly waking,
Hill and valley shaking,
'Till the sounds spreads wide around,
The Saxon's courage breaking,
Your foes on ev'ry side assailing,
Forward press with heart unfailing,
Till invaders learn with quailing,
Cambria ne'er can yield.

Thou who noble Cambria,
Know that freedom's cause is strongest,
Freedom's courage lasts the longest,
Ending but with death!
Freedom countless hosts can scatter,
Freedom stoutest mail can shatter,
Freeom thickest walls can batter,
Fate is in her breadth.

See they now are flying!
Dead are heap'd with dying!
Over might hath triumph'd right,
Our land to foes denying;
Upon their soil we never sought them,
Love of conquest hither brought them,
But this lesson we have taught them,
Cambria never yield!

CHAPTER V
Sir Matthew Cradock

The *Calendar of Patent Rolls* has an entry, dated 5 June 1483, which records a

> Commission to Thomas Fulford, knight ... and the sheriffs of Somerset and Devon to enquire into the complaint of Hervey Mathewe, master and owner of three parts of a ship called la Julyan of ... Brittany, and Nicholas Flymyng ... proprietor ... of the fourth part, that when divers merchants of Bridgwater had freighted the said ship ... at Luxburn in Portugal to take to Bridgwater, and on 10th May last it was lying at anchor off Ilfracome [when] one Matthew Cradock of Swansey in Wales, captain of a ship of war of the realm ... at the instigation of William Guyon and Maurice Abeynon of Ilfracombe, with other pirates entered into it and carried off gold, harness, wine, cords, mangonels, habiliments and other stuff to the value of 50 marks and put them and the ship to ransom for £50 for the payment of which the said Hervey and Nicholas were compelled to hand over the ship in pledge to certain merchants of Bridgwater, contrary to the ... truces between the King [of England] and ... the Duke of Brittany, and to cause restitution to be made and to arrest the offenders and bring them before the King and council.

The Bretons, Hervey and Nicholas, had every right to complain of piracy as England and France were not at war in 1483. It is, however, unlikely that any action would have been taken against Matthew and the 'other pirates' because

(1) the complainants were Bretons, and
(2) the incident may have had the tacit approval of the Yorkist, Richard, Duke of Gloucester and – since the death of his brother, King Edward IV – Protector of the Realm during the minority of Edward IV's two sons.

On 26th June, Richard usurped the throne to become King Richard III (the two young princes were incarcerated in the Tower and subsequently murdered). Then, in October, the exiled Lancastrian, Henry Tudor, set sail with 5,000 Bretons and 15 ships provided by the Duke of Brittany to lay claim to the English throne. The expedition, however, was aborted.

The piracy of 1483 raises the question of Matthew's age. If he had been born in *c*.1468 as is claimed, he would have been aged 15 in 1483, too young to have been 'captain of a ship of war of the realm'. It is for this reason that it would be better to accept *c*.1462 as the year of his birth. There is also the question of whether he was a Yorkist. In March 1486 (six months after Henry Tudor became King), Matthew was granted for life the offices of Constable of the castles of Caerphilly and Kenfig. One eminent historian has suggested that the grant was in line with Henry Tudor's policy of conciliating the Yorkists, and of winning over, by means of offices and emoluments, those among them likely to prove useful and amenable.

In 1488 Matthew leased Cogan Pill, near Cardiff, evidence that not only had his father died by the time of the deed, but that he had succeeded to his inheritance. The following year he is said to have married Alice, daughter of Philip Mansel of Oxwich Castle and Mabel, daughter of Griffith ap Nicholas of Dynefwr Castle, near Llandeilo. A staunch Lancastrian, Philip Mansel was the wealthiest and most influential of the Gower gentry, holding more fiefs than anyone else. Virtually nothing is known of Philip's daughter, Alice, other than that she gave birth to Matthew's only child, Margaret.

Steward of Gower

On 7th July 1491, Matthew was one of several men commissioned to raise a force from the lordships of Bishop Castle, Cardiff, Glamorgan, Morgannwg, Monmouth, Gower, Ilande, Usk and Caerleon against a threatened invasion by the King of France, and to raise and equip an expeditionary force to campaign in French territory. That same year, according to the Revd. J.M. Traherne (1860), he

> held the office of Steward of Gower (and Kilvey) ... the following year Sir Morgan de Kidwelly succeeded him as Steward of Gower ... Matthew resumed that office in 1497.

Sir Morgan de Kidwelly was definitely Steward of Gower in 1495, which to some extent supports the Revd. Traherne's statement above. A more recent authority maintains that Matthew was both Receiver and Steward of Gower from at least 1498 onwards. Matthew was certainly Steward in 1524 because, in that year, he testified as such in a dispute between the Lord of Gower, Charles Somerset, and certain tenants of the said lordship. Whether Matthew actually resumed the post in 1497 and held it, without interruption until 1526, is an issue that cannot be taken for granted.

During the time that he was Steward of Gower and Kilvey, Matthew held several other posts simultaneously. He was definitely Receiver of Gower in 1520, as he compiled the Receiver's account for that year. As Receiver he was accountable for all revenues that were due to the lord and, after deducting expenses such as the fees due to various officers, he was responsible for delivering the remaining revenue to the lord. In all probability Matthew was also Constable of Sweyneshe Castle, being responsible for the castle and its contents, including any prisoners in its gaol. He no doubt also held the office of chancellor, being responsible for issuing writs. As Steward he could claim a fee of £10, and £3 6s. 8d. for each of the other three offices – in total he could claim in fees £20 per annum.

The New Place

It is generally accepted that in the 1490s Matthew built – or rebuilt – the manor house that he referred to in his will as 'my new Place at Swainsey', which later became known as The Plas. The main block of The Plas is shaded in black on the plan. On the north face of the main block a porchway gave access to a cross-passage, to the east of which lay the hall, open to the rafters, with a large window and a fireplace on the north wall. Attached to the north-eastern corner of the hall stood a three-storeyed tower, the upper floors gained by way of a stair turret at the back of the hall chimney. West of the cross-passage there were service rooms on the ground floor, a great chamber on the first floor.

West of the main block lay the north and south wings (both hatched on the plan). The north wing enclosed the western side of a courtyard. To the north a wall with arched openings (not shown on the plan) separated the courtyard from the 'new gardens and a stable'. A gatehouse, flanked by outbuildings, occupied the eastern side of the courtyard, providing access to what was then Castle Bailey Street. A plaque above the gateway displayed Cradock's arms, which included three boars' heads, one

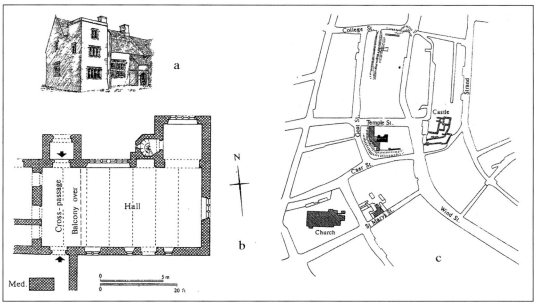

The Plas
a – as viewed from the north-east.   b– a plan of the ground floor.
c– its location in relation to ditches exposed by excavation

of them impaled with a sword, possibly a reminder of the huge boar killed by Matthew's ancestor, Jevan ap Cradock. It is unfortunate that when the gatehouse was demolished in *c*.1800 to make way for Temple Street (now a pedestrian way on the north side of Castle Gardens) no one troubled to sketch it for posterity. South of the main block the courtyard was enclosed by a wall with a wall-walk (probably a surviving section of the Outer Bailey wall) that led to an unusual octagonal tower. An orchard existed in the vicinity of the octagonal tower.

In his will Matthew referred to The Plas as his 'capital messuage' (a messuage being land with a dwelling on it). Prior to 1509, and after 1526 The Plas was undoubtedly his chief residence, a place where he conducted business and entertained men of means. Bards frequented The Plas, one of them, Iorwerth Fynglywyd (*fl.* 1500-25) and another, Rhys Brydydd, praised Matthew for his generous patronage of the bards, his valour and his hospitality.

Matthew was, without doubt, a wealthy landowner and his income increased dramatically following the death of his brother-in-law, Jenkyn Mansel of Oxwich Castle, in or soon after 1494. Jenkyn's eldest son, Rice, born 1487, was only a child at the time, and Matthew became both Rice's guardian and 'warden of the lands and tenements' of the Mansel estate. As warden, Matthew was entitled to pocket all profits from the estate until such time as Rice became of age at 21. It was also Matthew's responsibility to choose, as his brother-in-law would have done, a wife for Rice, and in 1502 he secured the marriage of Eleanor Basset, sole heiress of the late James Basset of Beaupre in Glamorgan. When the marriage took place nine years later, Eleanor's inheritance enlarged the Mansel estate.

That Rice proved a trusted member of the Cradock household is evidenced by the fact that in 1509 he had charge of two ships, the *Anthony Cradock* and the *Mary Cradock*; he was captain of the latter. However, two years after Rice reached maturity in 1508 the Lord of Gower, Charles Somerset, found it necessary to enquire about Rice's age, with the result that at an

> Inquisition taken at Sweyneshe … before Thomas ap Meurig, Coroner … in the presence of Matthew Cradock, esquire, warden of the lands and tenements of Rice Mansel, by oath of Jenkyn Franckelen and others … it is found that the aforesaid Rice was born at Oxwich on St. Paul's Day [25th January], 2nd [year of the reign of] Henry VII [1487] and that he came full of age on 25th January last past … Dated 26th April, 2nd Henry VIII [1510].

Deputy to Sir Charles Somerset

William Herbert II had died in possession of Gower; the lordship had then passed to his daughter, Elizabeth. When Elizabeth married Sir Charles Somerset in June 1492 her husband became Lord of Gower and, therefore, Matthew's lord and master. Matthew may not have been Steward of Gower during the early years of Sir Charles's tenure, but there are hints – questionable though they are – that from 1496 onwards Matthew was acting as Sir Charles's Deputy in matters pertaining to leases in the neighbouring lordship of Glamorgan, which at that time was Crown property. Matthew's position in authority improved in 1509, for in that year Sir Charles was appointed Sheriff of Glamorgan and Steward of Morgannwg. That is not to say Sir Charles carried out the duties relating to these offices – he simply pocketed the fees and appointed a deputy to do the work for him, and the Deputy was Matthew. That same year Matthew became the King's Receiver in both lordships, a post he held until 1524.

In order to carry out his responsibilities in Glamorgan and Morgannwg, it is likely that between 1509 and 1526 there were periods when Matthew did not reside at The Plas, which would explain why, for example, he refers to himself in 1515 as 'of Cardiff'. One may wonder how he coped with so many offices, but whereas he was Sir Charles's Deputy in Glamorgan, Morgannwg and Gower, so too would he have had his own deputies, as in Gower where the post of deputy-steward was well established. Nepotism and the fact that Rice Mansel appears to be working alongside Matthew in a dispute of 1524 are reasons to believe that Rice may have been Deputy-steward at that time.

Whatever Matthew's official status may have been prior to 1509, in 1504 he was pardoned of outlawry, meaning that he had failed to appear when summoned to court on three consecutive occasions and had, therefore been placed outside the law. The *Calendar of Patent Rolls* record that on

> February 6 … Matthewe Cradocke of London, alias of Swaynesey … alias of Sudeley, Co. Gloucester, gentleman, for not appearing before the above Thomas Brian and his fellows to answer Richard Gowele, citizen and mercer of London, touching a debt of 10 marks, and William Hody, knight, touching a trespass committed by him and John Seynaubyn of Chilton Tryvet, Co. Gloucester.

In 1213-14 England was at war with France. Both Matthew and Sir Charles had a part to play in this war. Matthew's ship, the *Mathue Cradocke* appears in a naval list of 1312, and he is described as a servant of Charles Somerset, Lord Herbert (of Raglan, Chepstow and Gower) and Lord Chamberlain (of England). The following year Matthew is described in another list as captain of the 240-ton *Mathue Cradocke*, crewed by 100 mariners and 100 men of the Lord Chamberlain's retinue. Another naval document, dated that same year, records that 195 men had manned his ship and that he, as captain, had been paid 18d. per day. The details of Matthew's contribution to the war at sea are unknown, but on one occasion at least he was up to his old tricks – piracy – for the French recorded that *Mathiew Cradot* and his accomplices had captured and robbed Nicholas de la Chesnaye and his partners, merchants of Rouen, of goods valued at 44,000 francs. As for Sir Charles, as a reward for his services in Flanders he was created First Earl of Worcester in February 1514.

Lady Katherine Gordon

A widower by 1517, Matthew married Lady Katherine Gordon, daughter of the Earl of Huntley and Gordon, and on 24th July that year she obtained a special licence from the King to dwell with Matthew in Wales. The reason for the licence was that Katherine was no ordinary woman. A relative of James IV of Scotland, she married in 1496 one Perkin Warbeck, a man who claimed to be one of the princes whom Richard III is supposed to have murdered in the Tower of London. In reality Perkin was the son of a Flemish boatman. Nevertheless, for six years he sorely troubled Henry Tudor, and on one occasion the King of Scotland invaded England in support of Perkin's claim to the throne. In 1497 Perkin was imprisoned in the Tower and, two years later, was executed for his part in a conspiracy.

The name Lady Katherine Gordon appears in a list of ladies who, in 1502, attended the marriage of Margaret, daughter of Henry Tudor, to James (Stuart) IV of Scotland (this union resulted in the Stuarts becoming Kings of England 101 years later). In *c*.1512 Katherine married James Strangeways, esquire, of Fyfelde in Berkshire. Shortly after he died in 1517 she married Matthew, and it is little wonder that a woman with her background should require the King's permission to reside in Wales. That Matthew had a strong affection for Katherine is evidenced by the terms of his will, and by the fact that it was his intention that in death they would lie together in the same elaborate tomb.

Knighthood and Retirement

At the time of his second marriage Matthew's social status was that of an esquire, but in a document dated 10th January 1520 he is referred to as a knight. Sir Matthew continued to be Charles Somerset's Deputy in Glamorgan, Morgannwg and Gower until after the death of Charles in 1526. He resigned from all his offices – save that of Constable of Kenfig Castle – shortly after Michaelmas that year, as evidenced by the fact that, as Receiver of Gower, he completed the Michaelmas accounts for that year. By then Somerset's son and heir, Henry, had succeeded to the Somerset estate to become the Second Earl of Worcester and Lord Herbert of Raglan, Chepstow and Gower. Evidence for this comes from a document, dated 8th October 1526, which shows that Matthew obtained from Earl Henry a lease on

> all manner [of] mines of coal now found, or that hereafter can be found … within the said Lordship of Gower and Kilvey.

The lease was for 80 years at an annual rent of £11. The income derived from this lease no doubt added to Sir Matthew's considerable wealth, the full extent of which is made evident by the terms of his will, dated 22nd January 1529. His death must have occurred between 6th June 1531, the date of a codicil, and 16th August 1531, when the will and the codicil were proved in London. Matthew made provisions for several religious institutions, the furthest being St. David's in the west and Lantarnam in Monmouthshire in the east. He also made provisions for numerous named persons, two of whom, John and Jankyn Frankeleyne, Sweyneshe burgesses, were bequeathed the coal lease. It can be assumed that by 1529 Matthew's brother and three sisters

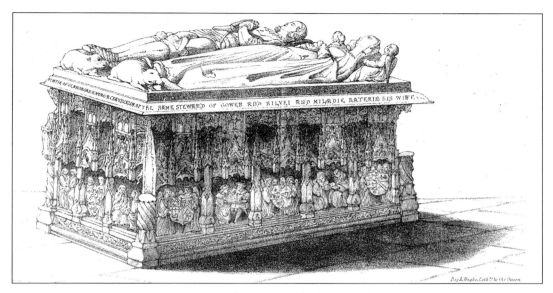

Sir Matthew Craddock's tomb

were all dead as none of them are mentioned in the will. Among the relatives who were handsomely provided for were his daughter, Margaret, his niece, Elizabeth Gibon (daughter of one of his sisters), his grandson, William Herbert (George's younger brother) and his great-grand-daughter, Katheryne (George's daughter) who must have been a child at the time even though the will refers to debts paid in connection with her (proposed?) marriage to Sir Roger Vaughan.

Matthew's wife, Dame Katherine Cradocke (formerly Dame Kateryne Gordon) fared well, for not only did she receive the £400 promised to her as her dowry, but also numerous objects of gold and silver, including a gold chain valued at £60 or more, as well as diamonds, pearls, a ruby and a sapphire. She also had, for the duration of her life, The Plas with all 'hangings, apparels, vessels and all other implements of household' that were there, as well as the 'farm called Corners Well', numerous cattle, 'all sheep … within the Lordship of Gower', the 'dairy in Gower called Forest Bychan' (Little Forest – possibly Fforest-fach), two of the 'best ambling horses with all their apparel', the manors of Dinas Powys and Llanedeyrn (both near Cardiff) and much more, all of which, following her death, was to pass 'to the use of' Matthew's grandsons, George and William Herbert. As the eldest grandson, George was to inherit the lion's share; that is, all

> lordships, manors, lands and tenements … within Glamorgan … Pembroke … [the] Lordship of Gower and in the town[s] of Cardiff and Swainsey, or elsewhere in Wales.

In the case of Cardiff, George was to inherit all 'messuage burgages … and tenements within the town' and franchise, including property at Cogan Pill and 'every piece of implements of household as [Matthew] left at the Blackfriars'. After the death of his mother, Margaret, and that of his stepmother, Katherine, he was to inherit much of what had been bequeathed to them, including The Plas and the manors of Dinas Powys and Llanedyrn. It was Matthew's wish that he should

> be buried in the Chapel of Saint Anne in Swansey in the North side of the Church there, which Chapel I [Matthew] caused to be newly builded and edified [and] that George Herbert … shall appoint lands and tenements of the yearly value of 20 nobles for maintaining and repairing of the said Chapel, and to find a priest to sing there for evermore for

the souls of himself, his wife, his ancestors and all Christian souls. It is no doubt due to these requirements that the chapel later became known as the Herbert Chapel. Matthew was laid to rest within this chapel under an elaborately-carved altar tomb made of Bath oolite, measuring approximately 3m. in length, 1m. in breadth and 1m. in height. Inscribed on the tomb were the words:

> here lieth Mathie Cradok, knight, sumetime depute unto the right honourable Charles, Earl of Warcet, in the Countie of Glamorgan and Morgan[nwg], Chauncelor of the same, Steward of Gower and Kilvei, and mi Ladi Katerin, his wife.

Clearly it was Matthew's intention that Lady Katherine should be interred with him, and on top of the tomb were two effigies, one of Matthew in armour, the other of Katherine in a costume of the period. Unfortunately, Katherine married Christopher Asheton, esquire, of Fyfelde in Berkshire, and although in her will she referred to Matthew as her 'dear and wellbeloved husband … deceased' she directed her 'body to be buried in the parish church of Fyfelde'. Katherine died in October 1537, and was probably interred in the church at Fyfelde where, on the north side of the chancel, there is a large, hollow square in the wall; this is called the Lady 'Gorgon's' monument. However, when the vault in the Herbert Chapel at Sweynesse was opened in 1840, five coffins presented themselves to view. One of the coffins had been presumably Matthew's; the other four contained the bodies of persons unknown. One hundred years later, the blitz of 1941 did irreparable damage to both St. Mary's Church and Matthew's tomb.

According to her will, Katherine had no great wealth to bequeath to anyone – 500 pence to be distributed among 500 of the poorest people in Berkshire being one of the largest bequests. Although she referred to 'my lands called Lannock' in Glamorgan, there was no mention in her will of The Plas, the manors of Dinas Powys and Llanedeyrn, or anything else that Matthew had left to her. Someone else had got their hands on all that.

CHAPTER VI
Sir George Herbert

It is generally accepted that George Herbert was born *c.*1500, possibly two or three years earlier, but there is reason to believe that he was born *c.*1495. There is, however, a problem with this in that if George's grandmother, Alice Mansel, had married Matthew Cradock early in 1489, their daughter, Margaret, would have been only six years old when she gave birth to George. The only way round this problem is to assume that George's grandmother, Alice, had married Matthew at least six years earlier than is generally accepted; this has to be so because Margaret, prior to her marriage to George's father, had married (or was betrothed to) John Malefont and he died young and childless between July 1493 and December 1495.

Nothing is known of George's early years until, as Steward of the Lordship of Abergavenny, his name appears in a deed dated 4th January 1516, by which time he must have been 21 and, therefore, born *c.*1495 or even earlier. George's appointment as Steward of Abergavenny may have had something to do with his father, Sir Richard Herbert, having held several offices in that lordship. It is also known that, in February 1515, Matthew Cradock and the Lord of Abergavenny, the 'Right Honourable Lord George Nevill, knight', entered into a pair of indentures (agreements). Both men, therefore, knew each other and it is likely that Matthew's influence may also have had something to do with George's appointment to the stewardship of Abergavenny, which he held until at least 1535, after which he appears to have held the deputy-stewardship until at least 1539.

George's marriage to Elizabeth Berkeley may also have been connected with the indentures of 1515, as Elizabeth was Lord George Nevill's niece (the daughter of his sister). Elizabeth was quite a catch as she had royal blood in her veins and was, therefore, superior in status to George. George may, however, have had some connection with royalty in that he is said to have been a gentleman waiter in the Queen's household, but there are historians who dispute this. In the 1530s he appears as one of the King's Esquires for the Body extraordinary, an appointment that did not require his continual attendance at court. When exactly he took this appointment is unknown.

In 1524 George succeeded Matthew as the King's Receiver of Glamorgan. The appointment may be attributed to the influence of his kinsman, Charles Somerset, Earl of Worcester, who had a close relationship with the King. George's suitability for the post is, however, questionable because, in 1532, complaints were brought against certain officers in the Lordship of Glamorgan relating to the embezzlement of money due to the King. George was not named as one of the officers, but as Receiver it was his responsibility to ensure that all money was accounted for. The fact that he failed in his duty suggests that either he was incompetent, or he was involved in the embezzlement.

In all probability George succeeded to the stewardship of Gower and Kilvey at Michaelmas 1526. He was certainly Steward the following year as he is referred to as such in a deed dated 2nd May 1527. He also succeeded his grandfather as Constable of Sweyneshe Castle, as well as Receiver and Chancellor of the lordship. With so many duties requiring his presence in Gower it would have been necessary for George to appoint a deputy-steward at Abergavenny, and his younger brother, William, appears as such in documents dated 1526, 1527, 1529 and 1534. Where George lived between 1526 and 1531 is unknown, but it is believed that after Matthew's death his chief residence was at Cogan Pill, near Cardiff, where there is a mansion house similar to The Plas, which he may have built as his arms are on the front porch. After Katherine Gordon's remarriage (prior to 1537) George was at liberty to take up residence at The Plas whenever his presence in Sweyneshe was required. He may even have been responsible for additions to The Plas as his arms were also displayed on the gatehouse, along with those of his grandfather. Several bards are known to have sung at The Plas once it had become his – Tomos ab Ieuan ap Rhys Brydydd, Iorwerth Fynglwyd, and his son, Rhisiart Fynglwyd, in c.1543.

Early Abuses

That George became Steward of Gower and Kilvey may have been due in part to Matthew's influence, presumably because Matthew considered him to be the right man for the job, if only for his forceful disposition. Matthew, of course, would have been aware of George's hot temper, but not so aware, perhaps, of his other shortcomings, at least not until they began to surface during his early years in office. In an age when men were obstreperous, quick to take offence and take the law into their own hands, it required a forceful figure to administer justice in a Marcher lordship. Such a man could expect criticism, and two years before his retirement Matthew himself had been accused of acting unlawfully against certain tenants in Gower, a charge from which he was exonerated. There is no evidence that George acted unlawfully during his early years as Steward of Gower, but in that part of the Lordship of Ewias Lacy that belonged to the Lord of Abergavenny, the tenants there complained to the Council in the Marches in 1527 about the misconduct of George's officers. George did nothing to rectify the situation, despite receiving several letters form the Council. Whether or not George's failure to respond until the Council ordered him to do so was due to incompetence or complicity is not known, but later evidence shows that he had scant regard for the Council in the Marches.

One year after Matthew's death the tell-tale signs of maladministration begin to surface in Gower, for on 1st September 1532 the principal men of Sweyneshe and Gower reached an agreement with Henry Somerset who, in exchange for 350 marks, not only confirmed the two de Breos charters of 1306, but agreed to remedy the malpractices of his officers. George was not mentioned by name, but it is obvious from the wording of several clauses that he was the root cause of a number of grievances in that he either authorized or tolerated the malpractices. The most prevalent abuse was to do with sureties. When men were formerly charged with an offence they were expected to find sureties who would guarantee their appearance in court; now they were expected to find sureties for their good behaviour as well, which was contrary to the customs of the lordship. Another complaint was that, when tenants were wrong-fully dispossessed of their land by other tenants, officers in the lordship were either turning a blind eye, or were themselves wrongfully dispossessing tenants of their land. Yet another cause for concern was that officers who made false accusations against tenants were not being dealt with. There were many other grievances inferred in the agreement, which Somerset promised would be rectified – but Somerset, being neglectful of his duties in the many lordships in his charge, appears to have done nothing, leaving George to carry on as he saw fit.

Within a few months of the agreement, the king's attorney, Thomas Holte, had cause to report on George's involvement in extortion and judicial murder, as well as his refusal to show anything other than contempt for the king's Council in the Marches. Holte stated that:

> George Herbert … steward of Gower … did take a young man … of the age of 16 years … a rich man's son dwelling thereby, and laid to his charge that [he] had stolen certain shipe [sheep?] from his own father, which his father utterly denied, and yet by means [threats or torture] the young man was caused to confess the felony. Upon which confession the said steward sent unto his father to bring him a great sum of money or else his son would be hanged. Whereupon his father complained to the Council in the Marches and … thereupon the Council awarded the King's letter to the said George Herbert, commanding him to respite the execution till the matter were examined before them. Upon which letter the said George would not appear before the Council, but … caused the young man to be hanged. And as the father informed the Council he [threatened] to hang him [as well] if he may take him.

The Act of Union

Anxious to curb the growing lawlessness in the Marches of Wales, Henry VIII appointed Rowland Lee, Bishop of Coventry and Lichfield, as Lord President of the Council in the Marches in 1534. Lee was ruthless in his dealings with felons, hanging, it is claimed, more than 5,000 of them in the course of six years, but Lee's hanging policy was no remedy for the root cause of the problem, which lay in the way justice was administered.

In England, Henry Somerset and his peers had no authority to deal with serious offences such as murder – that was the prerogative of the king – but in his Marcher lordships of Raglan, Chepstow and Gower, Somerset exercised royal jurisdiction, meaning he was at liberty to deal with felons as if he were the king; moreover, by the early 16th century, most Marcher lordships were in the hands of the Crown, and Somerset, as custodian of many of these lordships, exercised royal jurisdiction in these territories as well. Not that Somerset troubled himself unduly with judicial affairs – he simply pocketed the fees and appointed deputies to do the work for him. These deputies were, like George Herbert, notorious for their misconduct.

Henry VIII's answer to the problem was to have Parliament pass an act in July 1536, to deprive the Marcher lords of their right to royal jurisdiction. That same year Parliament passed the 'Act of Laws and Justice to be ministered in Wales in like form as it is in this [the English] realm', which later became known as the Act of Union. By this act Wales was to be 'incorporated, united and annexed' to England, the Marcher lordships were to be grouped to form new counties and Welsh law was to be abolished and replaced with English law.

These changes were not innovative. When Edward I conquered the independent princedoms of North and West Wales in 1282-3 he created six counties out of conquered territory – Anglesey, Caernarfon, Merioneth, Flint, Cardigan and what was then the relatively small County of Carmarthen. In these new counties (which, with the exception of Flintshire, formed the Principality of Wales, the personal property of the heir to the throne) Welsh law had been abolished and replaced with English criminal law and a civil law that was an admixture of Welsh and English.

Welsh law had survived in almost all the Marcher lordships. In Gower it had survived in the Welsh-speaking districts of *Supraboscus, Subboscus* and Kilvey. The Act of Union did away with the Welsh courts in these districts so that henceforth everyone in Gower – as in Wales as whole – became subject to English law. The act also provided for the creation of seven new counties, which was to be achieved by grouping neighbouring lordships. In the case of Gower it was joined to the lordships of Glamorgan and Morgannwg to form the new (pre-1974) County of Glamorgan. It can be assumed that in Gower, as elsewhere, few Welshmen lamented the abolition of Welsh law because successive generations of Marcher lords had used and abused native law as a means of making money. The view may have been, as it was elsewhere, that Welshmen were no longer second-class citizens in their own country; they were now on a par with their English neighbours.

Hastily devised, the Act of Union took seven years to implement. Nevertheless it should have brought about the removal of negligent men such as Somerset and dealt with the maladministration of the likes of George Herbert. Yet both men survived the changes that the act brought. Somerset retained his position in south-east Wales because the king permitted him (in name if nothing else) to keep 'the office of the justice of the whole of Glamorgan', for which he received a fee of £100 per annum. George, on the other hand, adapted to the changes.

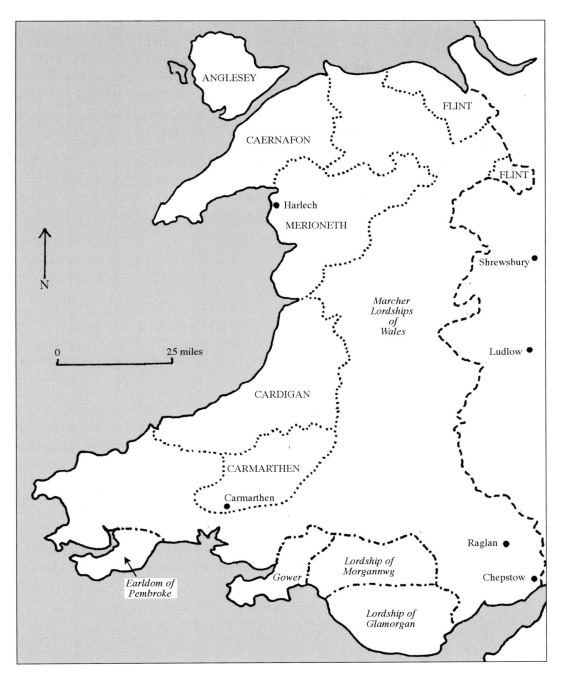

The counties of Wales prior to the Act of Union (1536-43).
With the exception of Flintshire they formed the Principality of Wales

George continued to administer justice as Somerset's Deputy until, in 1540, he became the first Sheriff of the new County of Glamorgan. He, then, advanced himself in what was, for Wales, a new avenue to power and influence. The act had brought a modicum of democracy to the country in that it required all counties to be represented in Parliament by a Knight of the Shire (later to be known as an MP). The first to be elected as such by the freeholders of the shire was, of course, George who, for his services, was knighted the following year. Thereafter, he became a JP, enforcing the law on the king's behalf at the County Quarter Sessions.

As Steward of Gower, George's responsibilities were reduced to safeguarding Somerset's interests as an absentee landlord; moreover, as Receiver, it was still his responsibility to ensure that anything due to the lord in the way of rents, tolls, mises and aids were accounted for, as well as the confiscated belongings of outlaws and condemned felons. In the Manor of Sweyneshe George's influence never waned, as evidenced by a petition, dated 1553, concerning bylaws:

> devised by John Fleming, Portreeve of the town of Sweyneshe, by the assent and consent of his brethren of the said town, by and through the advice and council of the Right Worshipful Sir George Herbert, Knight, Steward of the said town, for the common well-being of the said town and the inhabitants of the same.

The Act of 1536 brought benefits to the burgesses throughout Wales in that it permitted them to participate in the election of one burgess in every county town – except Harlech – to represent them in Parliament. In Glamorgan one burgess was elected to represent the County Town of Cardiff. Voting was restricted to burgesses – those of Cardiff and those of the other seven ancient boroughs within the county, including Sweyneshe and Loughor. The act may have given the Sweyneshe burgesses a taste of democracy, but that meant contributing to the elected burgess's expenses. Another expense brought about by the act was that of direct taxation to the Crown. In the Subsidy Assessment of 1543 – to which George was appointed as one of the commissioners – it was recorded that 111 householders in the borough of Sweyneshe were assessed as having sufficient means to be tax-payers. It is not known whether the 111 tax-payers were all burgesses, although it is likely that most of them were. What the assessment does reveal, however, is that approximately half of them bore unmistakably Welsh names.

The Dissolution of the Monasteries

By the Act of Supremacy, 1534, Henry VIII, frustrated by the Pope's unwillingness to dissolve his marriage to Catherine of Aragon (his first wife) declared himself to be the 'only Supreme Head of the Church of England'. Two years later he had Parliament to pass an act for dissolving nearly 400 monasteries throughout the realm, among them Neath and Margam abbeys. He did this for several reasons, one being that almost all the monasteries owed allegiance to either the heads of their orders, or directly to the

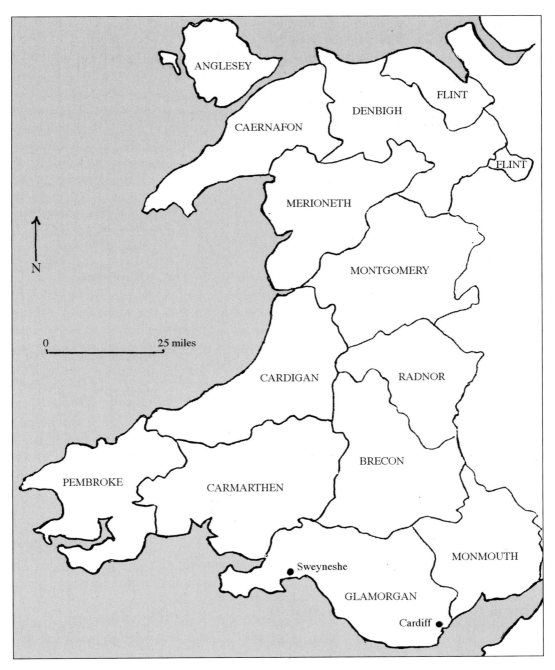

The counties of Wales after the Act of Union (1536-43)

Pope. What was more important was that many of the monasteries were wealthy; their property passed to the Crown.

Henry VIII had no desire for reform. He simply wanted the English church to be Catholic without the Pope. There were, however, those who had to be rewarded for their support in his break with Rome. So he allowed the Bible to be translated into English and permitted prayers to be uttered in the mother tongue, moves that were in harmony with growing national awareness, at least as far as the English were concerned. He also assented to the removal of sacred relics and images on the ground that they encouraged idolatry, but that was as far as he was prepared to go.

Henry was always in need of money, and men of means were aware that the day would come when he would sell off lands that had formerly belonged to the monasteries. Those who were far-sighted took steps to ensure they were in a favourable position to buy whatever would be on offer. The lands of Margam Abbey were undoubtedly the richest prize in West Glamorgan, but when it came to manoeuvring for a favourable position in respect of these lands, George was left standing by his uncle, Rice Mansel, because like the Herberts, the Mansels were a remarkable family when it came to enlarging their estate.

The Mansels appear to have settled in Gower during the reign of Edward I (1272-1307), but in what capacity is unknown until a document of 1400 refers to a Richard Mansel as lord of the tiny fief of Nicholaston and the tiny manor of Manselfield near Bishopston. The family fortune improved dramatically in c.1436-7 when of the last male member of the Penres family died, the reason being that, prior to that date, a Hugh Mansel had married Isabella, daughter of John Penres and sole heiress of the Penres estate, which included the fiefs of Penrice, Oxwich, Port Eynon, West Llangenydd and numerous parcels of land throughout the Lordship of Gower.

In c.1511 Rice Mansel married Eleanor Basset, sole heiress of Beaupre in Glamorgan; in 1527 he married his third wife, Cicely D'Abridgecourt. Rice had royal blood in his veins – his maternal grandmother had been the daughter of King Edward IV – but Cicely had royal connections as well. In c.1537 Princess Mary, daughter of Henry VIII (who became Queen of England in 1553) wrote a letter to her father's secretary, Thomas Cromwell, recommending to his

> lawful favour and goodness Sir Rice Mansel, this bearer [of the letter], for the said Sir Rice has married one of my gentlewomen who, for her long and acceptable service to me done [as a lady-in-waiting], I much esteem and honour. Wherefore, if you would at my desire, extend your goodness and favour to him … so that he might perceive his said suit … to take good effect.

It is believed that the 'suit' referred to in the letter relates to an application for a lease on the extensive Margam Abbey estate. This may well have been true because, that same year, Rice got his lease, and when the King made up his mind to sell, Rice was in a favourable position to purchase, between 1540 and 1558, almost the whole estate, thereby making himself one of the richest landowners in Glamorgan. These purchases may not have pleased George, who also lost out on the sale of the Neath Abbey estate, which is surprising because, in 1533, he and his eldest son, Mathew, had jointly acquired the stewardship of the Neath Abbey lands in Glamorgan.

Through agents, George managed to buy a few parcels of Margam Abbey lands. He also purchased the manor of Llandough in 1543, as well as the manors of Roath and Cardiff in 1545, all of which had belonged to Tewkesbury Abbey. In 1546 he purchased property at Llandaff that had been taken from the Franciscan and Dominican friars. He did well in Gower, too, because he anticipated what would be dissolved next. In 1540 Henry VIII dissolved the Order of St. John the Baptist, otherwise known as the Hospitallers. The Order held numerous properties in Gower, including the Church of St. John (St. John-juxta-Swansea) in High Street (now St. Matthew's, opposite the Tax Office). Since the 12th century the Order had several times been gifted property in and to the north of Sweyneshe, which collectively became known as the manor of Millwood. The greater part of this manor, which lay to the north of the Burlais Brook, also became the parish of St. John, although the parish Church of St. John remained within the parish of Sweyneshe. Rice Mansel acquired both the church and the manor of Millwood, whereas George acquired extensive property in the rising ground between the Burrows and Townhill, and also in the Sketty area (Milwodesketty – Millwood, Sketty), which in 1764 was referred to as the Barony of Sketty.

The Reformation

Henry VIII died in 1547 and his son, Edward VI (by Jane Seymour) was only nine years old when he succeeded to the throne. Edward and his chief advisors lent their support to those reformers who were soon to become known as Protestants – so named because they protested that not enough had been done to reform the Church of England and eradicate from it what they considered to be the false ideas of Catholicism. Edward may have been genuine in his support for reform, but his advisors were swayed by financial considerations, theirs as well the King's. Consequently, in the Act for the Dissolution of the Chantries, 1547, it was stipulated that:

> the King shall have and enjoy all such goods, chattels, jewels, plate, ornaments and other moveables … of every college, chantry, free chapel

that was to be dissolved. In Sweyneshe the Hospital of St. David's fell within the category of a chantry as the chaplains there were obliged to chant masses for the dead. The Hospital had been endowed with many possessions, and a survey carried out prior to the dissolution revealed that the person responsible for managing the Hospital's estate was none other than George Herbert. George was, therefore, in a favourable position to ascertain the more profitable assets of the estate, but his eventual purchase of these assets was connected with something else.

In 1549 Edward VI's Protestant advisors introduced the First Prayer Book in English, and also the Act of Uniformity to enforce its use. These changes sparked off a rebellion in Devon and Cornwall. The rebellion was crushed with the aid of Italian and German mercenaries. George was evidently involved in the campaign because the following year he was confirmed in the Hospital's possessions in recognition of his services against the rebels in the west.

St. Mary's Church

The dissolution of the Hospital of St. David's made George wealthy, and among his newly-acquired possession was the vicarage of St. Mary's Church (annexed to the Hospital at the time of its foundation in 1332), which made George a lay rector, having charge of the parish and a claim to all tithes, a portion of which he set aside as a stipend (salary) for a vicar of his choosing. Prior to 1549, St. Mary's was well endowed due to the generosity of its parishioners. Evidence for this comes from an inventory of 1549, which was presented to George in his capacity as a king's Commissioner. The inventory refers to many items of worth, including a canopy of cloth of gold, two silver chalices, several vestments in cloth of gold, Bruges satin, white damask or coloured velvet, as well as the lead on Sir Matthew Cradock's chapel. It can be assumed that all this property went to the Crown, as stipulated in the act, which also required the removal or destruction of

> all shrines, candlesticks, pictures and all other monuments of feigned miracles, pilgrimages, idolatry and superstition

and this would have included the altar and the rood screen that was situated in front of the singing gallery above the chancel. There is no record of the destruction a rood screen at St. Mary's; nor is there any record of the removal of an altar (regarded by Protestants as a relic of pre-Christian sacrifice), nor its replacement by a wooden communion table, around which parishioners gathered for a commemorative meal.

When Edward VI died in 1553, he was succeeded by his half-sister, Mary (daughter of Catherine of Aragon) and she, being an ardent Catholic, ordered the restoration of the Latin service, the rood screens and the altars, but here again there is no record of any of this activity taking place at St. Mary's. When Mary's Protestant half-sister, Elizabeth (daughter of Anne Boleyn), succeeded to the throne in 1558, out went the Latin service, the rood screens and the altars for the second time. On this occasion the records of St. Mary's are not silent, for the churchwardens' account for 1558 record a payment of 4d. to William Johns, the smith, for removing the rood screen, and a payment of 2s. 4d. to William the mason for removing two altars. The following year the accounts record a payment of 14d. to John Thomas for five 'posts for to make the table of the communion'.

More Dirty Dealings

The year 1549 and those that followed were to prove fruitful for George. On the 26th November 1549 Henry Somerset, Second Earl of Worcester, died and for the next seven years his widow, Countess Elizabeth, had custody of Gower during the minority of her son, William. On 10th September 1556 – three months prior to William succeeding to his father's estate – Countess Elizabeth granted to Sir George:

> five parcels of waste land and pasture in the manor of Trewyddfa ... whereof one parcel is called Fforest Trewyddfa ... one is called Penyllan [Penlan], another Dree Boeth [Treboeth], the third Gyn Goch and the fourth Pull y Llyn ... at the annual rent of 9s. 3d.

By 1650 the parcels were recorded as Fforest Trewyddfa, Penyllan (Penlan), Dree Poeth (Treboeth), Tir y doynaw (Tirdeunaw) and Cwm y gelly (Cwmgelly). Fforest Trewyddfa covered a large area and the timber derived from it must have been a saleable commodity, particularly to those in need of pit-props. The remaining four 'parcels of waste land and pasture' were profitable for a different reason in that they were rich in coal, and the grant stipulated that George had to render 'annually ... 4d. for every wey of coal ... taken from the said five parcels of land'. In short, George had done what his grandfather had done in 1526 when, shortly after the death of Charles Somerset, he had obtained a profitable coal lease.

Many years later (in 1595) Edward Somerset, Fourth Earl of Worcester, brought before the Court of Chancery a bill of complaint against George's grandson, Sir William Herbert, and others, claiming that since 1549 there had been

> wrongfully enclosed and encroached within the town and liberties of Swanzey divers parcels of waste of the said town and manor of Swanzey, and then claimed as freehold

by the persons who had carried out the encroachments. It appears that Edward's father had failed to keep an eye on his affairs, whereas George, his grandson and others had taken advantage of the situation to the extent that hundreds of acres throughout Gower had been lost. In the case of George's grandson, Earl Edward claimed that the

> said defendant, having subtly gotten into his hands a great number of court tolls, surveys, terriers and other evidence of right belonging to the complainant, thinks now by means utterly to extinguish and cover all ... abuses wrought by his late ancestors [meaning George primarily] who were indeed the only persons whose corruption or negligence have been the very principal ground ... of all the whole abuses there offered and executed.

Despite these underhanded dealings, George rose to high office in the judiciary, and the opportunity to do so came from an unexpected quarter.

The Rise to Power of a Younger Brother

George's younger brother, William, had only a small portion of his grandfather's possessions, but in true Herbert fashion he rose to a position of power and wealth. Prior to 1526 he had been in the service of Charles Somerset, First Earl of Worcester. By 1535 he had acquired certain offices in Glamorgan, and by 1547 had gained custody of several lordships in Monmouthshire. In 1549 he had been active in suppressing the rebellion in Devon and Cornwall. He then assisted Warwick in becoming Lord Protector in place of Jane Seymour's brother. As a reward for his services he was granted Seymour's confiscated lands in Wiltshire, as well as the Lordship of Glamorgan (the Vale). That same year he became Lord President of the Council in the Marches. The following year he was created Earl of Pembroke.

George, of course, benefitted from his younger brother's meteoric rise to power in that he became a member of the Council in the Marches, and remained so until at least the end of Mary's reign in 1558. It was probably due to his younger brother's influence that, in 1550, he was appointed Vice-admiral of South Wales, responsible for the coastline between the River Wye and the River Loughor. In 1552 he was appointed Sheriff of Glamorgan for the second time, a post he held for a year. He was already a JP in the counties of Flint, Radnor and Cardigan when, in 1554, he became a JP in Gloucestershire, Herefordshire, Shropshire and Worcestershire.

Other Family Members

George reached the peak of his career in the 1550s; at the same time he witnessed members of his immediate family make themselves known in the judicial and political affairs of Glamorgan. His eldest son, Mathew, became a JP, but appears to have died relatively young before the end of the decade. Mathew had eleven children, and is remembered as the father of two remarkable sons, William and John, the eldest of whom, William (later to be known as Sir William Herbert of Swanzey), served as a JP from 1554 onwards and was elected Knight of the Shire in 1559; the other son, John, became Second Secretary of State to both Elizabeth I and James I. Mathew's brother, William of Cogan Pill, was appointed Sheriff of Glamorgan in 1551 and served as Knight of the Shire in 1558. George's wife, Elizabeth, by whom he had six children, was still alive in 1547, and may also have been alive to witness the family's rise to prominence. She may also have come to accept that George could not be trusted, having at least one illegitimate child, a boy, referred to in documents of 1558 as William the Bastard, late of London and of Chepstow. In 1557 William the Bastard was old enough to bear arms.

Retainers and Feuds

To curb the power of the nobility and the gentry, Henry Tudor had strengthened the laws of Edward IV by forbidding great landowners to maintain private armies of retainers. Only genuine household servants were to receive livery: that is, provisions and uniforms. Henry did this not only to safeguard himself, but also to prevent great landowners from dominating their districts by force of arms. Whenever men of means broke the laws against livery, or were involved in breaches of the peace, Henry had them appear before his own council, which met in a room at Westminster Palace known as the Star Chamber, where heavy fines were imposed on offenders.

At the peak of his career, George, who had scant regard for higher authority, must have been of the opinion that the laws against livery did not apply to him, for in May 1555 an action was brought against him for retaining 48 men at Sweyneshe, and providing them with blue livery. There was nothing secretive about him having retainers, as they accompanied him in the performance of his duties. The action against him appears to have been dropped because, two months later, he was granted a royal licence to retain 40 gentlemen or yeomen, apart from his household servants and officers; moreover, his retainers were not uncouth ruffians, but young men from the most influential of families. That George had his way over retaining armed men can be explained by the fact that the Crown, when the need arose, depended upon the service of men such as George. Indeed, in 1544 the Crown had ordered that a large muster book be prepared, one that listed all men of means who could be relied upon to supply soldiers. The names of nine Glamorgan landowners appear in this book; they included Sir George Herbert, William Herbert (George's younger bother) and Sir Rice Mansel.

Feuds among the gentry of Glamorgan were common enough as, indeed, they were elsewhere, and great landowners continued to enlist the services of men who were often referred to as 'servants', though none – apart from George – went so far as to contravene the laws against livery. These servants were often tenant farmers, eager to uphold their lord's interests in the hope that, one day, they would receive favours. These servants often resorted to bully-boy tactics, their actions condoned, even encouraged by the men they served. The Herberts in particular had no qualms about their servants resorting to violence, and in this George was no exception.

In 1537 William Carne of Coety brought an action against both George and Sir Rice Mansel, accusing them of carrying out a murderous assault upon him at Cowbridge. Later that same year, Carne's younger brother, Roger, and his followers were involved in an affray with George's servants to the extent that sword-fighting took place and then arrows were exchanged, though to no great effect. Three years later, Roger Carne's cousin, John, was killed by the servants of Walter Herbert, George's cousin. There were undoubtedly many such clashes between the Glamorgan gentry and their respective servants, but the best documented feud to explode into armed conflict was the one between George Herbert and the Mansels, which erupted at Oxwich Castle in 1557.

It is possible that George developed an intense dislike for his kinsman, Rice Mansel, on account of his military prowess and his ever-growing influence in royal circles. In 1517, at the age of 30, Rice had been in Flanders in the service of his lord, Charles Somerset, and by 1526 he had been knighted. In 1535 he saw active service in Ireland as a senior officer in charge of 500 men. The following year he became Chamberlain of Chester. He succeeded George as Sheriff of Glamorgan in 1542.

Eleven years later he led a contingent of 500 men at the coronation of Queen Mary. That same year he was appointed Chamberlain and Chancellor of South Wales.

If there is doubt as to whether George bore enmity towards Sir Rice Mansel, there is certainly no question about his hostility towards Rice's eldest son, Edward, as an extant poem by Rhisiart ap Iorwerth calls upon the two men to make peace. At the time of the affray at Oxwich, Edward, who was 28 years old and married to Jane, daughter of the late Henry Somerset, Earl of Worcester, appears to have been residing at Oxwich Castle from where, presumably, he managed the Oxwich estate as a preliminary to succeeding to the whole Mansel estate when his father died.

Oxwich Castle – Scene of the Affray

There had been a castle at Oxwich as early as 1396, its exact location unknown. The present ruins – the remains of a fortified manor house – are believed to have been the work of Sir Rice Mansel, which he is said to have carried out between 1508 and the early 1520s. The castle is the only surviving example of a Tudor manor house within the bounds of the old Lordship of Gower. It consisted of a great hall block that stood more than 50 feet high, protected on the east by three tall towers. On the west lay a courtyard, bounded on the north by a wall (which no longer exists), on the south by a domestic wing (which later became a farmhouse) and on the west by a gateway, walls and at least one D-shaped tower. It was just outside the gateway that George and Edward Mansel clashed.

The gateway of Oxwich Castle where Ann Mansel fell, mortally wounded

The Affray of 1557

On 26th December 1557 a south-westerly gale howled, driving mighty, foam-flecked breakers against the Gower coastline. About mid-afternoon the gale drove a French vessel aground not far from Oxwich Church. Six crewmen made it ashore, and pretty soon the villagers of Oxwich were aboard the wreck, taking from it figs, raisin, almonds and wool, as well as timbers and anything else of worth, a welcome haul as England and France were at war at the time. All that had been seized was taken to Oxwich Castle up on the hill, where it was apportioned, everyone from the lord of the manor to the lowliest villager having a share.

Early the following day someone informed Sir George Herbert of what had happened. As Vice-admiral of the South Wales coast and as Steward of Gower, George had an interest in wrecks, and may even have considered what he would get from the wreck for himself. In haste he dispatched two of his gentlemen servants – William Hopkin Dawkin of Ilston and Harry Francklen of Sweyneshe – to take into custody the crew, cargo and ship. When the two gentlemen arrived at Oxwich they found the villagers were not prepared to hand over what they regarded as spoils of war, certainly not in the absence of a warrant. Unable to impose their will on the villagers, the two gentlemen left, though not without saying 'openly that they would bring more company on the morrow'.

Arriving back at The Plas in the early hours of the 28th, the two gentlemen reported to George, who flew into a rage and, rousing his retinue, marched the ten miles to Oxwich in the dark. With him were upwards of 20 servants and retainers, almost all of whom bore Welsh names. Some of them were gentlemen, some yeomen. One was a tailor, another a merchant, and with them came the vicar of St. Mary's Church.

At daybreak, George first called on the parsonage – a little beyond Oxwich Church – banging on the door until a woman lifted the latch. He pushed in, bursting into the bedchamber to find the parson, Richard Cosin, in his doublet and hose. According to some witnesses, the exchange was in Welsh; according to others, the parson said, in English, "I trust, Mr. Herbert, you will not take from us our own goods". Six pieces of figs and a horn of gunpowder were taken from the parson's outhouse and deposited in the church. Leaving a detachment there to guard what had been seized, George made his way uphill to Oxwich Castle, taking with him '18 persons having swords and bucklers [small, round shields]'.

One of the company, William Griffith, a guest at The Plas during the Christmas period, rode ahead and, on arriving at the castle, called out at the hall door, which a young man opened. Then George swaggered into the hall, demanding to see Edward Mansel, only to be told that Edward was at the house of Griffith ap Owen, steward of Oxwich. On learning that there were three French and one Flemish prisoner held at the castle, he ordered them to be taken to the church. He took no cargo, but said he would come again for that.

It was sunrise when George, with 17 persons in his train, made his way to Griffith ap Owen's mansion house at Slade Cross, by which time Griffith had already sent word to Edward Mansel. George arrived at the house in time to catch Griffith walking in the company of two French prisoners; he also witnessed Griffith's servants taking from the house a barrel of raisins, a sack of wool and three 'pieces' of figs. Griffith feigned surprise, saying, "How now, my lord. I had not thought to see you venture abroad in such foul weather."

"Had you done your duty as a true steward," George replied gruffly, "then had I no need to come." He, then, demanded that the prisoners and the goods should be handed over to him.

"Frenchmen's goods it is," Griffith asserted, "and our own, for such as took it ought to have it."

Disregarding what had been said, George ordered some of his men to search the house, and while they rifled through every room, he demanded to know the whereabouts of Edward Mansel. Griffith told him that Edward was at his aunt's house in Llandewi, adding that George should not strive with Edward, his kinsman, over such 'pilfrey' goods.

"He is but a boy and will never be a man," George sneered, and bragged that he would bind Edward 'like a boy and send him to his father like a cock'.

Not content with two forcible entries, George proceeded to demonstrate how heavy-handed he could be by ordering his men to rifle every house at and about Slade Cross, after which he made his way to Oxwich Green were he ordered his men to not only rifle the houses, but to force the tenants to use their own horses to convey the confiscated goods to the church. While all this was going on, George sat astride his horse, waiting for Edward Mansel to show up, knowing that he would have to pass the green to reach the castle. What he did not know was that Griffith ap Owen had sent word to Edward again, with the result that Edward made it to the castle by another route.

George was still near the green when Edward's aunt, Ann Mansel, arrived with several servants. She urged George not to contend with her nephew – his kinsman – over such pilfrey goods. "Tush! Tush!" replied George tersely. "It is not for that. I will not suffer my officers, who are as good gentlemen as your nephew, to be louted and misused at his hand. I will make him know the worst servant of my house that I send to do my commandment."

Ann suggested a compromise: if Edward would agree to providing an inventory of the goods held at the castle, would George stay his hand? George agreed and sent his guest, William Griffith, to parley with Edward, whom he found standing in the castle gateway in a truculent mood. Edward shouted that George Herbert had taken advantage of his absence to rifle his father's tenants, adding that had he company he would never have suffered it; now he would keep his father's house and die at the gates before he would allow George to enter by force. Despite all this, William Griffith managed to calm Edward down; he even got him to agree to compile an inventory, but under no circumstances would George be allowed to enter the castle.

William Griffith met George and Ann Mansel in the lane between the castle and the green. He told them that Edward was "well pleased that you come to the castle to receive an inventory of the goods," and that should have defused the situation. According to William Griffith, George 'willed his footmen to' return to the church while he spoke to Edward, but according to the testimony of others, George 'called away his servants in haste, who … left certain horses laden with certain stuff [goods] abroad, and resorted to the castle, leaving between the green and the castle four or five houses unrifled'. He also appears to have sent his lieutenant, William Hopkin Dawkin, to the church where 'divers … servants were keeping the prisoners and [the] stuff rifled'. Dawkin is said to have 'willed them [the servants] to come away forthwith to stand by their master', at which point the parson advised Dawkin 'to travel to pacify the matter', only to be told, by Dawkin, "that it was past his remedy."

George came within 12 metres of the castle in the company of his guest, William Griffith, and 13 of his servants and retainers, many of them wearing 'fens cotes' and 'privy cotes' (body armour, breastplates presumably) and armed with rapiers, swords and bucklers. Ahead, Edward Mansel, also armed with a sword and buckler, stood a little outside the castle gate. With him were tenants and servants, including Griffith ap Owen – up to 12 or 16 supporters according to one witness. However many there were, it appears that about four of them were in close attendance to Edward 'having fens cots', one of them armed with a gleyve (or glaive – a kind of spear with a curved cutting edge), the rest with swords and bucklers. The remaining supporters crowded the gate, armed with gleyves and possibly halberds (a halberd being a combined spear and battleaxe).

What happened next differs according to witnesses. George maintained later that he alighted and made towards Edward, intending to converse with him. Edward had his sword drawn when three of George's servants, fearing that Edward might strike, drew their swords and moved in front of George, at which point Edward and certain of his company attacked. Other witnesses claimed that immediately after dismounting, George and his company drew their swords and, without any words on their part, made towards the gate. Meanwhile, Ann Mansel alighted close to Edward and tried to push him within the gate, saying, "I pray you, cousin, get you in." Edward put his aunt behind him, then turned to see three of George's servants were almost upon him, namely William Herbert (George's bastard son), Watkin John ap Watkin and Harry Watkin. Taking a step forward, Edward drew his sword, shouting, "How now, are you come hither to rob and invade me?" He, then, struck at William Herbert; at the same time four of his company moved to support him.

In the affray that followed, Ann called upon her servants, Jenkyn William and others, to attend on Edward for his defence. Twice George offered to strike Edward, but it was William Herbert who wounded Edward in the arm. Many more would have been hurt or killed had it not been for George's guest, William Griffith, who turned Ann's 'horse athwart the gate between the two companies'. George yelled at him to take the horse away. It was then that George's servant, Watkin John ap Watkin, placed his 'sword in the buckler hand' and, taking up a stone, threw it; it struck Ann on the forehead. She fell, and those crowding the gate cried, "Murder, murder." George called off his men, commanding them to assemble about 12 metres away from the gate where 'he stayed awhile, then departed'.

Two men, one of them a cleric, pursued George to report that Ann Mansel had been slain, and that Watkin John ap Watkin was to blame, to which George replied that someone "within the gate had killed her." Watkin said nothing. Then, when they met

William Hopkin Dawkin, coming from the church with reinforcements, William Herbert told him that Ann Mansel had been slain.

But Ann was not dead. At an inquest held at Oxwich on 3rd January 1558 before Thomas ap Howell, Coroner, a jury of 19 men declared on oath that 'about 9 o'clock on the day of the affray, Ann had been struck by a stone of no great bigness', thrown 'with great force' by Watkin John ap Watkin, late of Sweyneshe, yeoman, serving man of Sir George Herbert. The stone was said to have caused a 'mortal wound in her forehead … of the breadth of two thumbs, and the depth even to the brain', with the result that Ann had languished for three days until 'she died of that aforesaid wound'. The jury also declared on oath that George and 12 of his servants and retinue were guilty of 'aiding and abetting … Watkin John ap Watkin to commit a felony', and that William Hopkin Dawkin and Harry Francklen had 'counselled and procured' George and his servants and retinue 'to injure' Edward Mansel. As to why the jury apportioned blame on Dawkin and Francklen, it has to be remembered that these two gentlemen were at Oxwich on the day preceding the affray. It is, therefore, obvious that they were the servants whom George referred to in his dialogue with Ann Mansel as being 'louted and misused at' Edward's hand. Dawkin and Francklen had evidently returned to The Plas in the early hours of the 28th December, complaining about their treatment at Oxwich the previous day.

There was more to come in that Sir Rice Mansel and his son, Edward, brought a bill of complaint against George and his servants and retinue, accusing them of riot and forcible entry into numerous properties. In April 1558 a commission of four Glamorgan gentlemen compiled the evidence given by witnesses on both sides. The case was then heard in the Star Chamber on 13th May that year, and the accused were found guilty

> of riotous and forcible entry … into one house of [the parson] Richard Cosin … the castle or mansion house of Sir Rice Mansel … the mansion house of one Griffith ap Owen [and] in divers and sundry houses of the tenants and servants of the said Sir Rice Mansel at and about Slade Cross and Oxwich Green.

The accused were also found guilty of 'riotous and heinous assault and affray' at the castle against Edward Mansel

> in which riot force and affray the said Edward Mansel was wounded and hurt. And one Ann Mansel, his aunt, then and there deadly wounded by [the] throwing of a stone by one Watkin John ap Watkin.

The court also declared that the

> French prisoners, merchandises, goods and chattels so spoiled, rifled and taken away [were the] lawful booty [of] Sir Rice Mansel and his tenants and servants.

It was stated that at

the end of the hearing [George had] openly confessed all the said riots … saying only such as … touched the death of the said Ann Mansel, with humble submission to the King [etc.].

The decision of the court was that, initially, George and those servants and retainers who were with him should be committed to the notorious Fleet Prison, 'there to remain until further order be taken' in respect of fines payable to the Sovereign, reparation to Sir Rice and his tenants for the 'lawful booty' that had been rifled, compensation to Edward for his injury and, finally, they were to pay the Mansel's costs 'for their suit in the court'. George was also ordered to

bring in to the court the residue of his said servants and retainers, now not present, for whose appearance he stands all ready bound that they may appear here in this court the first day of the next term to receive punishment for their offences.

It would appear that George and his men were heavily fined on 18th June 1558. As to the matter 'touching the death of the said Ann Mansel, the order thereof [was] reserved to the trial of the Laws of this Realm'. The outcome of this last trial is unclear. According to one local historian, Watkin John ap Watkin was pardoned of the killing of Ann Mansel on 19th September 1559.

The Final Years

Whatever the final outcome may have been, by 1560 George had been replaced as Steward and Receiver of Gower by none other than Edward Mansel; by this time, too, George's involvement in the judiciary seems also to have been terminated, as there is no evidence of his continued membership in the Council in the Marches during Elizabeth's reign (1558 – 1603).

Sir Rice Mansel died on 10th April 1559 and left in his will a year's wages and a coat to each and every one of his servants. He was succeeded by his son, Edward, who was knighted a few months later. Four years later, George appears as a generous benefactor of the poor of Sweyneshe, contributing 1s. towards poor-relief every Sunday in St. Mary's Church. His 1s. exceeded the contributions of other parishioners, but this was not an act of generosity on his part, but an obligation in that an act of 1563 made it compulsory for all householders to contribute to a poor-rate (the earliest form of Council Tax).

Little else can be said of George except that, at some point late in life, he is said to have married Dame Grace Bewring of London, widow of Geoffrey Newton, but in legal proceedings that took place after his death, his eldest grandson stated that he was never lawfully married to Dame Grace. One of the last references to George, prior to his death, is in a document, dated 15th June 1570, whereby he was summoned, along with William Herbert of Cardiff (also of Sweyneshe, his grandson, Mathew's eldest son), William Herbert of Cogan Pill (his son, Mathew's younger brother), Sir Edward Mansel and others, to furnish horses and arms for the Crown, possibly in connection with a rebellion in the north of England.

George died on 2nd September 1570, possibly in his mid-seventies. The bulk of his estate, including The Plas, passed to his eldest grandson, William (son of Mathew), who later became known as Sir William Herbert of Sweyneshe, despite the fact that by *c.*1582 his principal residence was at Cardiff where he had built a mansion house known as the Friary on the former monastic site of Grey Friars. Sir William became a leading figure in the judicial and political affairs of Glamorgan – a JP from 1554 onwards, five times Sheriff, twice elected Knight of the Shire, and Deputy-lieutenant from 1579 onwards. William also inherited his grandfather's temperament and tendency towards violence, for in his capacity as a JP he sent a letter in 1576 to Sir Edward Mansel concerning witnesses to be examined with regard to a recent affray at Cowbridge between his servants and those of Sir Edward; moreover, during the Cardiff riots of 1593-8, William gained notoriety, being accused of parading men in armour to overawe the bailiffs of the town and resorting to armed violence – but unlike his grandfather he did not fall from high office. He died childless in 1609, his estate passing to his younger brother, Nicholas, who also acquired Cogan Pill when his first cousin, George, died childless.

In Conclusion

In the 75 years following George Herbert's death, Sweyneshe and Gower witnessed a certain amount of change. Sweyneshe certainly benefitted from an increase in wealth, mainly from coal, and with a rise in the resident population there was a corresponding change in the town's housing, both in number and design, the housing within the town walls becoming congested. Equally significant is that, from 1584-5 onwards, the name Swanzey appears to have become the standardized spelling of the town's name, at least as far as the borough's accounts are concerned.

During this same period there were changes, too, in the religious sphere, which on a much larger scale were to plunge the realm into civil war. Three years into the war there returned to Swanzey a local man, a yeoman farmer, Philip Jones, to take up the appointment of Governor of the town and who later became Steward of Gower on behalf of Oliver Cromwell. Jones went on to become not only the most powerful man in South Wales, but also one of Cromwell's most trusted councillors, and as Philip, Lord Jones he became a member of Cromwell's equivalent of the House of Lords. During his 15 years in the service of Parliament, Jones accumulated a fortune. He made many enemies, too, which makes it difficult to ascertain whether, as a result of the numerous charges of misconduct that were brought against him – none of which were proved – he was a man wrongfully hounded by his enemies, or whether he was a very clever rogue.

---

* The Episcopal returns of 1563 record that there were in total 1,301 households in the Lordship of Gower and Kilvey. The figure is believed to have been only an estimate; nevertheless, when the figure is multiplied by five (the average number of persons per household), an estimate of the population of the lordship is arrived at – namely 6,500.

CHAPTER VII
Colonel Philip Jones (1)

Birthplace and Forefathers

Philip Jones was born in 1618 in a farmhouse known as Pen-y-waun, a mile to the north-west of Llangyfelach Church. In several documents he is referred to as the son of David Philip John ap Rees-hir, but to his Welsh-speaking neighbours he would have been known as Philip ap Dafydd ap Philip ap Siôn ap Rhys-hir. The reason for the difference is that in documents of the period – and in those of the preceding two centuries – the spelling of Welsh names was often anglicized and the 'ap' (meaning 'son of') was usually dropped. Philip had, however, like his father and grandfather before him, taken the name of his paternal great-grandfather, John – or Johnes, meaning John's son – as his surname. Philip and his immediate fore-fathers were freehold farmers; as such they saw themselves as gentlemen.

According to the antiquarian, Isaac Hamon, Philip's grandfather, Philip John ap Rees, was 'of Kellywooren' (Gelliwern) and owned 'Kelly wren ucha' (Gelliwern Fawr, the farm where he lived) 'Kelly wren issa' (Gelliwern Isaf) and 'Keven y forest' (Cefn Fforest Fawr) all of which are located near Pen-y-waun farm. 'Keven y forest' appears to have been an illegal acquisition because, in 1594, Philip John ap Rees was cited in a lawsuit as one of three men who had encroached on 300 acres of the Earl of Worcester's land in 'Keven y fforest', located to the north-west of Pen-y-waun farm. Despite the lawsuit, the Earl never regained his lost acres.

In his will, dated 1621, Philip John Prees (ap Rees) refers to at least seven properties. He must, therefore, have been a landowner of considerable worth. This is borne out by Isaac Hamon's statement that 'this Philip John ap Rees had a considerable estate of freehold till he shared it amongst his sons'. That he 'shared it amongst his sons' is surprising because, in 1543, an act had been passed, abol-ishing the Welsh system of partitionable inheritance (akin to gavelkind) in favour of the English system of primogeniture whereby an estate (or at least the bulk of it) passed to the eldest legitimate son. Yet in Gower, 80 years after the act had been passed, some landowners were still sharing their property equally between all their sons.

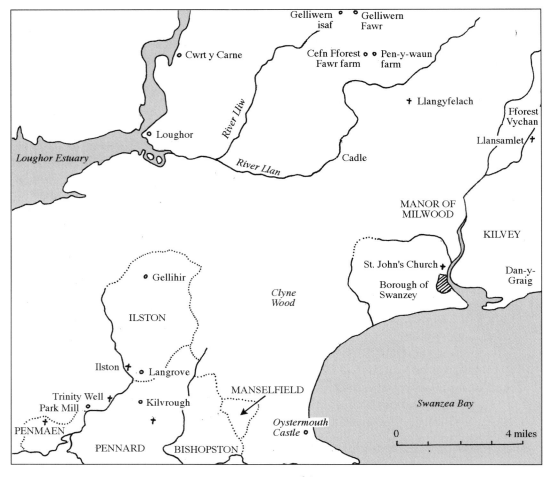

East Gower 1642–59

Philip Jones's father, David, had been one of six sons. David certainly had Pen-y-waun as his portion as Isaac Hamon refers to him as 'of Penywyn'. When he died in 1642, or perhaps a little later, David did not divide his estate between his three sons, but assigned Pen-y-waun to his eldest son, Philip Jones, and Philip's son and heir, Oliver, referred to it in his will as 'a messuage called Penywaun'. Sadly, the ruins of the farmhouse called Pen-y-waun Fawr were finally demolished in the year 2000.

Philip's Unrecorded Years

Although nothing is known of Philip Jones until 1645 when he was 27 years old, it is necessary to explore the world in which he lived, otherwise it will be difficult to grasp the circumstances that led to his remarkable rise to wealth and influence. That he was an able opportunist is indisputable, but the opportunity to advance himself had yet to present itself; until then he remains a nonentity and did not become a yeoman farmer until his father died in *c.*1642.

The Puritans

It can be assumed that his early life revolved around Pen-y-waun farm and, to a lesser extent, Llangyfelach Church because failure to attend Sunday service would have resulted in a heavy fine, even imprisonment. He must also have spent time acquiring an education, as his signature on later documents is bold, oozing with confidence, and certainly not that of an uneducated man. It would be reasonable to suppose that he received his education in England, as a neighbour's son, Marmaduke Matthews of Nydfwch, received his education at Oxford, albeit with the intention of becoming a cleric. Had Philip gone to a similar place of learning he would have discovered that the affairs of both church and state were closely connected, little realizing that one day he would have a role to play both in the affairs of state and in the propagation of Puritanism in South Wales.

Through his education Philip would have learned that when James I came to the throne in 1603, he alienated both the Catholics and the Protestant extremists known as the Puritans, so named because they wished to purify the Protestant Church of England of all trace of Catholicism. The majority of Puritans were Presbyterians, and what they desired was not simply a less ritualized form of worship with the emphasis on preaching, but a church in which bishops shared power with presbyters; that is, councils of elected ministers and lay-elders. James made it plain he would never agree to their desires. As head of the established Anglican/Protestant Church he needed his bishops to execute his wishes, and through them control his subjects. Consequently, the Puritans' position began to change from being a force within the Anglican Church to a force increasingly without.

Puritanism had first taken root in the towns of south-east England where commercial activities served as a vehicle for reforming ideas to be brought in from the Continent. Those who became Puritans still attended their parish church for Sunday services, but they also met in private houses for prayer, prophecy and discussion. They were, however, conspicuous by the fact that they dressed soberly, worked hard, shunned pleasurable activities, frequently used biblical phrases in their everyday speech and talked through their nose, a habit they took to America where it became the origin of the Yankee accent.

In Wales the Puritans were thin on the ground. Yet Philip Jones – even if he had not received his education in England – would still have picked up the bare essentials of Puritanism from the sermons that were preached at Llangyfelach Church. In 1580 a David Hopkins of Neath bequeathed money to pay itinerant 'lecturers' to give sermons in Welsh in the churches at Llangyfelach, Neath, Cadoxton and Swanzey. These sermons were usually delivered by zealous young graduates, and what those with Puritan sympathies had to say was as much political as religious. One of the most frequent quotations used by Puritan 'lecturers' came from Daniel, Chapter Three, verses 17–18, which state:

17. Our God whom we serve is able to deliver us from the burning fiery furnace, and He will deliver us out of thine hand, O King.
18. But if not, be it known unto thee, O King, we will not serve thy gods, nor worship the golden images which thou hast set up.

At Swanzey commercial contacts with London and Bristol would have exposed the townspeople to some Puritan influences. Stronger influences came from itinerant lecturers, and the borough accounts from 1613 onwards show that successive portreeves and aldermen paid itinerant preachers for their services out of the common coffer, and some of these preachers are known to have held Puritan views. That Puritanism gained a foothold in the town is evident in the parish register, which, from the 1630s onwards, shows a marked increase in the number of children given Old Testament names such as Isaac, Ruth and Rebecca. Such names were favoured by parents with Puritan sympathies.

In the Gower Peninsula there is definite evidence of Puritanism in the adjoining parishes of Penmen, Pennard and Ilston. The bishop of St. David's reported in 1636 that the vicar of Penmaen, Marmaduke Matthews (1606-83), a native of Llangyfelach parish, had preached 'against the keeping of all holy days', a view shared by others 'of profane opinion'. Two years later, when threatened with proceedings in the Court of High Commission, Matthews fled to America, but returned to Gower after the English realm had been torn apart by civil war – the King versus Parliament.

In 1642, the parishioners of neighbouring Pennard, 'having never had more than four services a year … and those by a man of very scandalous life', petitioned the authorities to appoint a Flintshire man, Ambrose Mostyn (1610-63), as 'a lecturer' because he was 'a man of goodly sort, and one who can preach in the Welsh and English tongues'. The authorities agreed to the request on the condition that the appointment would be 'at their own proper cost' and that Ambrose would 'preach every Lord's day in the forenoon and afternoon'. When civil war broke out a few months later, Ambrose fled to England rather than risk persecution in Royalist Gower.

As to the parish of Ilston, this (along with the northern part of Pennard) appears to have been a hotbed of radical reform, as several gentry families residing in the locality appear to have held Puritan views – the Dawkins of Kilvrough, the Prices of Gellihir and the Bowens of Langrove to name but a few. In 1641 the Ilston parishioners petitioned Parliament for the local clergyman, William Houghton, to be replaced by John Miles (1621-83) of Herefordshire. When civil war broke out the following year, John fled to England where, at much later date, he may have served as a chaplain in Oliver Cromwell's New Model Army.

Given time the Puritans would have broken away from the Anglican Church to become Presbyterians, Baptists, Independents and the like. In November 1639, William Wroth, rector of Llanfache, in Monmouthshire, founded the first Independent Church in Wales; three years later, a second Independent Church was established at Cardiff. There is even a suggestion that an Independent Church had been established at Swanzey prior to the outbreak of civil war, one that had been 'gathered at first by Mr. Ambrose Mostyn'. Philip Jones, on the other hand, would never have risen to wealth and power had it not been for the strife caused by one man.

Charles I (1625-49)

Crowned King in 1625, Charles soon found himself at odds with Parliament over taxation. Several times he dissolved Parliament to rule without it, once for a period of eleven years. Charles and his advisors proved ingenious when it came to creating new and excessive taxation, so much so that had King John been witness to their devices he would have applauded them. Charles was no lover of Puritans. His Archbishop of Canterbury, William Laud, was by today's definition a High Churchman, an Anglo-Catholic. Backed by Charles, Laud restored church ceremony to an extent that was considered unacceptable even to Protestants; he even tried to transform the communion table into an altar. Laud persecuted the Puritans to the extent that, during the greater part of Charles's reign, about 60,000 of them emigrated to America. He also caused the Presbyterian Scots to rebel. In 1640 Charles, being desperately short of money, recalled Parliament twice, the second of which – the Long Parliament – managed to undermine his position as King to a degree that he found unacceptable, and on 22nd August 1642 he declared war on the rebel majority in Parliament and on London, the capital which they controlled.

The First Civil War (1642-46)

One of the dividing lines between the warring factions was that of religion – Puritan sympathizers versus Protestants who favoured the Church of England as it existed, and also Catholics. On the ground, Parliament held London as well as the southern and eastern half of England, whereas Charles could command loyalty from the northern and western parts of the realm. In Wales the gentry by and large supported the King, and the lower orders followed the gentry's lead. There were, however, exceptions to this rule, the most notable being the English-speaking part of southern Pembrokeshire where Philip Herbert, Earl of Pembroke, and his tenants supported Parliament.

A New Magazine in the Townhall

At Swanzey the common attorney's accounts for 1642 record the cost incurred 'in making of the new magazine in the lower town hall', in total £2 19s. 1d. The 'New Castle' (built in *c.*1300) had long been neglected, as a survey of 1583 records 'the Castle of Swanzey, the buildings whereof are in decay'. Two years later the borough accounts record 'the Shirehall of Swanzey, being almost finished'. If this Shirehall was the Townhall frequently referred to in 17th-century documents, then it stood on the east side of Castle Square, its rear wall adjoining the west curtain wall of the 'New Castle' (the remains of the west curtain wall were finally demolished in 1774). The 17th-century Townhall or Shirehall consisted of (1) a guildhall and (2) a grand jury room, both on the first floor, which could be reached via an external stairway and a porch at the north end of the building. On the ground floor were several service rooms, one of which was converted into a magazine.

The Townhall as depicted in 1820.
The Dark house or gaol is marked A and consisted of several dark cells.
The doorway marked B may have led into a room that was converted
into a magazine in 1642

The Welsh – a Continual Sacrifice to the Sword

On 12th October, Charles left Shrewsbury to march on London with an army that was described as 'raw…unskilled and so unwilling … to fight'. A large proportion of his infantry had been recruited in Wales, and came, according to one eyewitness, 'in the same garments in which they left their native fields', armed 'with scythes, pitchforks and even sickles'. At Edgehill, near Warwick, they were intercepted by Parliamentary forces and badly mauled. Eyewitness accounts claimed that nearly 1,000 Welshmen fell that day, the field 'covered with the dead' of both England and Wales, among them Lieutenant-colonel William Herbert of Cogan Pill, MP for Cardiff. Despite the appalling loss, the King pressed on, reaching the outskirts of London on 12th November, where, in the face of overwhelming odds, he was forced to retire to Oxford.

It was said, towards the close of the First Civil War, that 'all Wales was the nursery of the King's infantry', and that the untrained and ill-equipped Welsh were 'a continual sacrifice to the sword'. Edgehill was only the start of it all because, while Charles marched on London, a second army, said to have been 7,000 strong, was raised in South Wales. Henry Somerset, Earl of Worcester, Lord of Gower and probably the richest man in the realm, is reputed to have spent £10,000 in raising this particular army. On or about 4th November, this South Walian army assembled at Cardiff, and 'with colours flying and drums beating' it set out to join forces with the King. Near Tewkesbury the army was intercepted by Parliamentary forces. The 'ragged and inexperienced' South Walians suffered badly – 2,500 dead, 1,200 taken prisoner and the rest 'sought safety in flight'.

Henry Somerset's eldest son, Edward, Lord Herbert, with the aid of his father's money, then raised 1,500 foot and 500 horse mainly from Monmouthshire. It had been Lord Herbert's intention to take Gloucester, but while his men encamped at Highnam, not far from the city, they were surprised by garrison troops and forced to surrender on 24th March 1643. The Parliamentary forces based at Gloucester continued to disrupt communications between South Wales and Oxford to the extent that, in August 1643, Charles postponed his advance on London in order to lay siege to the city; in this he was supported by Lord Herbert who, undeterred by the debacle at Highnam, raised yet another army from South Wales – 4,000 foot and 800 horse – again at his father's expense. The siege proved short-lived, for Gloucester was relieved by Parliamentary forces on 5th September.

Swanzey – 1643
The borough accounts for Swanzey record that in 1643

> There was paid in April last for my Lord Marquis of Worcester, his servants' diet & horse meat £10 9s. 4d. and 19s. 2d. more was paid for one night's entertainment to Sir Marmaduke Lloyd, all being £11 8s. 6d.

The entry shows that the Lord of Gower, Henry Somerset, had been created First Marquis of Worcester in recognition of his huge financial assistance to the King. The purpose of his visit was presumably to urge the townspeople to greater efforts. The Glamorgan gentry may have declared for Charles, but they were begrudging in their support, preferring to safeguard local interests rather than meet the needs of the King. For a start, Charles was desperately short of men, for not only had his Oxford army suffered heavy casualties, but its strength had been depleted still further by desertion and sickness. The need for more men could have been met, in part, by the county's trained bands: the militia made up of men who were socially and politically reliable.

> None of the meaner sort or servants, but only gentry, free-holders and good farmers, or their sons.

These men were grouped into bands relative to the hundred in which they lived. They were unlikely to have been trained, nor were they adequately armed, but despite these deficiencies they could still have been of use to Charles. Yet the Glamorgan

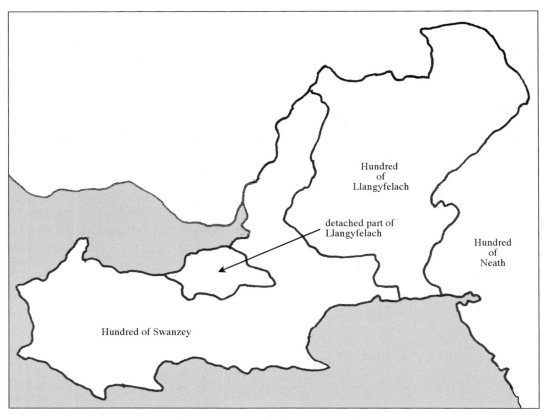

*The three most westerly hundreds of Glamorgan. That of Llangyfelach was
a predominantly Welsh-speaking area, as was the Hundred of Neath*

Commissioners of Array (those appointed to carry out the King's wishes within the county) would not dispatch its militia to Oxford for fear of enemy incursions. Rather, the Commissioners appear to have conscripted men from the lower orders – labourers, the unemployed, those with criminal records, even vagrants – and these men were certainly ill-equipped and untrained. This state of affairs was made evident in August when the Governor of Cardiff ordered the Commissioners of Array, Bussy Mansel of Briton Ferry, Walter Thomas of Swanzey and William Thomas of Dan-y-Graig to raise from the hundreds of Swanzey, Llangyfelach and Neath a further 60, 20 and 40 men respectively. On 13th August, William Thomas wrote to the Governor of Cardiff, protesting that

> their whole [Swanzey] band is already in service and so long continue under your command in the garrison.

In response to a rebuke from the Governor of Cardiff, Bussy Mansel, Walter Thomas and William Thomas then wrote, on 15th August:

We have done the uttermost … in accomplishing your orders for the raising of men in the hundred of Swanzey, yet could we not with all our industry find out of fit men but 40, the which number we have delivered into the hands of the high constables and herein closed sent [a] list of their names together with a list of 20 persons out of the hundred of Llangyfelach. We can [rest] assured that these parts are so gleaned of all spare people … that the husbandmen will be hardly able to manage their tillage, and thereby … a scarcity of grain will ensue.

The letter also makes it plain how poorly armed the conscripts were:

We received 12 bill staves for Mr William Gybbs which are carried by some of these men; more arms we could not get together upon so short summons. Neither do we conceive that the county will afford any worth the showing in the field.

Gun-runners at Swanzey

The last quote make it plain that there were no arms to spare in the county, which may have been true when the letter was written, but on 24th July the Commissioners of Array for Glamorgan entered into an agreement with two Frenchmen whereby the Frenchmen would ship to Swanzey

200 barrels of powder whereof 2 parts must be musket powder and a third cannon at 18d. per pound, the one with the other.
1,000 pound of match at 6d. per pound and 500 li. muskets and bandoliers of the best at 18s. musket and bandolier.

After the Frenchmen had evaded Parliamentary ships and landed the munitions, Robert Donnell of Swanzey was ordered to deliver 'all such muskets' to William Thomas, who was to test them, using a barrel of gunpowder and a quantity of match, and to distribute the muskets that were serviceable to the trained bands of the five most westerly hundreds. The unserviceable muskets were to be sent to Cardiff for distribution among the trained bands of the five eastern hundreds. It appears that the only weapons sent to the King's Oxford army were those that were loaned by men of means, for in a register of the Commissioners of Array, dated 18th August, it states:

A musketeer of the Civil War period

A perfect list of all such arms as have been lent by the gentlemen underwritten, for his Majesty's service ...

One gentlemen, William Thomas, loaned 6 muskets, 10 (pounds?) of powder and 15 blackbills. Another contributor was Marmaduke Matthews, former vicar of Penmaen, who had fled Gower at the onset of war. Evidently, Marmaduke had returned and, despite being a Puritan, loaned – possibly under duress – 15 muskets, 10 (pounds?) of powder and 2 clubs.

Contributions to the War Chest

When it came to contributing money the Glamorgan gentry were forthcoming, for in October £1,000 was levied on the county, £120 16s. 8d. of which was rated on the Swanzey hundred. Money could also be raised by sequestration; that is, confiscation of the estates of convicted 'separatists and persons disaffected unto his Majesty' the King. On 26th July, Bussy Mansel and William Thomas were ordered to sequestrate the estates of two members of the Gower gentry – Rowland Dawkin of Pennard and Jenkin Francklin of Ilston. The movables of these two men were to be sold and their lands and tenements set out to rent, but Mansel and Thomas appear to have been reluctant to act. However, sometime after 15th September, when Mansel and Thomas carried out their orders, both Dawkin and Francklin conformed and their estates were restored. At a subsequent date, Dawkin left Gower to become a colonel in the Parliamentary army.

Local Men of Note

Born in 1618, Rowland Dawkin of Kilvrough was a man of considerable landed wealth. His ancestry can be traced back to Sir William Langton of Kilvrough, who also held Langrove, Henllys and Gellihir. In 1305, Sir William stoutly opposed the tyrannical Lord of Gower, William de Breos VII, and in doing so,

> the said de Breos and others, with force of arms, did come to the house of Sir William Langton, at Kilvrough, and ... carried him to the said de Breos's castle ... of Oystermouth.

Three generations later, the family changed its name to Dawkin, and in subsequent centuries the family appears to have lost the greater part of its estate. Then, in 1534, George Herbert bought the Kilvrough lands; that same year, he sold Kilvrough to William (ap) Hopkin Dawkin (of Gellihir in Ilston) in part exchange for lands at Pant-y-Gwydr, Swanzey. Twenty-three years later, this William Hopkin Dawkin was involved in the affray at Oxwich; he was Rowland Dawkin's great-great-grandfather. Rowland, the eldest son of George Dawkin, married Mary, daughter of George Bowen of Langrove, by whom he had three sons and three daughters. The fact that his daughters – Rebecca, Priscilla and Ruth – all had biblical names is

Major-General Rowland Dawkin

reason to establish Rowland as a Puritan.

A neighbour of Rowland Dawkin, Jenkin Francklin, had descended from the Harry Francklen involved in the Oxwich affray. He was a gentleman, a free-holder with Puritan sympathies, as evidenced by the sequestration order and by the fact that, many years later, his name was written in the register of the Baptist church at Ilston.

Bussy Mansel, Walter Thomas and William Thomas have several times been mentioned as Commissioners of Array. In his early 20s, Bussy Mansel of Briton Ferry was the youngest of these three Royalists, the son of Arthur Mansel who was a grandson of Sir Edward Mansel of Oxwich. Bussy's mother, Jane, was the sole heiress of William Price, a coal magnate, and it was through his mother that Bussy inherited a manor house at Briton Ferry and coal interests in the Neath area. In Gower he was Lord of the manor of Millwood (the largest part of which lay within the parish of St. John, near Swanzey) where he also had a stake in coal. Bussy was not a staunch Royalist; he may even have had Puritan sympathies. In later years he twice transferred his allegiance to the winning side.

A staunch Royalist, Walter Thomas of Swanzey was the oldest of the trio, one who claimed descent from Einion ap Collwyn. He was a mercer and merchant, an exporter of iron and agricultural by-products. He also had a stake in coal in 'Clyne Fforest' in 1642, and in February 1643/44 he obtained the right to mine coal in the parishes of Swanzey and Llangyfelach. As Portreeve in 1615-6, Walter was responsible for initiating work at his own expense on the town's third quay. Walter was again Portreeve in 1625, and may have been Deputy-steward of Gower and Kilvey in 1631. He was certainly Steward on 1st October 1632 as he is referred to as such when he presided over the court leet on that date. He held the stewardship until 1644 when a Colonel Donnell replaced him.

According to some sources, William Thomas of Dan-y-Graig was a nephew of Walter Thomas. Other sources maintain that he was Walter's son, which is probably true because William is said to have become possessed of Dan-y-Graig as a result of his marriage to Catherine Mansel, Bussy Mansel's sister, and by this marriage he had a son (who died young) whom he named Walter, presumably after the man believed to have been his father. A staunch Royalist, William was an alderman with a considerable interest in coal, particularly in the Llansamlet area. In 1644 he became Sheriff of Glamorgan. At an unknown date his daughter, Ann, married Jeremy, the eldest son of the Puritan, Rowland Dawkin.

Threat from the West

At the close of 1642 the gentry of southern Pembrokeshire reported to Parliament that they held the towns of Pembroke, Tenby and Haverfordwest. No attempt was made by Royalist forces in West Wales to deal with this Parliamentary enclave until the Royalist commander, Richard Vaughan, Earl of Carbery (whose seat was at *Gelli Aur* – Golden Grove) decided to test the allegiance of the opposition. In August and September 1643 most of the gentry of southern Pembrokeshire and the towns of Tenby and Haverfordwest submitted peacefully. The town of Pembroke, on the other hand, with its stout walls, its castle and its resolute mayor, John Poyer, chose to resist. Carbery responded by establishing small garrisons in southern Pembrokeshire, thereby dispersing his forces to the extent that he did not feel strong enough to mount an assault on Pembroke.

The arrival of Parliamentary ships in Milford Haven in mid-February 1644 appears to have coincided with the time when Colonel Rowland Laugharne, of St. Brides in

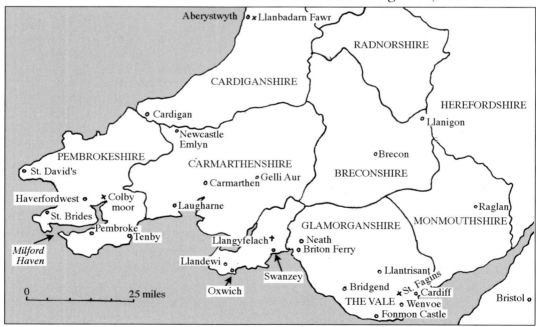

South Wales 1642-59

southern Pembrokeshire, took command of Parliamentary forces. With seamen to bolster his land forces, the young and energetic Laugharne, went on the offensive. By April he had taken control of Pembrokeshire as well as parts of Cardiganshire and Carmarthenshire. That same month the Earl of Carbery resigned his command. Events such as these caused consternation among the Swanzey burgesses, so much so that on 1st May they cancelled the court leet 'by reason of the troublesome times'. They even spent 16s. 6d. on repairing 'the turret in the castle', meaning, presumably, the half-round tower. More important still, Walter Thomas was made Governor of Swanzey, and later admitted that as such 'he did arm and array the inhabitants', which would have been easy for him to do because, three months later, it was reported that the Glamorgan trained bands had 800 arms, 784 of which were stored at Swanzey.

In May the Parliamentarian, Robert Moulton, on board the frigate *Lion,* in Milford Haven, wrote 'to the mayor and gentlemen of Swanzey', calling upon them to

> yield the town and garrison into the obedience of … Parliament, and in so doing you … shall be defended against Irish rebels, Papists, and those who seek to subvert liberties, and to destroy religion … Therefore, consider of it, and submit; for if you shall be obstinate, and spill any blood in resisting, you may not expect such favours as your neighbours have had. And this is the advice of your friend, who endeavours to preserve you, if you accept of his proffer; if not, I shall endeavour to keep you without trade.

The town's reply was:

> We cannot understand how we may … return you the name of gentlemen to your rude and rebellious paper … to will and require us forthwith to yield the town and garrison of Swanzey into the obedience of … Parliament. In defiance of … your traitorous summons, we send you this our fixed resolution, that we will neither yield town or garrison but will defend the same and our country against … your proud and insolent menacings … Subscribed by the High Sheriff, and most of the Gentlemen of Glamorganshire.

The High Sheriff of Glamorgan at that time may have been David Jenkins of Hensol, 'the Judge of the Mountains', but by the summer he had been replaced by William Thomas of Dan-y-Graig, who later declared that he had been compelled to carry out the duties of that office. As to Robert Moulton, he appears to have kept his word with regard to keeping the town 'without trade' because, at a later date, it was reported that Parliamentary ships had taken 'many of Swanzey boats and some of Cardiff'.

Colonel Sir Charles Gerard
Relief came to Swanzey and south-east Wales in the person of Sir Charles Gerard, described as of 'eminent courage and proved conduct in martial affairs'; he was also

ruthless. With 2,000 English and Welsh troops, Gerard swept through South Wales, winning back territory that Rowland Laugharne had taken from the Earl of Carbery, including Haverfordwest, which fell after some resistance on 22nd August. As a preliminary to besieging Pembroke and Tenby, Gerard implemented a scorched earth policy, driving off cattle and burning crops to deny the Parliamentarians in the besieged towns from foraging for food. London newspapers accused him of several massacres, none of which had any foundation.

Gerard's scorched earth policy in West Wales caused widespread indignation, as did the misconduct of his troops who plundered both town and countryside for supplies and booty. In Glamorgan he was hated for his demands for men and money, and for the way he rode roughshod over the gentry, several of whom he removed from high office, replacing them with men of his choosing. In Swanzey, Walter Thomas was relieved of his governorship of the town and replaced by Colonel Richard Donnell.

Rowland Laugharne

At the end of August, Gerard was recalled to engage his forces elsewhere. Three months later, Major-general Rowland Laugharne – after receiving reinforcements by sea – took the offensive again, quickly overrunning Pembrokeshire, but meeting stout resistance at Laugharne and Cardigan castles, both of which he subjected to bombardment before taking them by storm. A counter-attack on Cardigan by 2,000 Royalists in January 1645 resulted in bitter street fighting. Laugharne drove the Royalists out, forcing them to fall back on Newcastle Emlyn.

It was while Laugharne lay siege to Newcastle Emlyn that Gerard marched through mid-Wales to fall upon Laugharne's troops, taking them by surprise and overwhelming them by sheer weight of numbers. In the savage onslaught, Laugharne lost over 500 men, either killed or captured, and had to flee with his shattered remnants. The following day, Gerard entered Haverfordwest unopposed. On 8th May, Laugharne wrote to a Parliamentary commander in North Wales, saying:

> The enemy have become masters of the whole country excepting the garrisons of Pembroke and Tenby. I only have 400 foot and 120 horse … the enemy have 3,000 men … I ask you, the only friend … nearest at hand, to assist me by speedily sending a considerable party this way to divert the fury of the enemy, now ready to destroy us.

At Swanzey the borough accounts record:

Paid the ringer [of bells] the last of April for joy of the victory got by the general [Gerard] at Newcastle Emlyn.

Elsewhere in Glamorgan, Gerard's return caused consternation among the gentry, and this, coupled with the burdensome demands that had been repeatedly made upon the county, fostered a mood of open disaffection. When the King came to Cardiff at the end of July, to ascertain why his call for more men had not been met, he was presented with a list of demands, one of which was that Gerard should be relieved of his Welsh command. These demands were not presented to Charles by the gentry alone, but by the whole Glamorgan militia, which, when it assembled at Llantrisant on 1st August, adopted the title of the Peaceable Army. In the face of open disobedience, Charles had no recourse but to agree to the demands and leave. However, on 7th September, Charles sent troops to bring the Peaceable Army into line. When the opposing forces met outside Cardiff, the Peaceable Army backed down and agreed to disband. It, then, becomes apparent that one of the principal leaders of the Peaceable Army had been young Bussy Mansel. Bussy was relieved of his commission, but within ten days he was one of several who led the Army into Cardiff, where they forced the governor to surrender the castle to them.

The mood of the Peaceable Army may have been influenced by the disastrous defeat of Royalist forces at Nasby in June, and by the fall of Bristol to Parliament in September, but events in West Wales may have been another consideration. At the end of May, Gerard had left the region to deploy his troops elsewhere. Within two months of Gerard's departure, Laugharne had rebuilt his shattered army and, at the end of July, he led 1,000 men out of Pembroke. On the 1st August he clashed with 1,500 Royalists at Colby Moor, five miles outside Haverfordwest, and utterly defeated them. By the end of September almost the whole of West Wales had declared for Parliament. On 12th October, Laugharne rode into Carmarthen as a triumphant hero.

The manner in which Laugharne entered Swanzey is unknown, but it is likely to have been peaceful for the simple reason that the burgesses, like burgesses in other towns in West Wales, were for the most part lukewarm in their support for either King or Parliament. Few would have wanted to see their homes burnt, their families put at risk, or their livelihoods brought to ruin. The reply to Moulton's call to 'yield the town and garrison' in 1644 may have been defiant, but when the enemy drew near to Swanzey the following year the burgesses decided it was far better to accept the protection of approaching forces than to offer resistance and see their town suffer. That Laugharne entered Swanzey, probably in November, is made evident by the borough accounts for the financial year beginning Michaelmas (29th September) 1645, which record:

Paid for wine and beer for entertainment of General Laugharne – £1 0s. 4d.
Paid towards the delivery of a petition to Colonel-general Mansel – £1

The second entry relating to £1 was obviously made sometime after 17th November, as records show that on that date Bussy Mansel was appointed by Parliament 'to be Commander-in-Chief of all forces in the County of Glamorgan', by which time the gentry of Glamorgan had abandoned the King's cause.

These, then, are the events that led to a period known as the Interregnum (the interval between the reign of Charles I and Charles II). It was a period in which Philip Jones was to prosper.

Chapter VIII
Colonel Philip Jones (2)

At a hearing that took place *c*.1650 several unnamed persons tried to discredit Philip Jones by bringing a series of 'articles' against him. These 'articles' provide insight into his early years in office – for example, the first 'article' states that:

> in the beginning of the first war in South Wales, when Major-general Laugharne raised and levied forces for the Parliament, [Philip] having not above £10 per annum, left his own county and came to Pembrokeshire. Major-general Laugharne offered him a captain's place, which he refused, answering that it was against his conscience to fight and spill blood.

The second 'article' stated:

> That the said Jones refused Major-general Laugharne['s] convoy to guard him out of the enemy quarters [territory], but accepted rather of Gerard's pass procured by a grand malignant, one Mr Lloyd of Tryfool.

Philip gave no reply to the accusations, presumably because he was not present at the hearing, but on his behalf his associate, Rowland Dawkin, swore on oath that

> the first [article] he believed it false on the whole.

Rowland gave no reply to the second 'article', but it can be assumed that both 'articles' were false because (1) Gerard was not involved in the war in West Wales until May 1644 and (2) Laugharne did not attain the rank of Major-general until later that same year. In his thesis entitled 'Colonel Philip Jones 1618-74', published in *Trans. Cymm.* of 1966, A. G. Veysey states that Jones

> reappeared in Glamorgan when Parliamentary prospects began to take a turn for the better and quickly took a leading part in affairs as one of the commissioners sent from London … to arrange the pacification of the county in October 1645. There is little doubt that he had … been acting as an intermediary between the Glamorgan gentry

and Parliamentary officials after the dissatisfaction with the failing Royalist cause … His appointment as Governor of Swanzey and a commissioner … on 17th November that year were a reward for … persuading his native county to declare for Parliament. He had no military rank, which indicates that he had taken no part in the fighting, and his selection for these important posts reflects the obvious lack of sufficient gentry of … firm Parliamentary leanings … to fill the many vacant offices.

This assessment originates presumably, from a Memoir of the Members of the Parliament of 1658, which records that at the time of

the first of the wars he [Jones] had about fourteen or twenty pounds per annum [his income from Pen-y-waun farm] and improved his interest upon the account of the cause: first he was an agent for some Parliamenters in London, where, gaining acquaintance, and making good use of them, he became governor of a garrison, then a colonel.

Philip became a governor on 17th November (the same day that Bussy Mansel became Commander-in-Chief of Glamorgan forces), for on that day the House of Commons did

nominate and appoint Philip Jones, Esquire, to be Governor of the Garrison of Swanzey.

He then became Steward of Gower and Kilvey, being referred to as 'Steward and Governor of the town' at a Common Hall on 27th April 1646.

Philip wielded even more power as a member of the County Committee, which comprised of 15 or more of Parliament's most trusted supporters, among them Bussy Mansel, Colonel Rowland Dawkin and Philip's brother-in-law, John Price. As Committeemen, Philip and his associates were responsible for the financial and military affairs of the county; most of them were appointed JPs as well. The oldest surviving document relating to the County Committee concerns an ordinance of 1645, which Parliament passed for the maintenance of the Glamorgan militia, thereby raising the county's monthly contribution from £67 to £162. It was only a matter of time before Philip became the leading Committeeman not only for Glamorgan but for the whole of South Wales and Monmouthshire as well. So influential did he become that only his nominees – his 'creatures' as they were called – were appointed to important positions such as JPs, sheriffs and MPs.

A Royalist Backlash

With the exception of Raglan and Aberystwyth castles, all South Wales was under Parliament's control by January 1646. There were, however, rumblings of discontent in the Vale of Glamorgan, one reason being that men of small substance (Philip among them) had been placed on the County Committee in preference to men of higher social standing. Another grievance was that these men were imposing Puritanism upon the county. The situation was such that on 26th January, Bussy Mansel wrote to Laugharne requesting speedy assistance, but the Major-general – who, at the time, was laying siege to Aberystwyth Castle – did not respond.

The storm broke on 6th February when militiamen besieged Cardiff. Seven days later the Parliamentary garrison at Cardiff was forced to withdraw to the castle. Then, on 18th February, the militiamen were themselves obliged to leave the town and form up on a heath to the north; there they met Laugharne, who threw them into confusion and forced them back into the town. Two days later, as a result of negotiations, the militiamen were leaving the town when shots were exchanged. This led to a second engagement, and once again Laugharne was victorious.

Prior to Laugharne's involvement, a dispatch from Raglan Castle, dated 10th February, reported that Royalist troops 'are endeavouring to block up Cardiff' and 'are already in actual possession of Swanzey'. Further details of the situation at Swanzey are to be found in the 'articles' that were intended to discredit Philip Jones. The relevant 'article' states:

> That the said Jones, having a commission to be Governor of the Town of Swanzey, did, in the year 1646, leave a troop of 38 horse, commanded by Mr Edward Gwyn, to enter and take the said town, and possess themselves of all the magazines in the town and barkes [boats] that were in the Haven; so that, by reason of the said Jones's cowardly deportment, the enemy did then get the advantage of sending horse-loads [of munitions] thereof to the siege which was then laid by them before Cardiff.

Answering on behalf of Philip, Rowland Dawkin stated:

> that he knows Colonel Jones had a commission for the government of Swanzey [at] the time mentioned in the article; but at the time pretended in the article that Gwyn took the garrison, the Governor was not come to town, neither was it garrisoned by the Parliament forces till a fortnight after the insurrection of Cardiff was over [which ended 20th February]; and, though it be alleged in the article that by Colonel Jones's cowardly deportment, Gwyn possessed himself of all the magazines and provisions in the said town, to the great strengthening of the enemy, there was not any arms, ammunition, nor provision of the state, in the said town at the time.

While the town was in Royalist's hands, William Thomas and others laid siege to Briton Ferry House, home of Bussy Mansel, but the garrison there defeated the insurgents. William voluntarily surrendered to Laugharne on 25th February, by which time Swanzey had been restored to Parliamentary control. For his part in the siege and during the war, William had his estate sequestrated, but on 7th April he compounded (reached an agreement with Parliament) for his delinquency (a delinquent being someone who actively supported the King or assisted him with money), confessing that, being made Sheriff of Glamorgan in 1644, he had executed that office under the

Briton Ferry House, home of Bussy Mansel, 146 years after Royalists laid seige to it.

King's commission against the wishes of Parliament. He was fined £786 in September, but this was eventually reduced to £336.

In the case of Walter Thomas, he compounded on 9th April 1646, and did so through an agent due to 'his great weakness and age, being unable to stir in his bed without the assistance of two'. Walter confessed that he had been a Commissioner of Array for the King and that as 'Governor of Swansea he did arm and array the inhabitants'. On 7th August he was fined £400, but this was later reduced to £313. The punishment meted out to Walter and William Thomas appears to have been in accordance with the rules, but in the case of Henry Mansel of Llandewi there is a strong element of sleaze. At the hearing of *c.*1650 it was alleged in 'Article 7'

> That in the year 1646 the said Jones seized upon the writings [lease] of Mr Henry Mansel when his wife produced them before the Committee, forcing them from her; and then, to satisfy the gentlewoman, proposed that the writings be laid in the hands of Bussy Mansel, Esquire; the gentlewoman simply yielded thereto, the said Jones got a private order that the writings should be delivered unto him, which was done accordingly, so that now he enjoys the possession of … with the lands belonging to it.

Further details of the case are obscure, but in his thesis A.G. Veysey maintains that

> Henry Mansel of Llandewi, a former Commissioner of Array for the King ... had to appeal to the Committee for Compounding [in London] in September 1647 before Jones would surrender the lease of Llandewi Castle, which, Mansel complained, he had fraudulently obtained from the Glamorgan Committee. The Committee was later reprimanded for its 'unprecedented proceedings'.

A Spy at Swanzey

In March 1646, Charles surrendered to the Scots, his cause in England and Wales all but lost. Nevertheless, at the beginning of August the garrisons of six castles in Wales still held out on behalf of the King – Raglan in the south, the other five in the north. Elsewhere, staunch Royalists kept a wary eye on developments. At Swanzey a spy kept tabs of Colonel Philip Jones. In a letter to an eminent Royalist, dated 15th August and sent from the Nag's Head in Goat Street, the spy, James Jenkins, reported that

> All your friends here are well. Colonel Jones went out of the town on Wednesday last. He did what he could in this business. I hear there is 100 horse to wait on Colonel Mansel, and five companies of foot to remain in the garrison of Cardiff and Swanzey.

The Garrisons at Swanzey and Cardiff

Allegations of embezzlement are to be found among the list of 'articles' that were intended to discredit Philip Jones in *c.*1650. Article 8' stated:

> That, under the notion of being Governor of Swanzey, the said Jones levied divers sums of money and contributions; and having very few soldiers that were upon actual duty, he peremptorily commanded the townsmen to act as soldiers, and converted the aforesaid moneys to his own particular use, without there being any account to this day to the Committee of the County.

Answering on behalf of Philip, Rowland Dawkin

> said it's not true that ... Colonel Jones laid any taxation upon the county or levied any sums of money for the maintenance of his garrison; neither did he force the town to watch, but when the enemy had the field; nor ever receive any warrant from the Committee of the army till the 15 January 1647, and as for the number of soldiers, the mustering rolls will make it appear.

A similar allegation was made in 'Article 9', which relates to the time when Philip was Governor of Cardiff, a post to which he was appointed probably late in 1648. The relevant 'article' states:

> That whereas there is but sixscore foot [soldiers] allowed by the Establishment in the garrison of Cardiff; the said Jones, since he was commissioned Governor thereof, hath

entertained five companies, viz. his Own, Major Gawler's, Captain Morgan's, Captain Blethin's and Captain Nicholl's, ordering and aligning part of them to quarter in the County, to the prejudice of the well-affected.

Rowland Dawkin appears to have made no reply to 'Article 9', but the establishment of five companies at Cardiff and Swanzey had been decided upon long before Philip became Governor of Cardiff, as evidenced by the spy's letter of 1646.

Changes in the Burgess Body

At the Michaelmas court leet of 1646, Philip Jones was admitted to the borough as a burgess. More changes in the burgess body were to follow, changes that were in line with Parliament's policy of removing from positions of authority anyone who had espoused the King's cause. Consequently, on 6th January 1647 three Royalists – Walter Thomas, William Thomas and Leyshon Seys – were declared by a resolution of the Common Hall to be 'incapable of the place and privileges of Aldermen'. They were to be replaced by William Bayly, Richard Jones and Edward Bowen – all of whom were presumably Parliamentarians, but for reasons unknown Bowen's name was erased and only Bayly and Richard Jones were sworn in.

The Great House

It was necessary that, as Governor and Steward of Swanzey, Philip Jones should have a house fit for a man of his standing, and in February 1647 he purchased from a Royalist, Richard Seys, the Great House, which, in later records, was frequently referred to as 'in High Street below the gate'; that is, within the town walls. The house can be seen (marked 'J') on Samuel and Nathaniel Buck's engraving entitled *The East View of Swansea, 1748*. In his *Charters Granted to the Chief Borough of Swansea* (1867), G.G. Francis recalled:

The Great House, 100 years after Philip Jones bought it

> as a boy, being struck with the rich effect produced by the old oak panelling and carvings, covering the walls of some of the rooms.

The purchase of the Great House may have coincided with Philip's marriage to Jane, daughter of William Price of Gellihir, Esquire. The actual date of this marriage is unknown, but what is on record is that Jane bore four sons and five daughters. Two sons (John and Philip) and a daughter (Ann) are mentioned in a lease, dated 7th May 1649, which makes it possible to postulate that the marriage may have taken place in 1646, if not earlier. Jane's father, William Price, inherited Gellihir from his father, also William Price (second son of John Price of Cwrt y Carne, who had acquired the estate through his marriage to Elen Dawkin, grand-daughter of the William Hopkin Dawkin involved in the Oxwich affray). Despite being minor gentry, William Price was influential, he being Sheriff of Glamorgan in 1634; moreover, he appears to have had Puritan sympathies, residing as he did in that Gower enclave where Puritanism had taken root prior to the Civil War. It, therefore, seems likely that Jane's marriage may have been due in part to the religious convictions shared by her husband and her father. Her marriage may also have been the means of cementing an alliance between two influential men. Jane's brother, John Price, certainly benefited from his relationship with Philip, being selected for a number of important posts in the administration of South Wales, as well as becoming an MP on several occasions.

The purchase of the Great House was later seized upon as a means of discrediting Philip during the hearing of *c*.1650; the relevant 'article' states:

That the said Jones bought a new house of one Richard Seys, a delinquent, who is to this day so much favoured by the said Jones that, notwithstanding his being long since voted a delinquent, is not yet sequestered, and so has not yet compounded his estate with the Parliament; in which house the said Jones lived till his removal to the government of Cardiff.

In answer to the 'article', Rowland Dawkin

said it's true that Colonel Jones bought a house of Richard Seys in Swanzey, and [that he – Dawkin] was witness to the bargain; but believes that Seys was never protected from sequestration by the said Colonel Jones; but knows when Colonel Jones and others urged the Committee to prosecute effectually against several other delinquents, many of the Committee of Glamorgan refused, and said rigorous proceedings would incite the country.

Until 1966 it was commonly held that Philip Jones had been born in the Great House and not at Pen-y-waun. This view was the result of a letter, dated 1755, in which a distant relative of Jones maintained (albeit incorrectly) that Philip's 'grandfather and father lived in' this particular house. In his thesis of 1966 A.G. Veysey made it plain that the only Great House in High Street was the one Philip bought from Richard Seys.

Swanzey from the east as depicted by Francis Place in 1678 – 18 year.
Right of centre is the New Cast

The Fate of Swanzey Castle

On 3rd May 1647 Parliament gave orders for numerous castles throughout the realm to be 'disgarrisoned and the works slighted' so they could never again be used by Royalists. Among the works to be slighted was the 'New Castle' at Swanzey. It can be presumed that slighting would have involved the partial demolition of the east curtain wall and the N.E. Tower, as both the wall and the tower are depicted in a ruinous condition in Francis Place's pen and wash drawing of Swanzey in 1678.

What is noteworthy about the drawing is that it depicts a wall, which runs north-wards from the N.E. Tower to a smaller tower with a pyramid-shaped roof. This wall is believed to have been the east curtain wall of the Old Castle; if this is correct, the wall not only escaped slighting, but it appears to have been kept in a remarkably good condition. As to what happened to both castles after 1649, a survey of 1650 records that Matthew Davyes held a 99-year lease on

An ancient decayed building called the New Castle

and that Walter Thomas, Esquire, had

e restoration of the monarchy. Left of centre is the tower of St. Mary's.
hill dominates in the distance

Close-up of the New Castle from the above print

Two little gardens adjoining to the house of the said Walter called the Old Castle Gardens

In Francis Place's drawing the two little gardens are hidden from view by the Old Castle curtain wall referred to above.

The New Lord of Gower

Henry Somerset, First Marquis of Worcester and one of the King's staunchest supporters, had his estate confiscated by Parliament in 1646, the year of his death. On 5th May 1647, Parliament settled the Marquis's lands in Gloucestershire and Monmouthshire on Oliver Cromwell as a reward for his services during the Civil War. At an unrecorded date later that same year, Parliament added to Cromwell's good fortune by settling on him the Marquis's Lordship of Gower and Kilvey. So began a period in which Cromwell had a personal interest in the Borough of Swanzey; this not only brought Philip in direct contact with one of the most powerful men in the realm – he being Cromwell's Steward of Gower and Kilvey – but it also paved the way for Philip's remarkable rise to power.

The Second Civil War

In January 1648 Laugharne was summoned to London to answer allegations about his suspected involvement in Royalist plots, there to be detained on parole. That same month Parliament sent a Colonel Fleming to disband Laugharne's forces, for the most part without the pay that was owed to them. The Governor of Pembroke, John Poyer – who disagreed with Parliament's intention to disband Laugharne's forces – refused to co-operate, refused to hand over the castle and eventually drove Fleming out of town. In mid-March, Poyer declared for the King, soon to be joined by many of Laugharne's disaffected soldiers and by Colonel Rice Powell who, throughout the First Civil War, had been Laugharne's right-hand man. Poyer and Powell took control of Tenby, and later Carmarthen where, in the ensuing weeks, they were joined by Royalists from all over West Wales. They then marched towards Cardiff, confident that they would pick up more recruits along the way. On 5th May the *Perfect Diurnal* (a paper supporting Cromwell) reported:

> Just now we had intelligence that the enemy is at Neath and Swanzey.

The entry of Powell into Swanzey was later outlined in an 'article' that was meant to discredit Philip Jones; the 'article' stated:

> That Colonel Rice Powell, in February last, with a brace of pocket pistols, singly forced the said Jones [and] his sentinels from their standing at Swanzey, he being then personally in the garrison, and not making the least resistance, but permitted the said Colonel Powell to place sentinel of his own there when he first appeared against the Parliament, and so immediately Jones quit the town and fled to Herefordshire.

> In answer to the 'article', Rowland Dawkin stated

> That Colonel Powell in January or February 1648, according to His Excellency's orders, came to Swanzey and quartered two or three companies of foot, when he and the rest of the officers pretended that it was not safe for them to lay there unless they might put a guard on their own men, which accordingly they were suffered to do, as a thing

not prejudicial. But that Colonel Jones was in town when Powell came in, is not true; neither had Powell then declared against the Parliament, for then, upon the general's order, he [Powell] drew out of town within one week after his coming thither.

The point that Dawkin intended to make was that, yes, Colonel Powell had come to Swanzey in January or February 1648, being ordered to do so by His Excellency, Lord Fairfax, Commander-in-Chief of all Parliamentary forces, which was two to three months prior to when Powell changed sides by declaring against Parliament. In short, those who wished to discredit Philip Jones had confused Powell's lawful entry in January or February with an unlawful entry at the beginning of May.

Both Poyer and Powell were at St. Nicholas, near Cardiff, on 4th May. That same day they were joined by Laugharne who, having escaped from London, had presumably made his way to Pembroke, then travelled eastwards, stopping at Swanzey where the borough accounts record a payment of £4

> for grass that Major-general Laugharne [and] his troopers did make use of [the £4 being paid] to Mr Walter Thomas.

Also on 4th May, Colonel Thomas Horton arrived at St. Fagans – having forced marched his men from Brecon – and positioned them so as to block Powell's advance on Cardiff. The opposing forces were barely two miles apart. Yet for four days neither side offered battle. Laugharne, who had assumed command, had the advantage of numbers – 8,000 men, at least half of whom were inexperienced countrymen armed with farm implements. Colonel Horton, on the other hand, had 3,000 well-armed seasoned troops. What forced Laugharne to proceed against Horton was news that Oliver Cromwell was heading towards South Wales with several regiments. On the night of 7th – 8th May, Laugharne moved his forces into position near St. Fagans and offered battle around 8 o'clock in the morning. The Battle of St. Fagans was described by Horton in a letter to Lord Fairfax.

> On Monday morning ... the enemy advanced towards us ... we took the best ground ... About 60 men on horses charged once, but we beat them back, and after that none of the men on horses appeared again ... The enemy tell us they were 8,000. We had a sharp dispute with them for about two hours. Our men on horses charged the enemy, who were wholly routed ... Many of the enemy were slain [up to 200] ... We have taken 3,000 prisoners ... we have not lost many soldiers and not one of our officers.

So where was Philip at the time? In a letter, dated 6th May, Horton stated that

> Colonel Philip Jones, with his company [of foot soldiers] from Swanzey ... have been with us in all our march, and himself in many ways helpful to us.

So Philip had been with Horton 'in all [his] march', meaning from Brecon presumably, but it may have been a reference to earlier marches because, in late April,

Horton had advanced from Brecon into Carmarthenshire, only to meet stiff opposition from Colonel Rice Powell in the vicinity of Llandeilo, which forced him to retire to Brecon. It is also likely that Horton's presence in Carmarthenshire had prompted Laugharne to break his parole in London and join his comrades Poyer and Powell.

Laugharne – who had been wounded at St. Fagans – along with Poyer, Powell and the shattered remnants of their army, beat a hasty retreat westwards, followed by Horton who wrote a letter, dated 13th May, at Bridgend before moving on to Swanzey where the borough accounts record:

> Paid by Mr Portreeve, his order for the expense of ten horses of Colonel Horton – 15s.

Oliver Cromwell arrived at Swanzey on 19th May, evidence for which is to be found in the Minute Book of the Common Hall, which states:

> At which time came unto this town the truly honourable Oliver Cromwell, Esquire, Lieutenant General of all the forces of this Kingdom of England under the command of the Parliament, lord of this town, the Seignory of Gower, and manor of Kilvey … who gave unto the poor of this town to be set out at interest for the benefit and advantage of the said poor the sum of ten pounds and the sum is referred to the Portreeve … for the time being.

According to the *Perfect Diurnal*, Cromwell left Swanzey on 22nd May and marched 'to Carmarthen, and so to Tenby', arriving there on or about the 24th to find Horton laying siege to the town. Moving on, Cromwell besieged Pembroke, leaving Horton to deal with Tenby, which Colonel Rice Powell surrendered on the 31st. Two weeks later, Cromwell wrote a letter, informing Parliament about the situation at Pembroke; the relevant passage reads:

> we made an attempt to storm the castle but the ladders were too short … so the men could not get over. We lost a few men but I am confident the enemy lost more … we hope to take his water supply in two days.

The garrison at Pembroke surrendered on 11th July after a seven-week siege. Among those taken prisoner were Laugharne and his brother-in-law, John Poyer. These two men, along with Rice Powell, were court-martialled in London and sentenced to death the following year. However, Lord Fairfax decided that only one of them should die, the decision as to who being decided by lottery. On 24th August 1649 *The Moderate* newspaper reported that because

> the prisoners were unwilling to draw their own destiny, three lots were given into the hand of a child; [on] two of them was written 'Life given by God' and the other was a blank. The child gave the first [lot] to Colonel Powell, the second to Major-general Laugharne, in both [of] which life was written, and the third being a blank to Colonel Poyer.

Raising a Regiment of Foot

There had been many outbreaks of revolt during the summer of 1648 – two of them in North Wales – but the most serious threat came from Scotland. After the fall of Pembroke, Cromwell marched north to rout an invading Scottish army at Preston Moor. Meanwhile, at Swanzey, the County Committee drafted a letter, dated 10th August, informing London that, after Cromwell's

> departure out of the country … he left behind him, Colonel Horton and his regiment of horse, a troop of dragoons, and two companies of Colonel Pride and Colonel Deane's regiments, being all the foot he could leave us by reason of the [state of] affairs in the kingdom, which (we having in South Wales but two companies more upon establishment) was judged [to be necessary] by all that desired to preserve the peace of these counties.

What the committeemen feared was further unrest and decided to 'make up those four companies' of foot into 'a regiment consisting of a thousand men'. According to A.G. Veysey, Philip was appointed colonel of this regiment until it was disbanded in 1652, his pay being 12d. per day.

The Rump Parliament

The second Parliament that Charles had called in 1640 became known as the Long Parliament, due to the longevity of its existence. On the eve of the First Civil War some 300 members of this Parliament had chosen to oppose the King, the majority of them Presbyterians. Even so, by December 1648 the Presbyterian MPs were still prepared to share power with the King, despite the fact that Charles continued to plot their downfall. The Presbyterian MPs were hostile to their fellow-Puritans – the Independents, Baptists and several other sects – and had already struck a deal with Charles to suppress them; moreover, the Presbyterians fully intended to disband the army – and there was the rub.

The dominant element in the Parliamentary army were Independents. Any action on their part would be seen by them as self-defence, and in December that year they sent Colonel Pride to Westminster, where his soldiers prevented about 100 Presbyterian MPs from taking their seats and arrested a further 40 or so who resisted. As a result of what became known as Pride's Purge, the number of MPs was reduced to less than 100, about 60 of whom were Independents. This Rump (relic) of the Long Parliament – which relied on the army to survive – soon put the King on trial, the verdict being a foregone conclusion. On 30th January 1649, Charles was beheaded, his composure dignified to the very last.

The Commonwealth

The year 1649 marks the beginning of Philip's remarkable rise to greater wealth and influence. His course as an opportunist was set in that no sooner had Charles been executed than the Rump abolished both the monarchy and the House of Lords, declaring England a Commonwealth, to be ruled by the Commons (meaning the Rump) and a Council of State. As a minority regime that wanted to hold on to power indefinitely, the Rump relied on men such as Philip, whom they elevated to the extent that many years later (in May 1659) it was said of him that:

> for about ten years last past, [he] appeared the chief and only man to recommend and bring in persons to all places of authority, profit, or trust, ecclesiastical, military or civil, in South Wales … and had the chief governance and superintendency of all public affairs in South Wales.

Sequestration

Acting on the advice of Philip, the Rump passed the 'Act for the Sequestration of South Wales and Monmouthshire' on 23rd February 1649. By this act they appointed 39 commissioners to collect the fines, Philip being one of them. Almost immediately the commissioners were subjected to criticism inspired by Colonel Edward Freeman, Attorney-general for South Wales, who claimed that the estates of delinquents were being undervalued, the inference being that Philip and his associates were too lenient in their dealings with Royalists. Freeman – a hard-liner who was to become Philip's arch-enemy – made a determined attempt to have himself and men of his choosing as sequestration commissioners, but in this he was thwarted.

The Curse of Cromwell

The execution of Charles had caused outrage in Ireland, so much so that most of the English settlers and many native Irish declared for the late King's son and heir, Charles II. Parliament's answer to the problem was to send Cromwell. On or about 25th July he stopped at Swanzey – en route to Ireland – where the Book of Common Hall records:

> By the desire of us the aldermen of the town … there was provided for the Right Honourable Oliver Cromwell, Lord Lieutenant of Ireland and Lord of this town, and for all his followers, a dinner in the house of William Bayly, then Portreeve. Now, to defray the charge … towards that provision, we have thought fit to take ten pounds out of the town stock. And whereas the greatness of the charge of free quarters within the town was such … of horse and foot towards Ireland, that we were forced one night to entertain in the inns forty horse with some foot on the public charge … amounting to six pounds eight shillings, we see fit likewise to take the same out of the common stock of this town, all amounting to £16. 8s.

Cromwell spent nine months in Ireland where, in contrast to his usually humane treatment of prisoners and civilians, he was responsible for two massacres. He was, then, recalled to deal with the Scots, leaving others to mop up whatever opposition remained. It has to be said there have been many lords of Gower who were insensitive and merciless rogues, but none of them – not even King John – could match the

Portrait of Oliver Cromwell by Samuel Cooper, dated 1649.

barbarity and suffering that Cromwell inflicted on Ireland; nor have any lords of Gower established such a lengthy legacy of religious intolerance. In the course of three bloody years, Ireland lost up to one third of its people. Thousands were killed, and thousands more were either transported to the West Indies, or forced to settle elsewhere. Huge tracts of Irish land were then sold or given to a new wave of English and Scottish settlers.

Reinforcements

Whilst campaigning in Ireland, Cromwell received reinforcements, some of which passed through Swanzey. This is made evident by an acknowledgement from the then Portreeve, Mathew Francklin, which dated 19th January 1650 states:

that … 67 officers and soldiers [for] service of Ireland, under the command of Captain Nicholls [of the Cardiff garrison?] were quartered at Swanzey … in December last, for the space of five days, which after 8d. per day … was paid for their quarters, comes to the sum of £11 3s. 4d.

Propagation

There had been no serious attempt to Puritanize Wales until, in January 1650, proposals to do so came before the Rump. Philip's entry into Parliament as MP for Breconshire a few weeks later proved timely in that he was able to lend his support for the 'Act for the Propagation of the Gospel in Wales' to be passed on 25th February that same year. The act put Philip in a position of authority throughout South Wales; it also made him many enemies who would hound him persistently, not only during the three years that the act remained in force, but for many years to come.

The act had two principal aims: to eject Anglican clergymen from their livings on grounds of 'sufficiency' and replace them with 'godly and painful men' with Puritan views; to establish state-sponsored schools in which children would receive a Puritan education. Both aims were to be financed by the sequestered revenue of the Anglican Church; that is, what was due from property as well as tithes.

As a Commissioner, Philip was responsible for enforcing the act in South Wales, assisted by his trusty trio, Dawkin, Mansel and Price. It was their responsibility to examine Anglican ministers and, if necessary, eject them from their livings on grounds of delinquency, insufficiency (especially in regard to preaching) or morality. In South Wales 151 ministers were ejected, 20 of them in Glamorgan, among them Hugh Gore of Oxwich, Edward Gage of Rhosili and Dr. Gordon of Porteynon. Approvers were appointed to find suitable replacements, but in the course of three years only 12 new ministers are known to have been settled to livings in South Wales. These newcomers were not always welcome. When Morris Bidwell replaced Hopkin Morgan as vicar of St. Mary's in March 1653, the changeover upset at least one Royalist, Richard Seys, because five or six years later, when Bidwell died, Seys drew his sword in an attempt to prevent Bidwell's body being buried in the chancel of St. Mary's. Thwarted on this occasion, but still determined that his father's bones would not be corrupted by the close proximity of Bidwell's remains, Seys bought the chancel at St. John's from Bussy Mansel so that he could remove his father's bones from St. Mary's and re-inter them at St. John's.

In an attempt to remedy the shortage in replacement ministers, the commissioners had to resort to itinerant preachers. About 90 such preachers are known of have operated in Wales, often preaching at more than one church in a day, being supplied 'with fresh horses at every stage'. As with replacement ministers, the itinerants were not always welcome, especially in Glamorgan where they were looked upon as 'rambling teachers' and 'hackney preachers'.

Most replacement ministers and itinerant preachers accepted salaries derived from sequestered church revenue, but there was a growing number who refused state support. Baptists in particular were opposed to state sponsorship, and in this respect they operated outside the propagation act. One such minister was John Miles who, prior to the First Civil War, had been the official lecturer at Ilston in Gower.

Born in 1621, in the Welsh-speaking part of Herefordshire, John Miles became a Baptist in the spring of 1649 when he learned that what made Baptists different from other Puritans was their belief that faith was a matter of personal experience. The baptism of infants was to them a meaningless ceremony, for only those old enough to be committed believers should be baptized, usually by total immersion. At Ilston John established the first Particular Baptist church in Wales – Particular in that its members preferred to disassociate themselves from other denominations. By October that year his followers numbered 43, of whom 25 were women. By September 1651 John and his followers had established dependent congregations at Hay, Llantrisant, Carmarthen and Abergavenny. In 1657 he was officially appointed pastor of Ilston Church, thereby replacing the Anglican minister, William Houghton.

Tradition links John Miles with Trinity Well, a now ruined chapel in the secluded Ilston Valley. If John had been responsible for the chapel's construction in the days of Puritan rule, he would not have chosen the location for its seclusion, as he had nothing to fear from the authorities. There is, however, the view that Trinity Well may have been built by the Anglican minister, William Houghton, after his ejection from Ilston Church. Another view is that Trinity Well was established by John after the restoration of Charles II in 1660, the year William Houghton was restored to the living of Ilston. Whatever the truth, John Miles had one very important person in his congregation.

It has been assumed that Philip Jones had been an Independent, believing there should be no organized church, but that each congregation should be free to organize its own services. This assumption may have its origin in the fact that the Independents (later to become known as Congregationalists) constituted the majority of Puritans within Philip's sphere of influence. In 1659, when London pamphleteers felt free to criticize him, they labelled Philip both as a Presbyterian and an Independent, but they were misinformed, for the records show that on 1st December 1652 he became a Baptist. He was, in fact, one of 261 converts to join the Ilston group of congregations between October 1649 and August 1660.

It seems odd that Philip should become a Baptist – unless, of course, he really was a man with religious convictions and not as his critics saw him, an opportunist who made capital out of Puritan domination. Unlike the Independents (who had no rigid theology and were, therefore, tolerable to non-Puritans) the Baptists were detested, in part, because people wrongfully associated them with Anabaptists. For Philip to become a Baptist was to invite more criticism than he already endured.

In 1631 schooling took place 'in the town house', presumably the town house referred to in 1425 as 'next to the bridge of the fortress'. It is hardly surprising, therefore, that as the town house belonged to the burgesses the borough accounts should record payments for its upkeep. That year 2s. 6d. was spent on repairing the stairs; a further 6d. was paid to

> Thomas John, cooper, for setting up the bench in the hall and mending the loft and fastening the posts of the stairs of the school house.

The school must, therefore, have consisted of a hall in which there was at least one bench, whereas the stairway suggests that the loft may have been used as a dormitory; that said, there is still the question of what kind of school it was, whether it was private or endowed. There are no hints in the borough records to suggest that the Corporation financed the school beyond repairs to the town house.

When the propagation commissioners established a school at Swanzey in 1652, they authorized that £59 15s. 7d. should be spent on repairs to an existing building, though whether it was the town house is unknown. What is known is that this was a state-sponsored school – hitherto unheard of – the money coming from sequestered church property. When, on 17th March that year the commissioners appointed Moor Pye (the ejected Anglican minister of Llanfable in Monmouthshire) as master at Swanzey they awarded him a salary of £38 per annum, the money coming from sequestered church livings in Carmarthenshire. When Moor Pye left his post in 1654 to take up pastoral duties at Bishopston, he was replaced by Peter Meyrick, who held the post of schoolmaster until the restoration of the monarchy in 1660, after which the school closed, being denied further funding from sequestered church property.

Philip Jones would have been very much involved in the decision making relating to both propagation and the establishment of schools. What is worthy of comment is that he sanctioned the appointment of an ejected Anglican minister for the post of schoolmaster, and then, two years later, permitted the same minister to take up pastoral duties at Bishopston. Equally surprising is the fact that Hugh Gore, after he had been ejected from his living at Oxwich for delinquency, was allowed to set up a private school at Swanzey. This school – the location of which is unknown – is likely to have been favoured by Royalists. It may have closed in c.1660 when Hugh Gore left Swanzey to take up pastoral duties in Ireland. Hugh must have formed an attachment to Swanzey, for when, as Bishop of Waterford and Lismore, he returned to the town in 1682 he set up an endowed school in Goat Street for 20 sons 'of the poorer sort of burgesses'. This school survived into the 19th century, whereas the founder's name has been preserved in the name of Bishop Gore's School, Sketty.

New Aldermen at Swanzey

On 19th August 1650, David John, Robert Donnel and William John were deprived of their aldermanic status and replaced by Philip Jones, John Francklin, Thomas Williams and Mathew David. As a result of these new appointments there were now five Parliamentarians (the four named above, plus William Bayly) on the aldermanic council. The remaining seven alderman were time-honoured members, having served on the council since before the First Civil War. It is believed that at least two of the three men deprived of their status had been Royalist sympathizers.

Cromwell's Survey

On 27th August 1650 three men came together to carry out a survey of the Lordship of Gower and Kilvey on behalf of Oliver Cromwell – the intention being to record all that was due to the Lord General. The findings of these three men outside Swanzey is beyond the scope of this work, but in the borough the greatest property owner was William Herbert the Younger, great-great-great-grandson of Sir George Herbert. His father, William Herbert of Cogan Pill, had been killed at Edgehill in the King's service, whereas he was one of the few Herberts to espouse the Parliamentary cause. William the Younger owned The Plas, which apparently occupied the equivalent of $4\frac{1}{2}$ burgages within the Castle Bailey. The new garden and stable occupied roughly $1\frac{1}{4}$ burgages, The Plas and orchard 2, the Limehouse and Ton's Tower $1\frac{1}{4}$. In the Hearth Tax of 1670 The Plas is recorded as having 18 hearths. In total, William owned 40 tenements, the equivalent of some 20 whole burgages.

The second property magnate in Swansea was Walter Thomas, owner of 25 tenements, the equivalent of some 15 burgages. His principal residence was also in the Castle Bailey, on the north side of the thoroughfare. The Hearth Tax of 1670 records

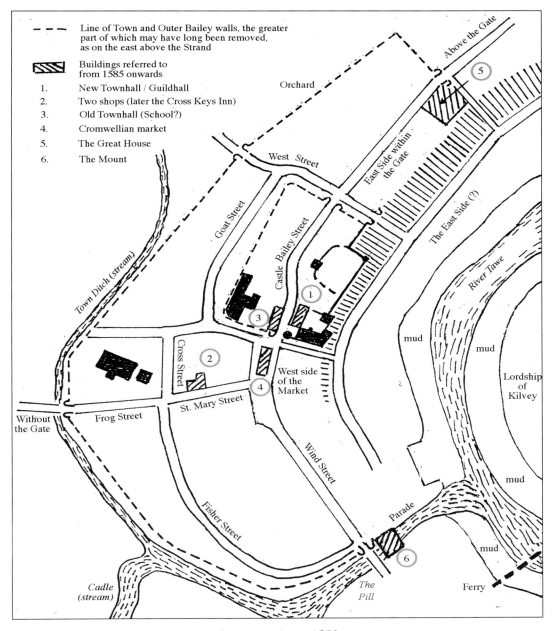

Legend:

- - - Line of Town and Outer Bailey walls, the greater part of which may have long been removed, as on the east above the Strand

▨ Buildings referred to from 1585 onwards

1. New Townhall / Guildhall
2. Two shops (later the Cross Keys Inn)
3. Old Townhall (School?)
4. Cromwellian market
5. The Great House
6. The Mount

Swanzey in c. *1650*

that this house had 12 hearths. Next came Richard Seys with 8 tenements, the equivalent of 8¼ burgages; his main residence was in 'The East Side Within the Gate', which probably refers to High Street. Surprisingly, William Thomas, despite his wealth, owned only three half burgages – two in Wind Street, one in Fisher Street.

A total of 196 tenements – be they whole, fractional parts of, or compact groups of burgages such as The Plas – are listed according to streets, or to areas that later gave their names to streets. Inside the town walls:

Goat Street had	38 tenements
The East Side Within the Gate	8 tenements (probably High Street)
Castle Bailey	17 tenements
The West Side of the Market	5 tenements
Wind Street	39 tenements
Fisher Street	12 tenements
Frog Street	6 tenements
Cross Street	11 tenements
Mary Street	7 tenements

Outside the town walls:

Above the Gate	17 tenements (upper High Street)
The East Side	12 tenements (probably the Strand)
Without the Gate	17 tenements (probably the Wassail gate)

The survey refers to several tenements that were not listed according to streets, such as the one held by Thomas David for £4 per annum; it consisted of

A Mansion house … in a street called Castle Bailey with a yard and outbuildings … called the Receiver's house.

When all the burgage shillings, or fractions thereof, that were due to Cromwell are totalled they equate with what may have originally been 145 whole burgages. The survey gives the names of 68 burgesses – possibly 72 – and that at a time when the population of the town is believed to have been around 1,600. The tenements owned by the heirs of three deceased burgesses are also listed, added to which six widows were also the owners of one or more tenements, though none of them were eligible to be burgesses on account of their sex. What is noteworthy is that William Bayly, who was definitely an alderman in 1650, does not feature in the survey as the owner of a burgage, but as a tenant of Walter Thomas, evidence that it was no longer necessary to own a burgage to become a burgess.

Many tenements were gardens, barns and other non-residential buildings, so it is difficult to calculate how many tenements actually relate to dwellings. The Poor Rate assessment of 1663 lists 133 dwellings, a figure that would not have included certain tenements in the survey, such as the parsonage and a building used by the common attorneys. Be that as it may, the Hearth Tax assessment of 1670 makes it clear that the largest dwellings in the town were situated in High Street, Castle Bailey Street, Wind Street and Mary Street. Smaller houses tended to dominate Goat Street, Cross Street and Frog Street.

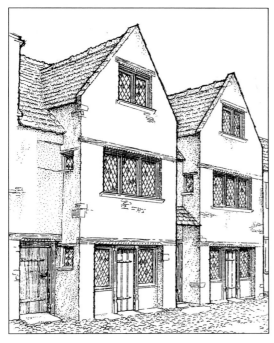

The Cross Keys Inn – street elevation restored to 17th century appearance when it served as two shops

Watercolour of the Old Post Office, Goat Street, as it stood until its demolition in c. *1830. The building had a 1620 date stone*

The survey makes no reference to shops, inns or other places of business; nor does it mention the Hospital of the Blessed St. David because, at the time of the survey, the main block is believed to have been converted into two shops. By the end of the century the same building had become the Cross Keys Inn. Other buildings that escaped mention were the Post Office in Goat Street, built in 1620, and the Custom House on the West Side of the Market, which certainly existed in 1573. No reference is made, moreover, to a curious structure known as the Mount, situated near the bottom of Wind Street. The Mount first appears in surviving borough accounts for the year 1632. Its purpose is a mystery. In the Bucks' engraving of 1748 it appears as a square, walled and crenellated structure similar to a small fort. In later drawings it is depicted as straddling the Pill, the water presumably culverted beneath it. In 1840 it was described as an 'ancient look-out for seamen'. It has also been suggested that in earlier times it may have served as an observation point for a gun emplacement on the nearby Parade (which is tree-lined on the Bucks' engraving). In 1804 the Mount was removed to make way for the Oystermouth Railway.

On the west bank of the Tawe there were two or more quays, which were probably no more than landing stages made of timber. There were also several small docks, some of which can be seen on the Bucks' engraving of 1748. They were rectangular excavations on the river bank, the sides revetted with timber, and large enough to accommodate just one sailing vessel. The earliest dock on record is to be found in the Common Attorneys' Account for 1624; it reads 'Received of Edmund Richard for making of the Dock by the Quay, 10s.'

Philip's Acquisitions

Philip appears to have had five tenements, the equivalent of 4¼ burgages, the Great House apparently occupying one whole burgage in 'The East Side Within the Gate'. He also held property that was separate from those listed according to streets. One such property was described as:

> A Mansion house and garden being in High Street in Swanzey and adjoining to the new dwelling house of the said Colonel Jones, value £2 per annum, which premises the tenant holds of the Lord General.

Further west, Philip had a five acre site for which he paid Cromwell £3 6s. 8d. yearly. The site was described as:

> A close pasture or meadow ground called the Orchard, lying near unto the High Street of Swanzey, enclosed with about an acre of the freehold of William Herbert, Esquire.

Philip also held a dozen properties outside the borough, most of them relatively small and let at rent. The largest outlying property was a 100 acre leasehold described as:

> Fforest vychan, alias issa, let to Philip Jones, Esquire, a Mansion-house with outbuildings thereto belonging and several closes of ground lying together about the house, and abutting on the river Mynrod [Fendrod] on the east, and the river Tawe on the west, and lands of Forest-ucha on the north and south ... Which premises he [Philip] holds by lease from the Lord General Cromwell, dated 7th May 1649, for 99 years, determinable on 3 lives, viz John Jones, Philip Jones and Ann Jones, his children, under a yearly rent of £30.

Outside Gower, in the Vale of Glamorgan, Philip held on lease the manors of Llancarvan, Wrinston, West Orchard and Michaelston-le-Pit. Not bad for a man of humble origin, and all accumulated in the space of five years. There are no hints as to how he acquired all this property.

Summary

Almost all that is known of Philip in the period 1645-50 is, in part, due to the appearance of his name in official documents and, in part, to what his critics had say, whereas the rebuttals of Rowland Dawkin are no more than what one would expect from a close associate. Throughout this early period he is to historians a rather shadowy figure, and this was apparent even to his contemporaries. As one of his critics declared, "Whoever his creatures might be, Colonel Jones was always beside the curtain." Only from 1651 onwards, when he walked the corridors of power at Westminster, does the character of the man begin to emerge; that said, as his wealth and influenced continued to increase, so too did the seriousness and number of charges that were brought against him.

CHAPTER IX
Colonel Philip Jones (3)

The Cromwellian Market

It was decided at a Common Hall in March 1646 'that there shall be forthwith a Market Hall erected and built' to provide cover in the Market Place, but nothing was done until, on 20th May 1651, it was resolved that instead of taking money:

> out of the public stock … the sum of sixty pounds shall be instantly rated … on the inhabitants of the said town, care being taken not to lay any part of the said rate upon any such poor people as have no subsistence besides their daily labour.

The Cromwellian Market as depicted by John Nixon in 1799

The Market Hall, which was completed the following year, consisted of a roof supported by ten stone pillars, the floor raised above the surrounding street level. Tradition has it that Cromwell contributed towards the cost, but there is no evidence to support this; nor is there any evidence to support the suggestion that Cromwell gifted lead – which had been stripped from St. David's Cathedral – to a certain gentleman of Swanzey, and that the 'gentleman' in turn presented the lead to the Corporation for use as a cover for the Market Hall roof.

Cromwell was definitely in Pembrokeshire in 1648 and 1649, and it is quite likely that, due to his connections with the General, Philip would have been present there on at least one of the occasions. It is, however, highly unlikely that Cromwell would have involved himself in blatant vandalism – but Jones! Among the Articles of Impeachment that were read out in Parliament in 1659, there is an allegation

> That he [Philip Jones] had disposed of the lead that covered the Cathedral of St. David's, which was valued at £300, to his own use.

The Complaints of Thomas Bowen

The outcome of the 1659 impeachment will be dealt with in due course; suffice to say there were repercussions relating to this matter as, indeed, there were repercussions concerning another occurrence of 1651, for the following year Thomas Bowen of Ilston, Gent., made an affidavit before the Lord Chief Justice of the Upper Bench. It was stated that, when Bowen appeared at Philip's house in Swanzey in July 1651 – he being charged with stealing a lamb – the Colonel in has capacity as a JP

> immediately reviled the deponent with divers bitter and unchristian expressions … and (having a great cane in his hand) pursued, assaulted and struck the said deponent therewith, and sent him to a nasty and loathsome dungeon or darkhouse; wherein the deponent had forthwith iron shackles and an iron bolt fastened on and to his legs and an iron chain; also the deponent was made fast and tied to a great block.

Guilty or not, Bowen had a lot to complain about: ill-treatment, imprisonment in the darkhouse on the ground floor of the Townhall and, as a convicted felon, had his goods seized and sold. Apart from the affidavit, Bowen also petitioned Cromwell for redress, but there is no record of the outcome of either of the proceedings.

Rebellion

If 1651 had been a bad year for Philip Jones, it proved a good one for Colonel Rowland Dawkin who, at the time, appears to have been Governor of Carmarthen and Tenby. In June that year a rebellion occurred in Cardiganshire. Rowland's success in dealing with the rebellion is to be found in a letter he sent to Philip. Extracts from the letter are as follows:

For the Hon. Col. Philip Jones
At Swanzey   Haste, haste, haste

Sir

To give you an account [of] how I hope it has pleased God … I marched from Carmarthen to Cardigan, and the party in rebellion in those parts marched near Llanbadarn Fawr to join with the rest of their friends; on Saturday morning, being yesterday, I marched from Cardigan with the horse and the foot towards the rebels and so continued marching together for some 14 miles; then I understood where the party were drawn together … being by this time two companies joined; thereupon I marched away with the horse, the foot not being able to keep pace with us. About 7 o'clock in the afternoon we discovered some 140 drawn up upon the top of a hill, and some of our scouts drawing near their body they fired near a dozen muskets, upon which we charged them up the hill and through the goodness of God immediately put them to rout. We lost no man, had but one run through the thigh, one horse killed and four more wounded.

There were killed upon the place 28 of them, many wounded and some 60 prisoners taken; some 50 may be fit to be sent somewhere out of the land, the rest are so wounded that I am confident they will not live three days.

… there is no doubt but these men were put on by the gentry, and especially by Captain Jones, the Floyds and the Jenkins, who kept a great racket up and down the county…Upon Tuesday next they intended to join all their party and have some from nearby Merionethshire. We hear Sir John Lewes's brother, one Major Lewes, headed this party we fell upon … was slain. I hope this will scatter all the rest…and prevent any design that may be afoot … to disturb the public peace … I desire to know what shall be done with the prisoners and remain yours really to serve you.

Rowland Dawkin

From my quarters near Llanbadarn, this Lord's day in the morning, being the 15th of June 1651.

Philip passed on the information to General Fleetwood. Two days later he sent a second letter to the General, extracts from which are as follows:

For your Hon. Lieut-general Fleetwood
at Somerset House
Haste, haste, haste, post haste

Dear Sir

I hope you have received mine of the 17th, giving an account of the Cardigan rebellion and through mercy the suppressing of it upon the 15th before. Since then I have received the gentlemen in the enclosed list of prisoners, against whom there will [be] a charge of treason … There are found among the common prisoners considerable freeholders … and these hint the design was general, and to have been ripe for weeks …

Indeed, Sir, I consider it exceedingly necessary to put these men upon a very speedy trial, and that in the North folk manner [the North of England – by court martial], for a jury will do no good in that county, where little [of the] Gospel has yet been …

Your very affectionate servant

Phil Jones

Swanzey, June 19, 1651.

The names of your prisoners:

Thomas Floyd, Esq	Mr. Reynold Jenkins
Capt. Richard Jones	Cornet Morgan Jenkins

The Humble Petition

As propagation commissioners, Philip and his associates attracted a great deal of criticism, which found expression in a petition that was presented to Parliament on 10th May 1652. The petition was allegedly signed by 15,000 persons, and among the leading sponsors were to be found a chancery official, John Gunter of Breconshire, and Philip's arch-enemy, Colonel Edward Freeman. It was claimed that the commissioners' wholesale ejection of the 'ancient clergy had created a 'famine of the word of God'. There were allegations, too, of unfair letting of sequestered livings, of allowing delinquents and scandalous ministers to preach, and of permitting unworthy men to become schoolmasters. More serious still were the high arrears in the commissioners' accounts, which exposed them to the charge of misappropriation of tithe revenue to the tune of between £20,000 and £100,000.

It was said in later years that the propagation officials were the nominees and friends of Philip Jones – in a word they were his 'creatures'. This, of course, was true in the sense that Philip would naturally appoint men of his choosing. It was also true in that his servant, John Creed, wrote the minutes at meetings in Glamorgan and Carmarthenshire; that his two brothers-in-law, John Price and Evan Lewis (who had married a sister of Philip's wife), served as treasurer and clerk respectively to the South Wales commissioners; that William Watkins of Llanigon, the former Royalist Receiver-general of South Wales – the man who was, or later became steward of Philip's ever-expanding estate – was clerk to the Brecon and Radnor commissioners. All four men appear to have 'made hay while the sun shines'.

Philip is known to have spent over £4,000 on purchasing property during the years 1650-52. Naturally, his enemies were to allege that some of this money (to say nothing of what has gone unrecorded) came from sequestered church property and tithes. In their view the high arrears in the commissioners' accounts was proof that Philip and his 'creatures' were pocketing huge sums of money. It has to be said, however, that the arrears may in part have been due to the unsettled conditions of the day, to the low rates at which sequestered livings were leased, and to the fact that many tenants fell into arrears with their rents. There is no evidence to support the view that Philip obtained any ecclesiastical revenue for his own personal use. He did, however, produce considerable sums of money to purchase secular estates in Gower and the Vale of Glamorgan.

In 1651, for example, Parliament put up for sale the Vale of Glamorgan manors of Llancarvan, Wrinston, West Orchard and Michaelston-le-Pit, which had originally belonged to the Marquis of Worcester. Philip had leased these manors from the Parliamentary Trustees since 1649, and within months of the sale he had not only purchased the manors, but he also bought the reversionary interest which Edward Somerset, heir to the Marquis of Worcester, claimed were his. The fact that the purchases were a legal and voluntary transaction meant that Edward Somerset surrendered his claim to the manors. Consequently, after the restoration of the monarchy in 1660, Edward failed in his attempts to reclaim what had belonged to his father.

A list of all the sequestered secular property that Philip purchased in the early 1650s is beyond the scope of this work; suffice to say these transactions were all legal. Philip also purchased a number of sequestered Church and Crown properties during the same period – the bishop's manors of Llandewi and Clase (Llangyfelach) in Gower being among them – but such properties he usually passed on to someone else; at a profit, of course.

It is possible that Philip foresaw that, should the monarchy be restored, then sequestered Church and Crown properties would be returned to their rightful owners. This was certainly the case for the messuages at St. Mary Hill, Pembrokeshire, and the Cilgerran weir in the same county, which Philip bought for £400. The messuages he resold to Griffith Bowen of Swanzey (one of his 'creatures') for £524 in 1654. After the return of Charles II six years later, the City of London reclaimed the St. Mary Hill property as its own, having bought it from Charles I prior to the Civil War. Not only did Bowen lose his investment, but he later failed in his attempt to obtain compensation; moreover, according to Bowen, Philip received £300 in rents as reimbursement to cover loss, which should have gone to Bowen, but which Philip kept for himself.

The Humble Petition remained a controversial subject for almost a year until it was overshadowed by other events, namely the expiry of the Propagation Act on 25th March 1653, the Rump's refusal to renew the act seven days later and by the political crisis that ensued. For their part in promoting the petition both Freeman and Gunter were arrested on Philip's orders and imprisoned briefly. Freeman subsequently lost his position as Attorney-general for South Wales, to be replaced by Edmund Jones of Buckland, a man later described as the Colonel's 'main agent and instrument in South Wales'.

The Dissolution of the Rump

By the beginning of 1653 the Rump Parliament had become renowned for its harshness towards Royalists, its stinginess towards the army which kept it in power, and also for its policy of governing the country by means of favouritism and bribery. Its refusal to renew the Propagation Act on 1st April 1653 was one of the main reasons why, on 20th April, Cromwell entered the House of Commons with soldiers and forcibly dissolved the Rump. This dramatic event, however, did nothing to resolve Cromwell's dilemma. He fully accepted that a parliament was necessary to curb the excesses of a ruler. He was also well aware that a free election would secure not only the return of a Royalist government, but also the restoration of the monarchy. In his opinion the only way to govern the country was to have a hand-picked assembly of Puritans with property. Consequently, he and his fellow army officers decided that lists of suitable men should be submitted by the Independent Puritan congregations. From these lists 144 'saints' were to be chosen by a council of army officers.

When the Nominated Assembly opened on 4th July 1653 it consisted officially of an assembly of 144 Saints; unofficially it was known as the Little Parliament. Historians, on the other hand, consistently refer to it as the Barebones Parliament, so named because one of its most active members bore the name of Praise-God Barebones. Six Saints were to represent Wales, Bussy Mansel being one of them. Monmouthshire – which was regarded as an English county – was represented by none other than Philip. During the six months that the Little Parliament sat, Cromwell became increasingly alarmed by the proposals of a radical minority and, on 12th December, the moderate majority dissolved Parliament and handed power over to him so that he became Lord Protector. Many years later it was said that Philip had been a member

> of the Little Parliament, which he helped to break and to advance the General [Cromwel], his master, to be Protector.

That he 'helped to break ... the Little Parliament' to thwart a radical minority is proof that he was a moderate. He may have been a radical with regard to propagation and the establishment of state-sponsored schools, but in a speech of 1657 he showed himself to be conservative in his outlook, declaring that it was 'expedient' to have a king as head of state even though the man he had in mind was Cromwell. He was never a rank and file MP. In the Little Parliament he had been a frontbencher, sitting with the most prominent of men. Four years later he was described as a bold speaker, and in subsequent parliaments he sat on most of the important committees, being knowledgeable on finance and matters relating to Wales.

The Protectorate

Soon after the dissolution of the Barebones Parliament, Cromwell accepted the army's proposal for a new form of government. The details were set out in a document known as the 'Instrument of Government' whereby the country would no longer be known as the Commonwealth, but as the Protectorate, governed by Cromwell as Lord Protector, a Council of State and a single House of Parliament consisting of 400 Puritans, from which Royalists and Presbyterians were excluded. Voting was restricted to the wealthier Puritans, and this resulted in the election of Philip Jones and Edmund Thomas of Wenvoe to represent Glamorgan, of John Price to represent Cardiff, and of Rowland Dawkin as one of two men to represent Carmarthenshire. The first Protectorate Parliament – otherwise known as the Convention – sat on 3rd September 1654, and straightaway there was trouble to the extent that nine days later Cromwell excluded 80 members from the House. Continued criticism of Cromwell and the 'Instrument of Government' resulted in Cromwell dissolving this Parliament on 22nd January 1655.

Corridors of Power

It was said in 1659 that Philip had been 'a Privy Councillor to the late Protector for about five years last past'. In fact Philip had been nominated a member of the Council of State at the end of April 1653 and remained as such until the end of the Protectorate. Whenever Parliament was in session he sat both as an MP and as a Councillor of State; whenever Parliament was in recess he and his fellow councillors of state continued to run the country until Parliament returned. With so much to do in London, it is little wonder that, in South Wales, it was said of him that 'whoever his creatures might be, Colonel Jones was always beside the curtain'.

A Pedigree, a Coat of Arms and a Son Named Oliver

By 1654 Philip had risen to great heights to say nothing of amassing a considerable estate. What he needed to confirm his standing in Wales was a pedigree. His English peers would have considered such a design ridiculous, but in Wales all Welshmen who considered themselves to be of worth had a pedigree, as did the *Advenae* who were of Norman and English descent. To satisfy his requirements, Philip turned to George Owen – York Herald – who provided him with not only a pedigree that stretched back to Gruffudd Gwyr (See Chapter III) and Maenarch, Lord of Brycheiniog (and beyond to Caradog Vraichvas who ruled between the Wye and the Severn), but also a coat of arms, impressions of which are preserved on several wax seals attached to letters he wrote. That same year (1654) Philip had his fourth son christened Oliver as a mark of respect to the Lord Protector. There is a tradition that Cromwell stood as one of the godparents, but there is no evidence to support this.

Philip Jones's Coat of Arms

Persistent Critics

Philip may have walked the corridors of power, but his enemies still hounded him like a pack of rabid dogs. Only two cases relating to their attacks may be sited here. The first relates to a pamphlet in which the originator, Basset Jones of Llanmihangel, near Cowbridge, claimed that it was his intention to acquaint Cromwell with the 'whole process and course of fraud, injuries and oppressions used by the said Colonel'. In response his Highness, the Lord Protector, gave instructions on 22nd March 1654 'that Colonel Jones be acquainted with' the petition of Basset Jones and 'that he give answer thereunto in writing'. From the details of this petition it appears that Basset Jones's father had a lease for 99 years on a messuage and lands in the manor of Wrinston, which he had obtained from the late Marquis of Worcester. Basset alleged that the property in question had been seized by Colonel Jones, using soldiers from the Cardiff garrison. Basset also pleaded with Cromwell not to turn his father over to the law, [he] having such woeful experience of the power and influence of the said Colonel.

In a written response to the allegation – which Cromwell received on 25th April – Philip admitted to having contracted for the manor, but denied 'using soldiers or any force, or' resorting to 'any breach of promise' to have Basset's father evicted from the said property, and claimed that he had

taken no other course to obtain [his] right than what was allowed and used by other purchases, and for satisfaction therefore [he had] put into Mr. Sadler's hands the whole proceeding from the beginning, and desire[d] nothing but the fruit thereof.

Basset's response was that the said answer of Colonel Jones] was 'evasive and impertinent'. It did him no good, for when the case was brought before the Council of State, the Council declared in Philip's favour, and continued to do so each time Basset appealed.

Another persistent critic was Alexander Griffith, the ejected Anglican vicar of Glasbury in Breconshire. An able publicist, Alexander wrote several pamphlets that were intended to persuade successive Parliaments to review the Propagation accounts. Alexander alleged that the amount of Propagation revenue at the disposal of the commissioners in South Wales and Monmouthshire was around £20,000 per annum, and that the greater part of this went into the pockets of the commissioners and their agents. What survives of the commissioners' accounts show that only about half the figure quoted by Alexander was actually raised; moreover, the commissioners themselves admitted that only half the revenue had been realized.

Under pressure, Cromwell gave orders for an investigation to take place, and on 30th August 1654 an act was passed to that effect. Philip proved his willingness to assist in the investigation by helping to draft the act and by placing his own supporters among the investigating commissioners. As one would expect, the investigating commissioners eventually 'passed' the Propagation accounts as correct at a meeting held at Neath on 10th August 1655. This, of course, did not silence Philip's critics.

The Rule of the Major-generals

After dissolving the First Protectorate Parliament in January 1655, Cromwell ruled the country with the aid of the Council of State. This led to widespread uprisings in March that year, which due to ill-prepared Royalist plans and government intelligence were soon crushed. An uprising was expected to take place in South Wales, but this never materialized, presumably because Philip and his associates kept a lid on the situation. Philip was, however, sent to Shropshire in March – where there had been trouble – to take command of Parliamentary forces there. Later that same month he went to another trouble spot in Yorkshire to 'perform a special service for the state'. It is unfortunate that the details of these missions have not survived.

Meanwhile, Colonel Rowland Dawkin had charge of the situation in South Wales, as evidenced by a letter from the Council of State, urging him to be diligent and watch strangers. The situation in other regions was such that JPs were refusing to enforce Cromwell's proclamations. Chaos loomed. A firm hand was needed. In October the country was divided into ten – later eleven – military districts, each under the command of a major-general. South Wales and Monmouthshire were placed temporarily under the command of Colonel Dawkin. Then, when Major-general James Berry took command of all Wales, Herefordshire and Shropshire in July the following year, Rowland Dawkin became one of his deputies, being described as a 'Deputy Major-general for … Glamorgan'.

One of the tasks of the major-generals was to enforce Puritan values as well as prevent unlawful assemblies, or assemblies in which Royalists might meet and plot. Numerous alehouses were closed, as were all theatres. Horse-racing, cock-fighting and bear-baiting were all banned. The Sabbath became a day in which it was forbidden to do anything except go to church, and laws against swearing, drunkenness and other vices were put into effect. There is little evidence as to how Glamorgan endured enforced Puritanism, but in Swanzey John Mofford was fined 5s. 'for setting sail upon the Sabbath Day out of this harbour'.

The Portuguese Affair

Another incident that demonstrates Cromwell's confidence in Philip is brought to light in a letter that Cromwell received from Dom. Rebell, the Ambassador of Portugal. In 1654 England and Portugal had entered into a treaty, but there were problems over certain clauses involving indemnity to be paid to English merchants. In the letter the Portuguese Ambassador reminds Cromwell that four commissioners (two from each nation) had been appointed to resolve the matter and, if they failed to reach an agreement, then he (Cromwell) was to elect an arbitrator out of his Council of State. Cromwell appointed Philip and the dispute was finally resolved in January 1656. In time, Philip's enemies accused him of accepting 'bribes and gratuities' from the London merchants who bene-fited from a decision he made in their favour.

The Quakers

In 1655 Marmaduke Matthews was appointed to the living of St. John's Church in High Street, and Philip had something to do with the appointment, but he had nothing to do with the arrival in Swanzey of a new form of Puritanism. The people who introduced this new teaching were members of the Society of Friends, whom outsiders referred to deri-sively as Quakers because they quaked for fear of the threatened punishment of God. In late September that year the town witnessed the arrival of John ap John, a Denbighshire yeoman, later to become known as 'the Apostle of Quakerism in Wales'. Anglican Protestants may have regarded the Quakers as just another Puritan sect, but to Puritans such as the Independents and the Baptists the Quakers were a source of annoyance because they challenged their views, and in this John ap John was typical of his kind.

Shortly after his arrival in Swanzey, John challenged Morris Bidwell, the Puritan minister of St. Mary's, as to whether he was a minister of Christ. John was immediately removed from the church and placed in custody overnight. The following morning he appeared before a magistrate to hear Bidwell demand that he should 'have the devil whipped out of' him. John made every effort to protest: he had not challenged Bidwell during his sermon, but afterwards and was, therefore, not guilty of any wrong-doing. However, each time John tried to declare his innocence Bidwell and another man either struck him or stopped his mouth with their hands. To make matters worse, John refused to provide security for his subsequent appearance in court and, on 8th October, he was sent to Cardiff gaol.

During his short stay at Swanzey, John ap John undoubtedly made a few converts, one of whom, William Bevan, a merchant, later gave his fellow converts a site in the town for a meeting house. The converts kept meticulous records of their ill-treatment at the hands of other residents in the town, usually for challenging either Bidwell or Marmaduke Matthews on matters pertaining to their convictions. The women converts were just as fearless and outspoken as the men, and several of them spent time in the 'dark house' for being too forthright. Elizabeth Holme, for example, was imprisoned in the 'dark house' on no less than five occasions. By 1658 the Puritan ministers had had enough and thereafter refused to bury Quakers in their churchyards. Although the Friends acquired a plot of land at Loughor for burying their dead, there is no evidence of any burials taking place there.

Cromwell's Charter

In his efforts to maintain control over a country in which the majority of the population was dissatisfied with Puritan rule, Cromwell introduced measures that would strengthen his hand in the boroughs. Initially, this involved placing government supporters in the majority on the aldermanic councils. This was certainly the case in Swanzey where, by 1st October 1655, there were seven pro-government supporters on the Council as opposed to five burgesses who had been aldermen since before the Civil War, none of whom are likely to have been staunch Royalists.

With a view to controlling troublesome and independently-minded burgesses, Cromwell then introduced new charters to the boroughs. In the case of Swanzey he increased his influence by granting a charter that resulted in the burgess body losing much of its say as to how the borough should be administered. Power was in fact vested in a smaller, more manageable 'Common Council', consisting of a 'Mayor, High Steward, Recorder, twelve Aldermen and twelve Capital Burgesses'. It can be assumed that Philip Jones had much to do with the wording of Cromwell's charter, even though it would appear from the text that the Lord Protector was granting the charter out of the good-ness of his heart, and that the 'Portreeve, Aldermen and Burgesses' had 'most humbly besought' the charter from him.

The title of Portreeve was replaced by that of Mayor, and the first man to hold the new title was the Portreeve, Lewis Jones, who was also to be the 'Coroner and Escheator', the 'Keeper of the Gaol', and the 'Clerk of the Market'. Lewis had to take the oath before he took up his duties as Swanzey's first Mayor. He then had to continue as Mayor until 29th September 1656. The election of his successor was to be as follows:

> The Mayor [Lewis Jones] and Aldermen and the rest of Common Council ... shall ... on the Monday before the nine and twentieth day of September ... assemble [in the Townhall] and name two fit and discreet ... Aldermen ... to be presented to the ... High Steward [or his deputy, who was to] choose one of the said two persons to be Mayor ... for one whole year [and the new mayor] shall on the Monday after such ... election be sworn [in] before the said High Steward ... or his Deputy.

That Philip had much to do with compiling Cromwell's Charter is borne out by the fact that it 'nominated' him 'to be the first [and only] High Steward' of Swanzey, giving him 'full power to appoint an able and fit person to be ... his Deputy in his absence'. The charter also made it possible for him to manipulate the composition of the Common Council – for example, the Mayor, Lewis Jones, was listed as an alderman, which means that in reality the aldermanic council had been reduced to eleven men.

Philip, on the other hand, was no longer an alderman as his place of the Common Council was assured by his appointment as High Steward. The man who replaced him was his associate, Rowland Dawkin. Four months previously, Rowland had not been an alderman, as evidenced by a document dated 1st October 1655. In Cromwell's Charter, however, Rowland heads a list of named aldermen, presumably because he was the senior man despite having less than four months experience. As to the 'twelve Capital Burgesses' who represented the burgess body, the men who topped this list were John Price and Even Lewis, Philip's brothers-in-law. Nominations such as these enabled Philip to dominate the Common Council.

Another important member of the Common Council was the Recorder, who had to be 'honest, able and discreet' and 'learned in the Laws of England'. John Gibbs, Esquire, was 'to be the first ... Recorder' and he was to remain in office 'so long as he shall well demeasne himself'. The recorder's knowledge of the law would have been invaluable because he, as well as the

> Mayor, High Steward or his Deputy, or any two of them [shall] have full power as [JPs] to hear and determine all ... pleas ... in the Guildhall ... on Monday and Thursday in every week.

Dating

The Charter is dated 26th February 1655. This is misleading. In Philip's day the first day of the year fell on the 25th March, and not the 1st January as it does today. Consequently, the year that should be applied to any date between the 1st January and the 25th March has often posed a problem for historians, many of whom have got round the problem by giving the date of the charter as 25th February 1655-6. In Philip's day the charter had been dated 26th February 1655 – which is correct – but by today's reckoning it was granted on 26th February 1656.

A Memorandum

Appended to the proceedings of a court leet held on 1st October 1655 was a memorandum to the effect

> that Lewis Jones, now Portreeve, was sworn [in as] Mayor … of Swanzey on the eighteenth day of March 1655, in the Town Hall, by Major General Dawkin and John Bowen, Esquires.

Here again the date is misleading. In Philip's day it would have been correct to date the occasion as 18th March 1655 as the last day of the year would have occurred six days later – on 24th March. Therefore, by today's reckoning Lewis Jones was sworn in on 18th March 1656. By right Lewis Jones should have been sworn in by the High Steward, Philip Jones. Presumably, Philip was out of town and it appears that Lewis Jones (the second senior alderman) was sworn in by the first and third senior aldermen, namely Rowland Dawkin and John Bowen. It has been suggested, however, that Bowen may have been Philip's Deputy-steward. If this were correct, then Bowen would have been both Deputy-steward and the third senior alderman.

Fonmon Castle

In May 1656 Philip entered into a series of property transactions which, according to his enemies, resulted in the purchase of 'a great estate with the money received for tithes in Wales'. These transactions were to cost Philip an incredible £11,083 over a two-year period. They involved the purchase of the Fonmon, Penmark and Llancadle manors in the Vale of Glamorgan, as well as the stately home of Fonmon Castle. The three manors and the castle had belonged to the Earl of Bolingbroke, whose landed interests were mainly in Bedfordshire and Oxfordshire. A loyal supporter of Parliament, Bolingbroke had got himself into financial difficulty to the extent that he had to sell off his Welsh estates to pay his debts. In March 1655 trustees were appointed to handle the sale.

Acting as Philip's agents, John Price and Edmund Jones of Buckland negotiated with the trustees. They also negotiated with over 60 creditors who, to cut their losses, assigned their share in the manors to Philip for only a fraction of its worth. At one point during the transactions it was necessary for Philip and John Price to borrow £2,000, which they repaid within six months. Then, to complete the purchase of these Welsh estates, a London lawyer is said to have received huge amounts of money 'in bags'.

Philip's enemies maintained that he had obtained the money through 'divers rewards, bribes and gratuities' in addition to pocketing propagation funds, but as a Councillor of State he is known to have received a salary of £1,000 per annum, as well as smaller salaries for the numerous offices and appointments that he held. He also received a regular income from renting property and from property deals. His total income, however, is unlikely to have covered the £15,800 he is known to have spent during the 15 years that he served as a government supporter, to say nothing of the purchases of which there is no record, or where records exist, no purchase price is given.

The Second Protectorate Parliament

During the summer of 1656 the major-generals worked hard to secure the return of a compliant House of Commons from which Royalists and Presbyterians were barred. In South Wales, Philip and Edmund Thomas of Wenvoe were returned for Glamorgan, John Price for Cardiff, Rowland Dawkin for Carmarthenshire and Evan Lewis for Breconshire. With government supporters such as these, Cromwell should have had a compliant House, but when the Second Protectorate Parliament met on 17th September nearly half the members – most of them Republicans – proved to be opposed to him; about 100 were excluded from the House. The MPs who remained came up with a proposition.

The Humble Petition and Advice

In February 1657 there were opening moves to persuade Cromwell to accept the Crown, but out of loyalty to, or fear of the Republican element in the army, he agonized over what he should do. In the meantime, Philip made a speech before the House in April, arguing that the title of King was

> not only expedient but in respect to a settlement necessary … for time and experience has grafted the name and office of King in the minds of the people.

The speech proved to be of no avail. Cromwell rejected the Crown, but agreed to a revised Humble Petition and Advice whereby his position as Lord Protector would become hereditary and Parliament would become two-chambered with the creation of an 'Other House' (the equivalent of today's House of Lords), consisting of 40 life members selected by him. On 26th June Cromwell was re-instated as Lord Protector with as much pomp and ceremony as if he had been crowned King. There can be little doubt that the revised petition had Philip's hand on it.

New Aldermen

Meanwhile, in Swanzey, the number of government supporters on the aldermanic council had increased, as evidenced by a list dated April 1657. Heading the list was the Mayor, John Daniels. He was followed by Colonel Philip Jones, one of his Highness's Council, and Major-general Rowland Dawkin. Fifth on the list was William Herbert, Esquire, the man who owned the largest number of burgages. It is possible that William had been pressurized into becoming an alderman by government supporters who desired a much larger majority on the aldermanic council. The reason for this postulation is that, as a man of wealth, William should have been an alderman at a much earlier date, but for reasons unknown this had not come about. What is also noteworthy about this list is that Philip, as High Steward, was already a member of the Common Council; now he was listed as an alderman as well. In total there were nine government supporters on the aldermanic council and only three who had been aldermen since before the Civil War.

Fonmon Leased

With the purchase of Fonmon Castle and the manors appertaining to it complete, Philip had a profitable estate at his disposal, one that would support him throughout his retirement. He did not, however, take up residence there due to commitments in London, which were to increase dramatically from December 1657 onwards. In October that year he, therefore, leased Fonmon Castle to one William Leicester for a period of five years. There was, unfortunately, one small problem in that Leicester had to evict the resident lessee, and oust him he did. The evicted lessee then resorted to law on the ground of 'force of arms' (trespass), but Leicester had the law on his side.

Comptroller

Philip was appointed Comptroller of His Highness's Household in December 1657, having charge of his master's finances and everything he owned. This was no mean appointment. In 1654 Parliament had assigned to Cromwell several royal properties, including Whitehall Palace, which he used as his principal residence, and Hampton Court, which he used as a weekend retreat. Both palaces contained costly furniture and works of art. Cromwell was evidently one of those people who trusted Philip implicitly, allowing him to handle the marriage settlement of his youngest daughter, Lady Francis Cromwell, in June the following year.

The Second Protectorate Parliament

After the pomp and ceremony of June 1657, there followed a parliamentary recess, during which time Cromwell selected 40 members to sit in the Other House, among them the Glamorgan MPs Philip Jones – whose title became Philip, Lord Jones – and Edmund Thomas. His selection of men such as these deprived him of their leadership in the House of Commons; it also exposed him to a wave of criticism, for when the Second Session of the Second Protectorate Parliament met on 27th January 1658 the excluded members who had been allowed to return launched so many attacks on the Other House that, on 4th February 1658, he was forced to dissolve Parliament yet again.

CHAPTER X
Colonel Philip Jones (4)

Most of what is known of Philip, Lord Jones comes from his critics, some of whom were determined to discredit and destroy him. It is rare that the appraisals of men less vindictive have survived. One such appraisal is to be found among the descriptive 'Memoirs of the Members of Parliament', preserved in the *Harleian Miscellany*. The author of the memoirs is unknown, but what he wrote about Philip at the close of 1657 is that:

> At the first of the wars he [Philip] had about seventeen to twenty pounds per annum [from Pen-y-waun farm], and improved his interest upon the account of the cause: first, he was an agent for some Parliamenters to London, where, gaining acquaintance and making good use of them, he became Governor of a garrison, then a Colonel, as also Steward of some of the Protector's lands in Wales, and one of the Long Parliament; after of the Little Parliament, which he helped to break and to advance the General, his master, to be Protector: for which goodly service himself was advanced to be one of his Council, and afterwards Comptroller of his Household or Court. He made hay while the sun shined, and has improved his interest and revenue in land, well begotten [no question] to three thousand pounds per annum, if not more. He is also very well qualified with self-denying principles to the Protector's will and pleasure, so as he is fit, no doubt, to rise yet higher, and to be taken out of the House to be a Lord, and to have a negative voice in the Other House. ...
>
> If part of the purchase-money [for the manors of Fonmon?] was not paid with the great bribe of about three thousand pounds, for which (as it is credibly reported) he has been privately questioned, he would do well to clear himself – being very much suspected – having gotten so great an estate in so short a time.

The author refers to Philip as 'very well qualified with self-denying principles'. The remark about 'self-denying principles' probably relates to denial of his own political interests in favour of 'the Protector's will and pleasure'; it certainly had nothing to do with denying himself wealth and influence. That he 'was fit ... to rise yet higher' in high office there can be no doubt, for not only did he 'improve his interest' from a yeoman farmer to become *Custos Rotulorum*, or ruler of South Wales, but on the political front he:

1) represented Breckonshire in the Rump Parliament from February 1650 to April 1653
2) represented Monmouthshire in the Little (Barebones) Parliament from July 1653 to December 1653
3) was one of two MPs to represent Glamorgan in the First Protectorate (Convention) Parliament from September 1654 to January 1655
4) was one of two MPs to represent Glamorgan in the First Session of the Second Protectorate Parliament from September 1656 until he was 'taken out of the House [of Commons] to be a Lord … in the Other House' in December 1657.

Most important of all he was a Privy Councillor, a member of the Council of State, from the end of April 1653 until the fall of Richard Cromwell's Protectorate in May 1659. That he owed much to Cromwell's influence cannot be disputed. He was an opportunist, one who had seized what was on offer back in 1645 when he became 'an agent for some Parliamenters to London'. It is tempting to speculate how much higher he could have gone, but his days as a grandee were numbered.

Cromwell's Second Charter to Swanzey

A supplementary charter was granted on 8th May 1658 to the Mayor, Aldermen and Burgesses of Swanzey, empowering them to

> nominate one able and discreet person of the said town … to be a Burgess of the Parliament.

In short, Swanzey was to have its first MP, whom it did not have to share with contributory boroughs. The charter is unique in that no other town in the Protectorate had such a charter from Cromwell, the purpose of which was to obtain the return of a Cromwellian supporter. Undoubtedly, Philip Jones had a lot to do with it, as Swanzey was a borough in which government supporters were in the majority on the aldermanic council. The 'able and discreet person' to be 'nominated' was William Foxwist, Esquire, and he was certainly not 'of the town'. Born in 1610, William Foxwist of Caernarfon studied and practised law until, in 1640, he represented his home town in the Long Parliament until excluded by Colonel Pride in December 1648. He also appears to have represented Anglesey in the Little Parliament of 1653, after which he served as a Deputy-judge of Assizes, sitting at Brecon in the Great Sessions. As the Member for Swanzey he did not take his seat in Richard Cromwell's Protectorate Parliament until January 1659. He proved to be a silent member, which supports the view that his selection had been the means by which Philip got a compliant Cromwellian supporter into Parliament. It was subsequently noticed by a Colonel Alured that there had been an irregularity in Foxwist's return, which suggests that no election had taken place. The proposed inquiry into the irregularity appears to have been suppressed.

Cromwell's Death

After the Second Protectorate Parliament had been dissolved in February 1658, Cromwell's health deteriorated until, succumbing to a malaria-type fever, he died aged 59 on 3rd September that year. According to the Rev. J. Prestwich, Cromwell was taken ill at Hampton Court – an ague – and after a week taken to Whitehall Palace where he died at three in the afternoon. His corpse was laid out and embalmed, but so ill-done that 'the body smelt so that it was obliged to be buried quickly' in a vault at Westminster Abbey. However, according to Whitelock's version of events:

> Immediately upon his death, the Council assembled, and being satisfied that the Protector had in his lifetime declared his son Richard should succeed him, the Council caused the same to be proclaimed in London … and they went [that] same day to Richard.

When news reached Swanzey a payment of 5s. was made 'for ringing the bells', and another 'to the musketeers and seamen [the sum of] 9s. … [and] for 14lbs. of powder at 12½d. per pound – 14s. 7d., and for match 2s. 3d.'

Four days after Cromwell's death, Philip wrote to Cromwell's other son, Henry, addressing him as:

His Excellency the Deputy of Ireland

May it please your Excellency,

We are now under the sad dispensation of the loss of your dear father, our lord and master; he has gone to Heaven embalmed with prayers and tears … God has been pleased to deny it, yet He has afforded us this mercy [as to David], that he has this day a son upon his throne … but he [the son] is not without great difficulties, which I hope the God of his father will carry him through … .

My Lord, your Excellency's most faithful and humble servant.

The son who was upon the throne was Richard Cromwell, the new Lord Protector, and now that Philip was Comptroller of what had become Richard's household, it fell to him to attend to the funeral arrangements. The fact that Oliver Cromwell's decomposing body had already been buried meant that for nearly three months a wood or wax effigy had to be used for the lying in state. The funeral, which proved to be a lavish affair, costing an incredible £60,000, took place on 23rd November and involved conveying an empty coffin to Westminster Abbey. In the grand procession Philip, Lord Jones, took his place among 'the peers whose trains were all borne'.

Richard's Parliament

In his letter to Henry Cromwell, Philip referred to the 'great difficulties' that Richard had to face. The root of these difficulties was not so much that the country at large was fed up with Puritan rule, but that the Puritans were hopelessly divided. Oliver Cromwell had kept the lid on the situation by his strength of character and by the fact that he could rely on the army to support him. Richard could command no such respect from the army and was, therefore, in no position to enforce his will on the opposing factions.

To make matters worse, when Richard's Parliament met on 27th January 1659, many of the MPs who had supported Richard's father were not there to support him, being replaced by men hostile to the Protectorate. In South Wales, for example, John Price still held Cardiff, but Rowland Dawkin no longer represented Carmarthen, being displaced by a member of the opposition, David Morgan of Abergwili. Glamorgan fell to Evan Seys of Boverton, also a member of the opposition, and both he and David Morgan soon aligned themselves with Philip's arch-enemy, Colonel Edward Freeman, MP for Leominster. Philip and Edmund, Lord Thomas of Wenvoe were no longer MPs as both men were members of the Other House, though they were still members of the Council of State. Yet another of Philip's political associates, Edmund Jones of Buckland – who was described as the Colonel's 'main agent and instrument in South Wales' – was expelled from Parliament on a trumped-up charge of delinquency. There was even an attempt to oust William Foxwist, Swanzey's first MP, on the ground that there appeared to be no election return from the sheriff.

Philip and another Privy Councillor, John Thurloe, remained close to Richard Cromwell. In later years, Thurloe recalled that army officers had objected to the fact that

> his Highness was lead only by the advice of Mr Comptroller and myself, and that he would do nothing without us.

Philip must have been anticipating trouble for both Richard Cromwell and himself because, at a later date, he admitted

> that he received pay for himself and his soldiers, before 25th March 1659, and salaries for services since the year 1642.

It is tempting to speculate on what 'salaries for services' were owing to him since 1642, the year the Civil War started, but that is to digress from the fact that Philip was evidently making sure that any money due to himself and his garrison troops would be paid before impending trouble put it beyond his reach. The trouble that he anticipated is easily identified, for in March 1659 the opposition, led by Colonel Freeman, had renewed its attacks on him, prompting a Royalist to remark that:

> our Commonwealth men began to snarl at Colonel Jones … accusing him of the receipt of above £100,000 in Wales for which he has not [accounted for]

What the Royalist referred to was an incident that took place in the presence of Richard Cromwell, whereby David Morgan, MP for Carmarthen, and a former propagation official, accused Philip of having bought 'a great house with the money received for tithes in Wales'. The House of Commons chose Colonel Freeman and the

Glamorgan MP, Evan Seys, to investigate the allegation, which they no doubt proceeded to do with vigour, but they were prevented from completing their task by another opposing faction.

Army officers under General Fleetwood forced Richard Cromwell to dissolve Parliament on 22nd April and recall the Rump, the 42 surviving members of which assembled 15 days later. On 24th May Richard acknowledged that the Protectorate was at an end, by which time a liberated press was already criticising him and those who, for 'worldly honours and carnal interest', had stood by him as advisors. Referring to Philip Jones, a London pamphlet asked:

Whether a knave or a coward had most honesty? And whether both centred in one, born to £51 per annum (bred according to the Welsh mountains) which in ten years he has multiplied to £5,000 per annum.

The pamphlet labelled him a

debaucher of both Protectors [a man who] sacrilegiously robbed God's house to build himself sumptuous palaces ... an oppressor of his country, a parliament-breaker, a corrupter and debaucher of members of the last Parliament; a Presbyterian, an Independent, a Cavalier [Royalist], a defrauder of the public revenue [and a] thorough-past Protectorian.

More was to come in that the Rump invited anyone with a grievance against Protectorate officials to present their petitions. The complaints of the aggrieved in South Wales appeared in the *Petitions and Articles of Impeachment*. This petition, containing 20 articles, was read out in the House on 18th May by Bledri Morgan, a former Carmarthenshire sequestration official, who out of a 'sense of suffering ... of himself ... by the greatness and potency of Colonel Philip Jones' had aligned himself with Colonel Freeman and John Gunter, as evidenced by the fact that their names appear in Articles 10 and 20 in connection with their 'persecution' at Philip's hand.

The Articles of Impeachment

The petition rendered Philip subject to impeachment, the object of which was to show him to be unfit for high office. Article One stated:

that the said Colonel Philip Jones, for about ten years last past, appeared the chief and only man to recommend and bring in persons to all places of authority, profit or trust, ecclesiastical, military or civil in South Wales, being a privy councillor to the late Protector for about five year last past, and having had chief governance and superior tendency of all public affairs in South Wales, under the said Protector; who, contrary to several Ordinances and Acts of this Parliament ... recommended, nominated and brought into authority there, divers notorious Cavaliers in Arms, compound delinquents and other disaffected persons.

In all, Bledri Morgan listed the names of 28 Royalists whom Philip had favoured for appointments as officials so that they:

> being sensible of his friendship, declared a resolution to protect his person and estate if Charles Stuart and his party should prevail.

Among the Royalists listed was Richard Vaughan, Earl of Carbery, who, it was alleged, had shared with Philip the revenue from the Original Seals in South Wales. It was also alleged that Philip had persuaded his fellow councillors to grant a pass to one of Carbery's servants, permitting him to travel to Paris the previous year. After the return of Charles Stuart, Carbery was appointed Lord-Lieutenant of all Wales and was, therefore, in a position to 'protect' Philip, though whether he actually did so is unknown. What is known is that a number of Royalists were nominated by Philip to a variety of posts, and one of them remained loyal to him to the very end.

Article 14 charges Philip with seizing:

> one shipfull of plate, valuables and jewels, of the value of £20,000 at least, cast ashore on the coast of Glamorgan in the year 1649 [the year he was appointed a Collector of Prize Goods] and that he had disposed of the lead that covered the Cathedral of St. David's, which was valued at £300, to his own use, against the great trust reposed in him.

Article 17 stated that Colonel Philip Jones is said to:

> have deported himself in a cowardly manner at Cardiff, Ely Bridge, St. Fagans, contrary to his honour and dignity.
>
> Few can show the like improvement of estate, having in about ten years' time, brought £8 per annum to about £5,000 per annum. The said Philip Jones having no trade, nor any visible means to accomplish the same, having £1,000 per annum stipend as a Privy Councillor, which, with an overplus, he did expend in the support of himself and his family, who lived at exceedingly high rates.

The remaining articles relate to propagation, sequestration, assault and wrongful imprisonment, seizure of goods and estates, perversion of justice, the protection of murderers and perjurers, and defrauding public revenue.

Philip's Response

If Bledri Morgan thought he had Philip on the run, then he had miscalculated. As a former Rump MP, Philip was present in the House on 23rd May, and

> standing up in his seat, made answer to the petition of Bledri Morgan, Gent., and to the articles to the said petition annexed, denied the particulars and cleared himself, and desired that the House would be pleased to put the business into a speedy way of examination.

The 'business' was referred to a committee of 31 members, most of them Republicans and, therefore, opponents. On 26th May they ordered:

That persons undermentioned do personally appear before the said committee, at Speaker's Chamber, Westminster, on this day three weeks peremptory, to testify of the truth of the said articles.

Sixty-four witnesses were called, the majority from Gower. Some were long-standing complainants such as Elizabeth Mansel, late of Llandewi, now of Swanzey, and Thomas Bowen of Ilston; others were associates who, as men in office, were expected to testify on oath. On the designated day only 40 witnesses appeared before the Committee. Soon after the hearing, Bledri complained in a second petition:

That the said Colonel made use of his privilege as Member of Parliament to sit at the said committee covered; and by his bold and unseemly deportment to daunt and discourage the evidence produced against him … And many witnesses [24 in all], though summoned, by reason of his potency are afraid to appear.

Then, out of sheer malice, Bledri proposed in the same petition:

That the said Colonel and his adherents, whose names are here under written, be exempted from pardon [which the Rump was considering for all Protectorate supporters] and himself suspended from sitting in this Parliament until the whole charge against him be fully examined, and in the mean time to give sufficient security to attend your Honours' judgement therein.

As to those whose names were 'under written' and were, therefore, listed by Bledri as the 'agents, instruments and adherents of Colonel Jones', evidence was to 'be produced against them all', among them Rowland Dawkin, John Price, Evan Lewis, Jenkin Franklin of Ilston, Jenkin Dawkin (Rowland's son), William Watkins (Philip's steward) and Edmund Jones.

A Letter of Hope

It would appear that Philip had an agent in the enemy camp, or at least in a place where his opponents' consternation could be observed, for on 13th June – two days before the 40 witnesses appeared before the Committee – someone who signed his name GR wrote:

To the Honourable Philip, Lord Jones thereto

My Lord

Your adversaries are much discouraged how to proceed upon Wednesday against you because their clamorous witnesses are not yet come up. Bledri Morgan would have a mōcon to put off that day; but John Gunter resolves to have the business of the office of Port fines examined, and their main work is to engage Blagrave on their side, who intend (as you say) a grant from Pembroke for it; the Lord Carbery being but an intruder, having obtained his grant from the [late] King at Oxford; and having performed that, they intend immediately to petition the Parliament to abolish the office; and they intend to serve the Earl of Carbery, and the same day they will go on with the Article concerning the privy seal, which they say your Lordship procured for Sir Henry Vaughan to clear his delinquency. I believe they are hopeful for the Portugal business … and they say they have the deaf, blind and the lame to prosecute the business. Did I but know your Lordship's resolution, I would pump John Gunter whether he is to be withdrawn to desert ym. I know he is selfish, and will be soon possessed with an Agrigentinion Squincy; but I know he is dangerous to be dealt with … and I dare not venture without abundance of … direction. My Lord be not discouraged. Wait the Lord's leisure and doubt not but [that] He will protect you in your innocency, and you have but their sanballast against you, whom the Lord will at last disperse with the spirit of division among themselves.

More Trouble

Even though his enemies were failing to provide sufficient evidence to support their allegations, they were still making Philip a controversial figure, so much so that Richard Cromwell declared that the whole business caused 'trouble in his [Richard's] household'. This may be the reason why Philip left Whitehall Palace and took up lodgings in the Strand with a Mr. Machornist. His enemies then tried to involve one of Mr. Machornist's servant girls in a plot to pin a charge of bribery on Philip. The girl, Jane Sanders, appears to have been lured to the house of David Morgan, MP for Carmarthen, who with the aid of his wife (who absolutely loathed Philip), Bledri Morgan and John Gunter, promised Jane a 'piece to buy her a pair of gloves', employment in the service of Morgan's wife, sums of money and even marriage with her employer if she would swear that she had witnessed Philip hand over £300 to a 'person with red hair' for not appearing as a witness before the Parliamentary Committee. Jane spiritedly refused to be involved in the plot, for "it was untrue," she said. Morgan's wife then 'called her [a] slatt and bid her go out of her house, which she was forced to do though it was 11 o'clock at night'.

Bledri and his associates were not the only ones to pursue Philip, for a leading Royalist was informed in May that Colonel Jones had been approached with the view of winning him over to their cause, perhaps not for the first time, as the report stated that the Colonel

seems more ready to assist the King [because he is] ruined beyond all recovery if the Commonwealth be [re]established, [he being] accountable for £137,000 to the state.

It seems likely that Philip came to an arrangement with the Royalists, though the details are unknown.

The restoration of the Rump (22nd April) and, more significantly, the Commonwealth (24th May) led to a purge of all Protectorians in high office. By the beginning of July, Philip had been removed from the County Committee and from his governorship of Cardiff Castle, being replaced in the latter instance by a man whom he had personally 'put out of authority' at an earlier date. His leading associates – bar one – all received similar treatment. Rowland Dawkin, for example, was relieved of his governorship of the Tenby garrison and probably the Carmarthen garrison as well. The only man to remain in high office was Bussy Mansel, whose past performance in the Barebones Parliament made him acceptable to the Rump. Bussy was a survivor: as early as April 1659 he had been in contact with Charles Stuart as a prelude to his return.

In July there were uprisings throughout the Commonwealth, which were not suppressed until late August. In Swanzey, Cromwell's charters were discarded, the title of Mayor dropped, and at the Michaelmas court leet William Jones was sworn in as Portreeve. In September, too, Philip was fined for non-attendance at Parliament and probably cashiered. The reason for his non-attendance was that, at some point prior to the fine, he had gone to ground rather than suffer the ongoing attacks of his enemies. He did not return to Wales, but took up residence with his brother-in-law, John Price, who had property in East Barnet, Hertfordshire, where he could keep an eye on developments in London. It was in his interest to lie low: he had foreseen the 'great difficulties' that Richard Cromwell had to face; he knew first hand how bitterly divided both the Puritans and the Republicans were; he knew, too, that it was only a matter of time before the monarchy returned in the person of Charles Stuart.

By the end of summer the Rump had returned to governing in a high-handed manner, but when, on 12th October, it dismissed General Lambert from his command the army dissolved the Rump the following day. Such was the division and confusion that ensued, the army was obliged to reinstate the Rump on 26th December. Even then the governance of the country remained in turmoil. A strong hand was needed, and the only man in a position to restore order was General Monck, Commander-in-Chief of Commonwealth forces in Scotland. On 2nd January 1660 Monck led his forces south, arriving in London early in February to find the Rump extremely unpopular and unfit to govern. Monck's answer to the problem was to demand, on 21st February, that the Presbyterians who had been excluded from Parliament in 1648 be reinstated, thereby ensuring a moderate majority in the House, a majority that would favour the return of Charles Stuart. He also called for new elections.

Prior to dissolving itself on 16th March, the reformed Long Parliament issued commissions for the county militia and assessment committees. Among those appointed to be committeemen in Glamorgan were Philip, Rowland Dawkin, John Price and Colonel Edward Freeman. How Philip and Freeman sat on committee meetings together can only be left to the imagination, especially as Freeman had recently been re-appointed Attorney General for South Wales; moreover, the day before the Long Parliament dissolved itself it passed an act to re-open investigations into the propagation funds. On 5th April the Council of State, then, appointed commissioners to carry out the investigation, one of whom was Colonel Freeman. As it turned out both Philip's return to office and the investigation were soon terminated by yet another important event.

The Restoration of Charles Stuart

The elections that took place on 25th April secured the return of candidates who favoured the restoration of the monarchy in the person of Charles Stuart. Despite a ban, many Royalists were among the candidates, and on General Monck's authority they were allowed to take their seats. It was also Monck's decision that all peers should take their place in the resurrected House of Lords. Monck then communicated to Parliament the terms of Charles Stuart's return from exile, which were embodied in a carefully worded document known as the Declaration of Breda. In short, Charles acknowledged Parliament's right to govern; in return Parliament proclaimed him King on 8th May. Charles landed at Dover on the 25th and, escorted by Monck, arrived in London two days later. News of Charles's return was received with enthusiasm by the majority of the population. In Swanzey the Portreeve recorded:

> Paid at Mr Leyshon Seys his house and at the Wine Tavern in the entertainment of Colonel Freeman and several other gentlemen that accompanied myself and the aldermen in the solemn proclaiming of his most gracious Majesty Charles the second to be King of England, Scotland ... and Ireland, which was performed on the 11th of May 1660, the expense in both places was £4.7.0.

The Common Attorneys' Account also records charges for reading the proclamation, for ringing the bells and for bonfires and beer. What is noteworthy about the payment to Leyshon Seys is that the man who made the entry, William Jones, had been sworn in at the Michaelmas 1659 court leet as Portreeve – not Mayor – presumably because, by then, the burgesses had dispensed with Cromwell's charters and reverted to their former privileges.

So what had been Philip's position with regard to the burgesses riding themselves of a charter that he had helped to draft? Did he acquiesce, knowing that the days of Puritan rule were numbered? Or did the burgesses take advantage of his absence when political chaos caused him to go to ground? Whatever the truth, Cromwell's charters had become irrelevant; they may even have become a liability in that the restored Rump might react against a town that had been supportive of Cromwell's Protectorate. In all probability, getting rid of incriminating charters is just another example of how Swanzey changed sides in the face of adversity.

Of course, once the charters had been put aside, Philip would have lost his position as High Steward of the Town, but that would not have effected his position as Steward of Gower and Kilvey. When exactly he ceased to be Richard Cromwell's Steward is not known, but it is likely to have been sometime after the Restoration in May 1660, when the Royalist William Thomas of Dan-y-graig replaced him.

One thing is certain, Philip's removal from the stewardship of Gower had nothing to do with maladministration. Indeed, Swanzey had benefitted during the 15 years or so that Philip had been Steward and Governor of the town. The coal trade had increased, the poor had been provided for and the streets had been paved extensively, on one occasion for a distance of 1,426 yards moreover, the town could boast a covered market, two schools, one of them state sponsored, and for a short while it had its own MP.

The Act of Indemnity and Oblivion

On 18th June Bledri Morgan petitioned Parliament to have Philip's name on a list of 20 officials who were to be exempt from the proposed Act of Indemnity and Oblivion, but in this he was unsuccessful, presumably because there were too many men in the House who were not Philip's enemies. This did not mean that Philip would be free from prosecution once the act came into force, or that the property he had accumulated would not be taken from him. Philip had been a leading propagation commissioner, a principal supporter of the Protectorate, a man against whom numerous allegations had been made. His position was precarious to say the least and his survival depended on his connection with men in high places, Royalists in particular. This appears to be made evident by a curious receipt preserved among the Fonmon papers.

> August 24, 1660
>
> Received the day and year above, written of Colonel Philip Jones for the use of … the Right Honourable the Lord Gerard, one of the Gentlemen of his Majesty's bedchamber, the sum of five hundred and twenty pounds. I do hereby oblige myself to procure such a discharge and acquaintance from him, the said Lord Gerard, to him, the said Colonel Jones, as shall be thought necessary for his security. Witness my hand the day and year above written.
>
> £520   Richard Mason

Who Richard Mason was is unknown, but Lord Gerard was none other than the man who had twice forced Laugharne to take refuge in Pembroke Castle. It is believed that the receipt was for money paid to Gerard for services rendered, namely that he obtained a pardon for Philip under the Act of Indemnity, which came into force in August. Whatever the truth, Philip received a pardon on 19th November.

Acquisitions – Retained and Lost

At a hearing in 1662, Philip admitted:

> that he had purchased some lands and fee-farm rents belonging to the late King, Bishops, Deans and Chaplains in the Counties of Carmarthen, Glamorgan and Pembroke; and received so much of the profits thereof as he could get, until the 1st June 1660. And pleaded settlement of account and the Act of Oblivion; which were eventually allowed.

By his own admission Philip had held onto his acquisitions until at least 1st June 1660. What he did in the months that followed may be summed up in the words of A.G. Veysey:

> In accordance with the terms of the Restoration Settlement he surrendered the sequestered property he had acquired.

That meant all property that had formerly belonged to the Crown, the Church, or to Royalists such as the late Judge David Jenkins of Hensol. He also had to forego all

> Property in the Seignory of Gower [that had been] leased to him by Oliver Cromwell [and also] several fee farm rents in the counties of Carmarthen, Pembroke and Glamorgan.

What remained in his possession far outweighed his losses because

> The Act of Indemnity … confirmed the holdings of all bona fide purchases of land; [that is, land] legally acquired in ordinary transactions.

Philip retained possessions of the several lordships, castle and manors of Fonmon, Penmark and Llancadle, which he had bought from the Earl of Bolingbroke; the manors of Llancarvon, Wrinston, West Orchard and Michaelston-le-pit, which had formerly belonged to the late Marquis of Worcester; manors, lands and tenements in at least seven Gower parishes, and in the town, parish or liberties of Swanzey. Philip's principal 'creatures' and associates also survived the Restoration Settlement with their acquisitions more or less intact. According to A.G. Veysey:

> John Price remained on his estate at East Barnet, William Watkins at the house he had built, some said with propagation funds, at Penyrwrlodd near Llanigon in Breckonshire. [At the same time Watkins] continued to serve Jones as steward of his estate, being rewarded by him with property at Cwrt Coleman, Glamorgan. Rowland Dawkin also succeeded in retaining the estate he had acquired

in Gower, as did John Price, including the manor of Talybont (once the grange of Cwrt y Carnau held by Neath Abbey), which they shared. As to Edmund Thomas of Wenvoe, he ended up with an estate that was later valued as twice that of Philip Jones. For both men and for their associates – bar one – there could be no place for them as yet in Restoration politics, nor in the administrative and judicial affairs of Glamorgan. Bussy Mansel was the one exception, for not only did he retain his estate, but following the election of April 1660 he had, as MP for Cardiff, taken his seat in the Convention Parliament until its dissolution at the end of the year, after which his pre-eminence in local affairs was eclipsed by the return of the established gentry to positions of authority.

That should have been the end of the story, leaving the reader to decide whether Philip's associates and 'creatures' were a bunch or reprobates and, more importantly, whether Philip was a man who made enemies on account of his ever increasing wealth and influence, or whether he was a very clever rogue.

But there was more to come.

Chapter XI
Colonel Philip Jones (5)

The period following the Reformation was a dangerous time for leading Protectorians, not because Charles II desired revenge, but because Royalists who had suffered under Puritan rule wanted to settle old scores. Many leading Protectorate officials were hunted down, especially those who had signed the death warrant of Charles I. It mattered not whether these regicides were alive or dead: they were tried and punished, even posthumously. On 12th January 1661 – the 12th anniversary of the execution of the late King – Cromwell's corpse was exhumed, posthumously hanged and decapitated. Everywhere prominent Royalists were out to reclaim their confiscated estates.

In Gower, Edward Somerset, Marquis of Worcester, had re-established himself and he, like Cromwell, had every intention of installing men of his choosing in places of authority. In the manor of Swanzey, William Thomas was succeeded by his father, Walter Thomas, as Steward at Michaelmas 1661. Edward's choice of men is reflected in other areas as well. In his *Contributions towards a History of Gower* L.W. Dillwyn lists the names of eleven burgesses who were aldermen at Michaelmas 1661. When this list is compared with the list that has survived from 1657 it becomes evident that three men had been relieved of their aldermanic status – Philip Jones, Rowland Dawkin and Mathew David. They had been replaced by two Royalists, William Thomas and Leyshon Seys who had also been sworn in as Portreeve.

There is no reason to doubt that these changes were in accordance with the wishes of Edward Somerset. In the two years following the Restoration, Edward had relentlessly hounded Philip over the four manors of Llancarvan, Wrinston, West Orchard and Michaelston-le-Pit, first by petitioning the King, then by introducing a private act in the House of Lords, and finally by taking legal action in the Chancery Court. Edward may have failed on all three counts, but there were others pressing to have Philip brought to court.

The Cavalier Parliament that first sat on 8th May 1661 still had a score to settle with former Protectorate officials, despite the pardons that had been issued in accordance with the Act of Indemnity. In the spring of 1662 the Attorney General, Sir Geoffrey Palmer, was ordered to carry out an investigation into the whole business of finance during the Interregnum. There were two commissions, the first to gather information on the collection and administration of all taxes, rents, fines and propagation funds. The second commission had the task of examining sequestered church livings and ecclesiastical administration; among the commissioners were Colonel Freeman and John Gunter. The findings of these commissions led to 352 former officials in South Wales being prosecuted for illegally receiving public revenue, among them Philip, Rowland Dawkin, John Price and Evan Lewis, but no charges were brought against Bussy Mansel. When Philip appeared in court he

> denied all charges of illegally receiving taxes [etc., but] admitted that he had with others to superintend the coining of 32 tons of bullion … that he had purchased some lands and fee-farm rents belonging to the late King, Bishops, Deans, Chaplains in the counties of Carmarthen, Glamorgan and Pembroke; and received so much profits thereof as he could get until the 1st June 1660.

The commissioners had great difficulty in finding the evidence needed to complete their investigation, especially with regard to propagation funds. More than nine years had passed since the propagation period and, as A.G. Veysey explains:

> the great chain of influence and control which had stretched through his [Philip's] agents into every county of South Wales remained hidden among the vast numbers of minor officials who were accused at the same time. Those prosecuted denied the charges, like John Prosser, who in reply to allegations of embezzlement of Propagation funds in Radnorshire, maintained that a 'most sad and lamentable fire' in March 1659 had destroyed his house and papers – all except the Quietus given him by the commissioners appointed to examine the Propagation accounts at Neath in 1655. Little could now be proved in the face of a general desire to forget past events so that the prosecutions were subsequently dropped.

That should have been an end to the matter, but in October 1662 Philip was accused at the Pembroke Quarter Sessions of stealing 17 tons of lead from the roof of St. David's Cathedral, but once again the charge appears to have been dropped.

Religious Persecution

Prior to the Restoration, Charles Stuart had issued the Declaration of Breda, whereby he expressed religious tolerance with the words

> a liberty to tender consciences [and that] no man shall be disquieted or called in[to] question for differences.

He also stated in the Declaration that he would

> consent to such act[s] of Parliament as ... shall be offered to us for the full granting [of] indulgence.

Initially there was no action taken against Puritans, but there were many Anglican clergymen who had been ejected from their livings and who now wanted their livings restored to them. In Gower, William Houghton was restored to his former living at Ilston Church on 23rd July 1660. Tradition has it that John Miles and his fellow Baptists then moved to Trinity Well in the secluded Ilston Valley. There are, however, those who maintain that Miles and his congregation relocated to Swanzey.

John Miles's ejection cannot be construed as persecution – that was yet to come – for although Charles desired toleration, the Cavalier Parliament had every intention of restoring the supremacy of the Church of England and, if necessary, making life difficult for those who did not conform; hence the terms Nonconformists and later Dissenters (those who refused to comply with the dictates of the established church).

The first to suffer locally were the Quakers who were detested by fellow Puritans and Anglicans alike because

(1) they believed that all earthly officials, both political and religious, were corrupt and undeserving of respect and obedience,
(2) they refused to pay tithes and
(3) they refused to take the oath of allegiance and supremacy when required to do so by magistrates.

In short, they were considered to be subversive troublemakers. Their persecution in eastern Glamorgan began in February 1661. Then, towards the end of the year, trouble erupted in Swanzey when the Portreeve, Leyshon Seys, accompanied by armed men, broke up a Quaker meeting and imprisoned all the men.

Other denominations were left unmolested. Marmaduke Matthews, for instance, continued to hold his living at St. John's and Daniel Higgs continued to officiate at Port Eynon. The crunch came on 19th May 1662 when the Cavalier Parliament passed the Act of Uniformity, whereby all ministers had to take the oath of loyalty to the King, be ordained by a bishop, and agree to use the new Anglican Book of Common Prayer. Puritans such as Matthews and Higgs were given three months to conform. Both refused; both were ejected from their livings.

Puritan laymen were also expected to conform, firstly by taking the oath, which most of them did, but their failure to conform in other areas led to them being haled before the archdeacon's consistory court at Carmarthen. Philip was summoned there on three separate occasions for failing to attend church. This suggests that he still resided to some extent at Swanzey, as Gower was part of the Diocese of St. David, whereas Fonmon was in the Diocese of Llandaff. Other laymen to appear before the consistory court were Jenkin Francklin and Matthew David, the latter a former alderman who appeared before the archdeacon on two occasions for failing to attend church. Rowland Dawkin appeared at Carmarthen on four occasions for refusing to have his children baptized in the parish church. In all 96 persons from Swanzey and Gower were haled before the consistory court on one or more occasions between 1662 and 1668.

In 1663 the Baptist leader, John Miles, emigrated to America, influenced no doubt by one of his congregation, Griffith Bowen, who had sailed to the New World in 1638 and returned the following year. John set out in the company of about 15 of his followers from the parishes of Rhosili, Llandewi, Penmaen and Bishopston. After a three month voyage he landed at Boston, Massachusetts, and eventually founded a settlement that he and his followers called Swanzey, which in 1675 was attacked by Indians. Meanwhile, back in Gower, Lewis Thomas had taken over the leadership of the Baptists who remained, meeting in several Swanzey homes, and later at Llodrau Brith farm, three miles out of town.

Puritans who remained in Swanzey and Gower after the departure of John Miles were to find themselves up against even tougher restrictions. In 1664 Parliament passed the Conventicle Act, whereby five persons or more over and above household members were forbidden to assemble for religious purposes (conventicles) unless it was in accordance with the Anglican Prayer Book. Anyone in breach of the act risked three months imprisonment or a £5 fine. A second offence could result in the penalty being doubled. A third offence could mean transportation for seven years.

Parliament went a step further in 1665 when it introduced the Five Mile Act, whereby ejected Puritan ministers were forbidden to venture within five miles of any city, town or borough, or dwell within any parish in which they had previously ministered. Yet despite these acts at least four Puritan ministers continued to hold conventicles in Swanzey, among them Daniel Higgs, the ejected minister of Port Eynon, Lewis Thomas, the Baptist leader, and William Bevan, the Quaker leader who was summoned to the consistory court for failing to attend church and for holding conventicles. Undoubtedly the best known Puritan minister to carry on regardless was Marmaduke Matthews, the ejected Independent minister of St. John's. Marmaduke appeared before the consistory court for holding conventicles on no less than three occasions without having to endure the horrors of transportation. Indeed, Marmaduke continued to preach in Swanzey until his death in 1683. He was described by Edward Calamy in his *An Account of the Ministers Ejected, Volume II*, as a

> very pious, zealous man [who] went from house to house to instruct the inhabitants of the town ... [He] preached at a little chapel at the end of the town by the connivance of the magistrates ... [and] would often go on market-day to the country people and speak to them about spiritual matters.

How did Marmaduke get away with it? 'By the connivance of the magistrates' so it was said. It seems that the authorities within the lordship were lax when it came to dealing with Nonconformists, so much so that William Lucy, Bishop of St. David's, wrote to the Deputy-lieutenant of Glamorgan on 8th March 1666, complaining that nothing had been done to eradicate the Dissenters at Llangyfelach, whom he considered to be 'dangerous … and an affront to established religion' – to no avail because seven years later he had cause to complain of their continued existence.

So why were the authorities so lax? In the case of Swanzey, it has been estimated that the population in 1662 stood at 1,690, the figure coming from calculations based of data taken from the parish registers of baptisms, marriages and burials. In a census conducted by Archbishop Sheldon in 1676 the number of adult Nonconformists in Swanzey was recorded as 292, a figure that may well be too low, as it was the Archbishop's intention to minimize the numerical strength of Nonconformists. All things considered it is, therefore, likely that the Nonconformists in Swanzey constituted almost a third of the population. Fifteen years of Puritan rule would have been largely responsible for that, and the man at the centre of it all was, of course, Colonel Philip Jones.

The Latter Years

In October 1662 the five-year lease on Fonmon Castle expired, permitting Philip to take up residence there. In the decade that followed, Philip appears to have kept a low profile,

> the calm … interrupted [according A.G. Veysey] only by the claims of two London mercers in 1670 for payment for goods supplied for Oliver Cromwell's funeral.

It was during this period of relative calm that he enlarged Fonmon Castle by adding to it the north wing. He could certainly afford the luxury as the income from his estate was in excess of £1,000 per annum, which put him among the twelve wealthiest landowners in the county. As a squire he was accepted into the ranks of the Glamorgan gentry, his offspring marrying into the most influential of families. Had it been otherwise, Philip would not have been appointed Sheriff of Glamorgan in November 1671, nor would he have been a JP from August 1672 onwards. It was probably during the post Restoration period that he had his portrait painted, which, with his cane and sword, depicts him more of a Royalist than a Puritan.

Philip maintained contact with many of his former associates, as evidenced by the fact that he and John Price were both present at the post-nuptial settlement of the son of Edmund Thomas of Wenvoe. In Philip's will John Price, Evan Lewis and Edmund Jones of Buckland were trustees, empowered to pay his debts with the estate rents of the manors of Penmark, West Orchard and lands in Penmark, Llancarvan, St. Athan and Porthkerry. William Watkins, the former Royalist Receiver General of South Wales, whom he had appointed steward of his estate, and whom he rewarded with property at Cwrt Coleman in Glamorgan, remained loyal to him to the very end.

Philip's Will

In his will, dated 15th April 1673, Philip refers to 'several deeds of lease and release, dated 5th and 6th March 1672, between me on the one part and Edmund Jones, Herbert Evans, John Price, Evan Lewis and David Evans [who had been Philip's Under-sheriff in 1671] … the said persons' being nominated by him as 'trustees' for the payment of his debts.

To his 'dear and loving wife, Jane Jones', he bequeathed 'the several lordships, castle and manors of Fonmon and Llancadle … for and during her natural life, in lieu of [a] dower', which proved to be for a period of four years as Jane died in 1678. To his daughter Priscilla he bequeathed £1,500, and to Jane and Katherine £1,000 each 'for

Portrait of Philip Jones when he would have been about fifty

their respective portions, to be paid in one, two and three years respectively'. The two daughters, Ann and Elizabeth, had died before the will had been written, Elizabeth in 1672.

Philip's sons, Samuel and Philip, had also died prior to the will, Samuel in 1671. To his youngest son, Oliver, Philip bequeathed all his 'manors, lands and tenements [etc.] situated in the parishes of Llangyfelach, Llanrhidian, Oystermouth, Llanmadoc and in the town, parish and liberty of Swanzey'. All other property he bequeathed to his eldest son, John, which after the death of his mother in 1678 included 'the several lordships, castle and manors of Fonmon and Llancadle'.

In the final paragraph Philip directed that I 'do appoint my dear and loving wife, Jane Jones, and John Jones, my son, to be joint executors, and do leave my personal estate to them to pay my debts and funeral expenses'. Among the three witnesses was his trusted steward, William Watkins.

Epilogue

Philip died on 5th September 1674, aged 56, leaving many to ponder whether he had been a man who – because he had risen from a humble background to become one of the most powerful men in the country – had been unjustly hounded by fellow Puritans, or whether he had been a very clever rogue, one who had covered his tracks well. There had undoubtedly been men in office who had pocketed both public revenue and propagation funds. The question was whether he had been one of them? He certainly 'made hay while the sun shined'. Yet none of the allegations that were made against him were ever proved.

In the reign of Charles I, Philip had little hope of raising his status beyond that of a yeoman farmer, or of improving 'his interest and revenue in land', but when a revolutionary government held sway his aspirations, his drive and his ability could not be constrained. Did that make him one of those men who, in revolutionary circumstances, seized any opportunity to claw their way to the top? Or had he really been a man with religious convictions, one who refused 'to fight and spill blood' because 'it was against his conscience'.

If there is one thing that can be said in Philip's favour – as far as the records are concerned – it is that he did not kill anyone. If he had, his enemies would have made an issue of it. It can also be said to his credit that he does not appear to have been harsh in his dealings with Royalists – he obviously favoured some of them – but could he have been farsighted enough to know that one day the situation might change, that Charles Stuart could return and that there would be a day of reckoning.

Historians of more recent times have labelled Colonel Philip Jones as 'a great opportunist, a trafficker in Welsh sequestration, the most resourceful Puritan layman in the whole of Wales'. That he rose to high office is one of the intriguing things about him, as is the fact that he survived numerous allegations, several investigations, even impeachment. As to the man himself, he will always remain 'beside the curtain'.

Philip was buried in the chancel at Penmark Church. He was succeeded by his son, John, whose second wife was the daughter of Sir Thomas Bloodworth, Knight, sometime Mayor of London and an MP. John was knighted in 1677 and died on 15th October the following year. He was succeeded by his younger brother, Oliver. It appears that in 1681 Oliver had cause for concern, believing that Parliament would reopen investigations into the missing propagation funds. Fearing that he would be ruined, he wrote to the man who had been his father's steward, William Watkins, who reassured him, in a letter dated 4th September 1681, that he was 'perfectly safe' on account of his father

> being free from any such debts [because he had] answered this charge in the Exchequer near 20 years since, and nothing could be found against his answer.

South block of Fonmon Castle

In the first part of the letter, William Watkins wrote:

Sir,
Last night I received yours, 30 miles from London, and therefore could not sooner return you an answer, which I am very sorry for, least you should think that any harm can befall you in the matter you mention. You may rest assured that your father never received a shilling of the tithe-money. I have reason to know it, for I transcribed the accounts of those officers, and remember well that he told me and others that he had acted in the business at his own charge, and never took of the money to the value of a pint of wine. This was his very expression, and I know he was to be believed.

Chapter XII
Gabriel Powell (1)

During the early part of his life Gabriel Powell appears to have been – if what he had to say of himself is to be believed – a loyal and efficient Steward of the Lordship of Gower and Kilvey, but in his latter years, when the rural setting of the Tawe Valley had given way to the smoke and grime of industrialization, this tall, beak-nosed, irascible man devoted himself to defending the privileges of the Swansea burgesses; in doing so he obstructed all attempts by industrialists to improve and enlarge the harbour. He also thwarted moves to improve the appearance of the town and provide the amenities that were required of a fashionable resort. Gabriel may not have wielded widespread power and influence as did Philip Jones, but locally his word was law. When he died the *Gloucester Journal* referred to him in his obituary as 'King of Swansea'.

[Note – Gabriel was referred to as 'King of Swansea', not 'Swanzey', and it is fitting at this point to explain why. Since its appearance as 'Sweynesse' in a charter of c.1170 there have been at least 80 known variations in the way the town's name has been spelt. In documents relating to the latter half of the 17th century the spelling of 'Swanzey' was common enough, and remained so well into the 18th century. Indeed, in a letter dated 1720, Gabriel refers to the town as 'Swanzey', but by 1750 the spelling had been superseded by two different forms – 'Swansey' and 'Swansea'. For reasons unknown it was the 'Swansea' spelling that prevailed at the time of Gabriel's demise, a spelling that has remained unchanged to the present day.]

Early 18th Century
Born on 8th May 1710, Gabriel Powell grew up in a world not unlike that of Philip Jones prior to the Civil War. The old order of church and state had re-established itself. The same family still possessed the Lordship of Gower and Kilvey, although, from 1682 onwards, successive heads of the family held the title of Duke of Beaufort. In Swansea the burgesses continued to exercise their ancient privileges. In the lordship as a whole, country life remained virtually unchanged, a backwater in which the peasantry still endured grinding poverty. Landowners and entrepreneurs, on the other hand,

grew wealthier as a result of the ever-increasing coal trade. This trade was very apparent to visitors, one of whom, Daniel Defoe (author of *Robinson Crusoe*) wrote in *A Tour of England and Wales* (1722) that:

> Swansea is also a sea-port, and a very considerable town for trade, with a very great trade in coals and culm [small coal and dust] which they export to all parts of Somerset, Devon and Cornwall, and even to Ireland; so that sometimes may be seen a hundred sails of ships at a time loading coals here; which greatly enriches the country, and particularly this town.

The Powell Family

Gabriel came from a family of Breconshire gentry who claimed descent from Maenarch, Lord of Brycheiniog. His great-great-grandfather, John ap Howell (d.1626), had been the first in the family to adopt Powell as a surname, which he achieved by dropping the 'a' in ap, the 'H' in Howell and joining what remained to form Powell. Gabriel's father, Gabriel Powell of Pennant (1676 – 1735) had been a lawyer; at the age of 20 he had married the daughter of a Swansea burgess, which resulted in his admittance to the borough the following year. Gabriel Powell of Pennant became Portreeve in 1705, 1713 and 1726, but his greatest advancement came in *c.*1708 when he was appointed Steward of Gower and Kilvey, a post he held almost continuously until his death in 1735; it was a post that benefited his son and namesake enormously.

Gabriel the Younger was the second eldest of three sons. His elder brother, John (1704-69), became a Swansea burgess in 1728, an alderman in 1731 and Portreeve on three occasions, viz: 1733-4, 1743-4 and 1746-7. The advancement of both John and Gabriel the Younger had undoubtedly been due to their father's influence, and both sons had the benefit of training in law, the former as a lawyer, the latter as a solicitor.

In 1739 John Powell married Elizabeth, widow of Thomas Herbert (d.1736), owner of The Plas and numerous properties in Swansea, Cardiff and Glamorgan. The marriage proved short-lived, for Elizabeth died in July that year. Her infant son,

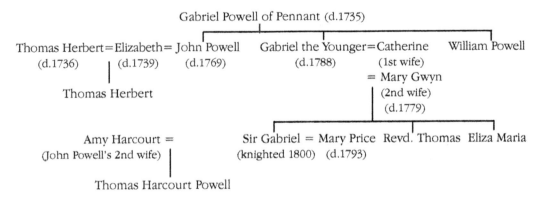

Gabriel Powell's family tree

Thomas, whom she had by her first husband, died in February 1740, thereby ending the Herberts' connection with Swansea. There followed a lawsuit between Elizabeth's sister and a Roger Powell of Energlyn (no relation to John and Gabriel Powell) that lasted some 25 years. Roger Powell based his claim on the fact that he was the son of Ann Powell, the maternal aunt of Elizabeth's first husband, Thomas Herbert (d.1736).

In September 1732, Gabriel the Younger was admitted to the freedom of the borough at the age of 22, which in itself is unsurprising as he was the son of a burgess (although, as Steward, his father had the final word on the matter), but the very day he gained the freedom he was also made an alderman as well; this was undoubtedly due to his father's influence. Exactly a year later both he and his bother, John, were nominated for the post of Portreeve; his father selected John on this occasion. Three months later Gabriel's first wife, Catherine, died without issue (the date of their marriage is unknown). Gabriel was nominated for the post of Portreeve again at Michaelmas 1735, but failed to be selected for the second time.

Early Days in Office

When his father died in December 1735, Gabriel succeeded him as Steward of Gower and Kilvey, being selected for the post by his lord and master, the Duke of Beaufort, probably on the recommendation of Gabriel's father. Although only 25 at the time, Gabriel was well qualified for the office: he was a solicitor and, in a letter to the Duke, he stated that his father had taken 'some pains to make' him 'thoroughly acquainted with' the Duke's interests; that is, in the lordship as a whole and in the demesne manors, including the manorial borough of Swansea. Unlike earlier stewards such as George Herbert, Gabriel received no salary and little in the way of fees and perquisites (perks), which was why all who were appointed to the post had to be men of means. In short, holding the stewardship had become an honour. In Gabriel's case, he still practised as a solicitor, his fees for the legal services he rendered to men of means being sufficient for him to be reasonably well off.

By right the Swansea Corporation should have complimented Gabriel with the office of Recorder at the time the Duke appointed him Steward, but the Corporation awarded him the lowly office of town clerk instead, possibly due to his unpopularity. He obviously resented the slight because, sometime after his appointment to the recordership in 1746, he tampered with the Corporation records, altering the words 'Town Clerk' to 'Recorder'. He then amended the records in such a way as to suggest that the Duke himself had appointed him to the recordership and not the Corporation.

Within six months of his appointment to Steward, Gabriel was accused of failing to safeguard the Duke's interests in the manor of Trewyddfa. The Duke's Receiver maintained that he had not collected rent from certain tenants for pasturing their live-stock on the commons. Gabriel wasted no time in vindicating himself, and did so by quoting recorded events that went back to the days of George Herbert.

Gabriel would appear to have been desirous to hold several offices simultane-ously, which he achieved in the latter part of his life. He must surely have coveted the office of portreeve, and at Michaelmas 1740 he was appointed to the post. However, on this occasion it can be assumed that he ceased to be Steward, if only temporarily, and for the next 12 months someone else held the stewardship, possibly his elder brother, John.

Boundary Disputes

One of Gabriel's duties as Steward was to ensure that the Duke's pastures, meadows and woodlands were not encroached upon. The tenants of Gower were notorious for moving their boundaries further afield, then claiming the enclosed land as theirs. Large scale encroachment of wasteland had occurred between 1549 and 1578 when the administration of the lordship under George Herbert and his successor, Sir Edward Mansel, had been either lax or corrupt, as a result of which the earls of Worcester had lost over 3,400 acres. Encroachment of wasteland for agricultural purposes was one thing, but in Gabriel's day there were tenants who had an eye of what lay beneath the soil.

Coal

The situation with regard to coal is summed up perfectly in the Gower Society's publication *Gabriel Powell's Survey of Gower 1764*; the relevant passage reads:

> Most of the known and potential coal resources lay under what had been the agriculturally less productive parts of the Lordship of Gower and Kilvey, the greater part being in the Welshry areas, and here the commons were more extensive than in other parts of the lordship … no one had any illusions about the considerable value of these commons and the minerals below them.

The Duke claimed all minerals beneath wasteland, copyhold tenancies and highways. Anyone who wished to mine and sell coal from beneath these areas had to obtain from the Duke a lease, for which they paid 4d. for every *wey* (about five tons) of coal mined. It is hardly surprising, therefore, that tenants encroached upon adjacent commons; nor is it surprising that boundary disputes were common. In Gabriel's opinion the worst offenders were Thomas Price of Penllergaer and old Robert Popkin of Fforest. Both men were landowners of note; both had a considerable interest in coal. The Gower Society's *Survey of Gower 1764* refers to several boundary disputes between Gabriel and his opponents Price and Popkin. Only two of these disputes will be cited here. The first concerns Popkin; it took place in 1750. In a letter to the Duke, Gabriel wrote:

> As I rode out this morning I observed a deep trench carried up for twelve or fifteen yards along the side of the highway at a place called Dyvnant [modern Dunvant] within your grace's manor of Gower Subboscus. Upon enquiring how it came to be done, the workmen informed me that they were employed to do it by Mr Robert Popkin, who was about carrying up a coal level from thence under the adjoining tenement.

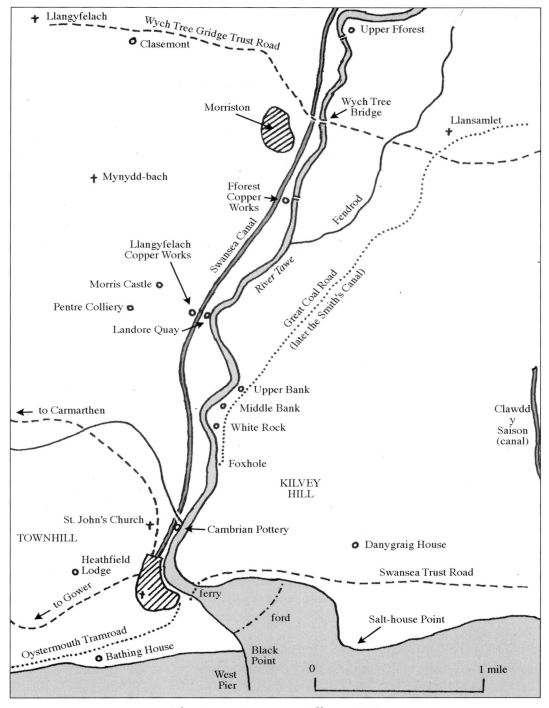

The Lower Swansea Valley c.*1800*

As to Price, a court action in 1753 seemed likely to stand or fall on whether trees had been cut down within the boundaries of an alleged highway, which ran near Price's mansion at Penllergaer and the ancient estate of Nidfwch. Gabriel had been shown:

> the spot which Mr Price's witnesses marked as the places where Mr Price's witnesses had cut or remembered the cutting of trees on. I carefully sought them in the presence of two others. I pulled up the turf, I poked the ground afterwards with a knife and could not find the least footstep [?] of an old stump, not even a root of any size.

In the days of Philip Jones coal mined in Gower had been used locally for domestic purposes, or 'sold to sea', but in Gabriel's lifetime it was also used to fuel the growth of a new industry.

Copper Smelting

It required between 18 and 20 tons of coal to smelt four tons of copper ore to produce one ton of copper. It, therefore, made sense to ship the ore to where coal could be mined in abundance, such as the Lower Swansea Valley, which also had the advantage of a river that, at high tide, was navigable as far as Morriston, the boats being towed upriver by teams of horses. The Llangyfelach Copperworks – one of the first to be established in the Lower Swansea Valley – stood adjacent to what is now Neath Road, between Cwm Level Road and Siloh Road. In 1717 Dr John Lane of Bristol took out a lease on 'the site of the other old copper works at Landore' from Robert Popkin of Fforest, who was to supply the works with both coal and culm. In 1724 Dr Lane brought in Robert Morris of Shropshire to manage the works. Two years later Lane became bankrupt as result of a bad investment elsewhere, with the result that:

> old Popkin of Fforest locked up the copper works, though he had no preference beyond other creditors for more than a year's rent.

The situation was resolved when Richard Lockwood took over the business, which in time became known as Morris, Lockwood & Co., but in 1728 a new problem arose in that Popkin failed to provide quality coal in sufficient quantity. Acting on the advice of Gabriel's father, Morris – who dubbed Popkin 'the old Fox' and wished he 'would only die, or be good humoured' – obtained coal from a neighbouring colliery. Popkin was furious and refused to supply iron from his forge at Upper Fforest, but he was soon made to grovel.

The success of the Llangyfelach Works can be attributed to Morris, who spent time in Cornwall securing supplies of ore, which came in 60 ton boats to be offloaded at a nearby quay on the Tawe, the quay probably consisting of timber-revetted earth. In Morris's absence his wife, Margaret, managed the business. She paid the men's wages, dealt with correspondence and 'used to go to the works to see if all things went on well'. She must have been a remarkable woman to have held her own in an age when women were expected to stay at home.

Another copperworks came into existence when, in 1720, a Swansea Quaker, James Griffiths, took out a lease on a plot of land on the Strand (immediately below what is now High Street Station) called 'Mr Sey's … Coal Bank', and also a piece of waste to the west. Griffiths planned to build a copperworks on the site, being *encouraged* to do so and financially backed by another Quaker, Silvanus Bevan, and Gabriel's father (d.1735). The venture was opposed by several persons on the ground that smoke from the works would be harmful to 'the inhabitants of Swansea'. One such person was Robert Popkin, whom Gabriel's father referred to as 'a cunning crafty person', one who had encroached on the lands of 'my Lord Duke and his other neighbours'. Despite the opposition, 'Griffiths & Co's Copper Works' came into being. The Business suffered a series of setbacks until Robert Morris took over the works in 1735. It finally stopped working in 1745, but its closure did not deter others from establishing copperworks further inland.

In 1736 four Bristol merchants entered into an agreement with Bussy Mansel of Margam (not the Bussy Mansel of the Civil War period) to erect 'one new copper

Fforest Copper Works in 1791.
The Beaufort Bridge on the right was constructed c.1760 and demolished in 1969.
It has been replaced by the steel bridge that can be seen today

The Buck brothers East View
Places of note are, from left to right, A – the Beaufort Arms; B – the Pill; C – the New Quay; D – C
H – the Old Postern; I – Gabriel Powell's house; J – the Great House (beyond which stood the N

smelting house' within three years at White Rock, Foxhole, on the east bank of the Tawe. The Foxhole site had several advantages, one being that coal and culm from Mansel's colliery at Llansamlet could be conveyed by packhorses (and later horse-drawn carts) down Mansel's Great Coal Road to the site. A second advantage was that Mansel had a newly-built 'dock or quay at White Rock', which the Bristol merchants could use for offloading ore.

The last of the early copperworks came into existence in the 1740s, when Robert Morris established the Fforest Copperworks on the west bank of the Tawe, near the present-day Beaufort Bridge below Morriston. Quarrels over the price and poor quality of coal supplied by Robert Popkin – and possibly Thomas Price as well – led to Morris mining his own coal. His best known mining venture – the Clyndu Level – was remarkable in that coal from this level was supplied to the Fforest work by an underground canal (the name of which has survived as Clyndu Street, Morriston). Morris's mining ventures obviously pleased Gabriel Powell because, in 1753, he wrote to the Duke, saying that:

sea as it appeared in 1748.
...th Castle; E – the tower of St. Mary's; F – the New Castle; G – the summer house of G.V. Vernon;
...e of the town) and K – some of the docks mentioned in 17th and 18th century documents

Mr Morris has at last been so fortunate as to discover the Great Penvilia Coal Vein in its full perfection at the bottom of Trewyddfa Common, just above the copperworks, which will in all probability yield great profit …

Almost a year later Gabriel wrote:

Mr Morris has at last got his new pit down and again works at his level, so he is out of Popkin's and Price's power.

But Thomas Price had other ideas and

took so much pains in stopping the air from Mr Morris's [coal] works and did it so effectually that he has for the present entirely destroyed his own – worse – the workmen that were imprisoned were employed [by Mr Morris] to keep open the air hole, which Mr Price did so effectually shut up, that the poor fellows lost their lives.

Gabriel indicted Price's workmen on behalf of 'Mr Lockwood & Co. for smoking their works'. The following day he succeeded in winning two cases for the Duke against Robert Popkin. His adversary in court had been Gruffydd Price, son and heir of Thomas Price. As a barrister, Gruffydd Price stood as Gabriel's rival in a number of court actions. Little wonder then that Gabriel wrote to the Duke, informing him of his success and adding somewhat gleefully:

> I hope it will cure him [Popkin] of his rashness, and convince Mr [Gruffydd] Price that he may possibly be mistaken in his law.

Gabriel's Private Life

In July 1740 Gabriel married his second wife, Mary, daughter of Thomas Gwyn, Esq., of Gwempa in Carmarthenshire, and Elizabeth, sole heiress of Richard Middleton, Esq., of Middleton Hall, also in Carmarthenshire. It was through her mother that Mary claimed descent from William Thomas of Danygraig and Catherine, sister of Bussy Mansel of Briton Ferry, who were her great-great-grandparents. Mary bore three children: Gabriel (b.1753), Thomas (b.1755) and Elizabeth Maria.

As to where Gabriel and Mary lived, this appear to have been in High Street below the gate, the house apparently close to the Great House of Colonel Philip Jones (which, by 1755, was no longer in the possession of the Joneses). Gabriel's house had been handed down from father to son, though why it should have passed to Gabriel in preference to his older brother is unknown. The house can be seen on the Bucks' engraving of 1748, which depicts three laid out gardens sloping to the Strand. Above the centre garden is Gabriel's house, easily identified as one that is both large and imposing. In the Gower Society's *Survey of Gower 1764* Bernard Morris described the house as

> having a double-saddle roof running parallel with High Street … The window layout is symmetrical each side of a large staircase window, and taken with the location of the chimneys on the end walls, suggests that the house had four rooms on each of its two floors, arranged around what was probably an imposing central staircase, plus an attic for servants and perhaps basement rooms.

Further details of the house appeared in *The Cambrian* (a weekly newspaper) on 14th April 1804. The article reads:

> TO BE LET, FURNISHED,
> A SPACIOUS HOUSE, in HIGH STREET, SWANSEA, containing three large parlours with a kitchen, on the ground-floor; four bed-chambers, two with closets, on the first-floor; and five in the attic; together with a large Walled Garden; also Stables and Coach-house if desired: formerly in the occupation of Gabriel Powell, Esq. deceased, and lately of Mr Thomas Lynch.

In 1744 Gabriel came into possession of Ty Gwyn farm (demolished in the 1950s, the site buried beneath Singleton Hospital), though he did not live there. He also had a stable in Cross Street, kept pigs on the adjacent wasteland, held a lease on a 'coal bank on the Strand from 1735 onwards, and according to a

> lease dated the 26th of March 1753 [he held] all that parcel of land [as did Philip Jones] called the Orchard Close, for 21 years at the yearly rent of £5.

Letters

Gabriel wrote numerous letters to successive dukes of Beaufort, many of which have survived. Apart from business matters, these letters contain a great deal of information about Gabriel, who saw himself as a fearless and diligent defender of his lord's interests. He was a serious man who liked to have all his own way – which made him unpopular – and would totally ignore the views of those who were not in agreement with him. He could read Latin and had a remarkable knowledge of local history, which must have been useful to him both as Steward and as a solicitor.

His letters reveal that he was not office-bound, but a man keen to be out and about, especially in matters relating to boundary disputes and encroachments, added to which he appears to have had remarkably good intelligence on local affairs, which he obviously obtained by way of informers, be they workmen or men of means. As a result of this intelligence he was able to respond swiftly to encroachments. He often spent time in London, residing at George's Coffee House, near Temple Bar, where he mixed with members of the legal profession. On his way to or from London he would call at the Duke's mansion at Badmington in Gloucestershire. On occasion he travelled to Hereford, as in 1750 and 1755 when he is known to have been present at the Assizes.

Gabriel was a stickler for detail, both in his work and in less formal matters such as reporting what he did with a sturgeon weighing 123 pounds (which must have come from Swansea Bay), or the dimensions of a young whale stranded near Whiteford Point, Llanmadog – '65 feet in length, 17 feet in height … and 7 feet from eye to eye' with 'a bruise on the head', which the locals took five hours to kill with hatchets.

The Methodist Revival

Gabriel lived in a world of change, much of it brought about by industrialization, which effected him both as Steward and as a solicitor, as evidenced by the contents of his letters. Yet he appears to have been unaffected by the Methodist revival that took place under his very nose, one that transcended denominational boundaries and led to mass conversions and the establishment of religious societies. As with Puritanism, Methodism originated within the Anglican Church. Initially, its aim was to counter the sleepy, intellectual aspects of the established church by appealing to the emotions of sinners.

With his knowledge of the past, Gabriel would have been aware that religion had moved on from the Civil War period when men were prepared to die for what they believed. Intolerance, even hate, had given way to mutual acceptance, even cooperation in some areas. If the Church of England had become tepid, then Non-conformists – after 30 years of persecution (1660-89) – had become circumspect, content to maintain their numbers by passing on their beliefs to those born within their respective denominations rather than by the conversion of outsiders. The calm acceptance had begun with the Toleration Act of May 1689, which permitted Non-conformists to worship under licence in their own chapels as well as in private houses. The Swansea Independents were one of the first Non-conformist communities in Wales to build their own chapel, and are reputed to have done so in 1788, a year before the act came into force. Nine years later, when the chapel proved too small to meet their needs, the Independents built a larger building on the site of the present-day Unitarian Chapel in High Street. The smaller chapel passed to the Baptists.

The Independents built another chapel at Gellionnen in 1692. By 1715 they had a chapel in Swansea with an average attendance of 250; a chapel at Cwmllynfell with a congregation of around 600, and their fellow believers at Cilibion and Pitton in the Gower Peninsula boasted an average attendance of 200. The Independents who met at Neath, Blaen-gwrach and Tirdwncyn Farm (near Llangyfelach Church) had an average attendance of 1,006. How many of this particular group actually met at Tirdwncyn Farm is unknown. Their number must have been considerable as Llangyfelach was a hotbed of Nonconformist activity, and yet, surprisingly, the Tirdwncyn members did not build their chapel at Mynydd-bach until 1762.

The new, High Street, Independent Chapel of 1697.
The site is now occupied by a Unitarian Chapel

There are no attendance figures for the Swansea Baptists who met, presumably, in the former Independent chapel, which some sources claim stood in a small court on the east side of High Street above the gate. Nor are there figures for the Swansea Quakers, though they undoubtedly had a meeting place in the town, possibly on the Strand, below what is now High Street Station. Estimates relating to the Baptists and Quakers in Swansea during the early 18th century suggest that they both had memberships of less than 100.

Methodism first made its appearance in the mid-1730s. In South Wales its leading exponent was the fiery young preacher Howell Harris of Trevecka, who came to Swansea and Gower on numerous occasions from 1738 until shortly before his death in 1773. He came at the invitation of both Anglican and Nonconformist ministers, the latter being particularly enthusiastic to hear his emotional preaching, which invariably led to instant conversions and testimony meetings. Howell made numerous converts from among the colliers at Llansamlet, the converts meeting at farms until they built Salem Chapel in 1782-3. On one occasion in 1763 he preached on the outskirts of Swansea to a crowd of 4,000. On another occasion outside Swansea a drunk made three attempts to shoot him with a pistol, which repeatedly misfired. Harris told the man to aim in another direction; this time the pistol fired. Later, the drunk was found dead in a limekiln – 'divine retribution' it was said.

Howell was on extremely good terms with John Wesley, one of the leading exponents of Methodism in England, and actively encouraged him to visit Wales in support of his work. Both men were staunch Anglicans; both saw their work as a means of reforming the Church of England. Neither wanted Methodism to become a sect separate from the established church. The two men, however, differed on a point of doctrine. Howell accepted the teaching of John Calvin, a 16th-century French theologian. He believed in predestination – that God had, from the beginning, decided who would be saved and for such (the elect) Christ had died. John Wesley, on the other hand, followed the teaching of Jacobus Arminius, a 16th-century Dutch theologian, who maintained that salvation was available to all who accepted it – the Arminian view. In time these differences were to result in a division in Wales – of Welsh Calvinistic Methodists and of English Wesleyan Methodists, the latter being strongest in what were then English-speaking areas.

Division loomed on another front. In the 1740s many Methodists talked of separating from the established church, even though both Howell Harris and John Wesley were opposed to schism. The wishes of these two men prevailed until the closing decades of the century, by which time moves were in progress that would make schism inevitable. In 1789 Selina, the elderly dowager Countess of Huntingdon, founded a Calvinistic Methodist chapel on the site of the present-day Exchange Buildings in Adelaide Street. That same year the Wesleyan Methodists built a chapel in Goat Street. Ten years later another Calvinistic Methodist chapel was established at Crug-y-glas, an eminence behind The Old Duke public house at the top end of High Street. The Wesleyans were the fist to secede from the established church and did so in 1795. Sixteen years later the Welsh Methodists followed suit. By then the Nonconformists had adopted much of the Methodist's form of worship.

Circulating Schools

At roughly the same time as the Methodist revival the Anglican Church was actively engaged in establishing charity schools, which became known as the Welsh Circulating Schools (1737-77). There had been charity schools in the preceding 100 years, but the Welsh Circulating Schools that were established by Griffith Jones, vicar of Llanddowror, were exceptional in that they were more successful and longer lasting than those that had preceded them. There were several reasons for their success: they were free, they operated during the winter months and they taught in the mother tongue, be it Welsh or English.

In Gower, Jones established a number of Welsh-language schools on the fringes of Swansea – at Olchfa, Dunvant and at Pentre Estyl in the parish of St. John, at Penlan and numerous other places in the parish of Llangyfelach, as well as in the parishes of Llansamlet and Llangwig. English-speaking schools were concentrated in the Gower Peninsula. One English-speaking school was set up in Swansea, but it closed within two or three years. Pupils were taught to read the Bible and other religious literature. Jones's schools, therefore, had a part to play in the revival.

There were other schools in Swansea during the time of Gabriel Powell and – with the exception of Bishop Gore's grammar school – they were all short-lived, but the one that left its mark on Swansea was the Theological College of the Presbyterians. It stood on the south side of West Street and eventually gave its name to a section of that thoroughfare – College Street.

St. Mary's Church

As an Anglican, Gabriel may have come close to losing his life one Sunday in May 1739. At the time, much needed repairs were being carried out on St. Mary's Church. It was customary for the congregation to wait outside until the arrival of the minister. Fortunately the minister was late, for

> the roof of the middle isle … unexpectedly fell in … just before Divine Service began, by which particular instance of Divine guidance the lives of many people were saved, and only one person wounded.

The chancel had remained intact, but the nave required more than just a new roof, for on inspection it was found that:

> the pillars that supported the roof are so decayed that they must be taken down and rebuilt. And upon a moderate computation of able and experienced workmen the charge of rebuilding the same will amount to twelve hundred and sixty pounds.

*St. Mary's Church, a century after Thomas
Woodward rebuilt the nave following
a roof collapse in 1739*

It was decided that the work should be done as cheaply as possible. The man commissioned to rebuild the whole nave was Thomas Woodward of Worcester, and he did it for £640. The result was a rather plain nave, smaller than the one it replaced. Changes and extensions were carried out over the years, as in *c*.1785 when Gabriel obtained leave to build a vestry at his own expense, but Woodward's work was to prove a constant source of trouble for a long time to come.

The Townhall

Another building in need of repair was the Townhall. In 1734 part of the first floor was 'boarded and ceiled', meaning presumably the walls were boarded and the rafters concealed from view. Ten years later the Corporation purchased 20,000 'tile stones' to re-roof the building. It was probably about this time that the windows and doors were modernized.

The Gregorian Calendar

Another great change that took place in Gabriel's lifetime was the adoption by Britain of the Gregorian Calendar. As of 2nd September 1752 the first day of the year no longer fell on Annunciation Day, 25th March, as it had for centuries, but fell on 1st January, thereby bringing Britain in line with the rest of Europe.

Impressment

Life in 18th-century Gower was far from idyllic. In the peninsula smuggling was a way of life, involving all levels of society from gentry to farm labourers. In Swansea it would have been unwise to walk the unlit streets at night. In 1753 there were 51 licensed premises in the town, many of them in the Strand, and not only were they full of drunks and prostitutes, but in the pitch-black alleyways there was always the risk of attack by footpads, or worse – press-gangs.

Armed with a warrant, a pressmaster – usually a junior naval officer – had power to impress anyone 'who used the sea', and if the person 'who used the sea' resisted, the pressmaster usually had about ten naval ratings to enforce his warrant. Persons exempt from impressment were those in possession of a protection certificate, and also civilians who did not 'use the sea' – at least, those were the rules, but they were not always adhered to. It is known, for example, that a press-gang burst in on a Baptist meeting at Swansea in 1706, probably at the instigation of someone who disliked them. Fortunately the Baptists had been forewarned and the men made good their escape. A more detailed account of impressment appeared in *The Cambrian* on 21st February 1862. The account concerned an event that occurred in 1760.

> During the American [seven year] War, Mr John Voss, esq., of Nicholaston … was returning from Swansea with a neighbour called John Smith, a very powerful man. Coming over the sands, near Swansea, they were met by a press-gang, consisting of 12 sailors and a lieutenant … As Smith wore sailors clothes the 'gang' endeavoured to seize him. Mr Voss demanded of the officer his authority, which the gentleman refused … [saying] "You, Sir … had better take your departure when you skin is whole."
>
> "I," said Mr Voss, "am determined to see justice done and will protect this man, and will do so in spite of your swaggering threats …"
>
> The officer … shouted to his men and they rushed to obey, but a terrific blow from Smith stretched the foremost on the ground … the next received the same – and now the lieutenant, with drawn cutlass, strode up. Mr Voss at once leaped from his horse and ran up to his friend, and back to back they fought … They kept a slow retreat and gained Bryn Mill, when the lieutenant got behind Mr Voss and with his cutlass cut down his bold antagonist's shoulder … but the next moment the officer lay stretched on the sand from a fierce blow dealt him by his foe …
>
> Mr Voss scorned to yield … and encouraging Smith, that worthy fought like a lion, and sailor after sailor measured his length on the sand … The officer and his troop were astonished and mad … and wildly they rushed at their determined antagonists; but, lo! soon affairs took a different turn, for Mr Voss's brother and two more came running up … when the 'gang' saw them they took to their heels … the Gowerians … took the wounded victor to Swansea, where he had his wounds dressed.

How much of the story is true is debatable, as the article was written 102 years after the event, but John Voss certainly lived at the time; moreover, the article states that:

> Very soon after [the event] the vessel to which the press-gang … belonged became wrecked off Pwlldu [which may well be true, but what is certainly a fabrication is the claim] that all perished except one [pressed man] … from Plymouth [also that when Mr Voss] visited the scene of the disaster [he turned over a corpse] and lo! it was the body of the lieutenant with whom he had … fought.

The article is undoubtedly linked to an event recorded in naval documents concerning the court martial of pressmaster, Lieutenant James Gaborian. These documents state that, on the morning of 28th November 1760, two Admiralty tenders (probably cutters of about 60 tons) lay in the shelter of Mumbles Head: the *Caesar* under Lieutenant Gaborian, and the *Reeves*, the officer of which had overall command of both vessels. Little can be said about the *Reeves*, but the *Caesar* had at least 65 impressed men in its hold, the hatches of which were battened down. Sailing on a spring tide, the tenders headed out to sea, their destination Portsmouth. In increasingly rough weather the vessels made little headway, and by 2 o'clock in the afternoon Gaborian received an order to turn back, but wind and waves drove the *Caesar* onto the rocks below Pwlldu Head, where it became wedged in a cleft now known as Caesar's Hole.

Swamped by breakers, terrified by the sound of seawater surging into the gullies all around, the crew clambered onto pitted rocks, leaving the prisoners screaming in the ship's hold. Those who made it ashore said nothing of the prisoners trapped and at the mercy of an incoming tide. It is hardly surprising, therefore, that when people from all over Gower gathered the following morning to witness the wreck they were amazed to see bodies both in the water and on the rocks. In all 97 bodies were retrieved and buried in a mass grave (Gravesend) near Pwlldu Head. According to Lloyd's List, 65 men and three women had drowned, but when Gaborian faced a court martial in January 1761 for the loss of his ship, no one considered it worthwhile to record any reference to those who had perished. What is on record is that Gaborian was acquitted and blame apportioned to bad weather, the ship and the ship's pilot.

The Townhill Enclosure

Gabriel always put the Duke's interests first. That is not to say he neglected the interests of the burgesses. As a solicitor he successfully defended the Corporation's rights in many a court action against parties other than the Duke. In matters involving both the Duke and the Corporation there appears to have been an acceptance on the part of the burgesses to avoid confrontation, which is hardly surprising as none of them would have been admitted to the borough unless Gabriel or his father had considered them acceptable. Indeed, as a privileged group the Duke, Gabriel and the burgesses were quite capable of working together for the common good – for example, shortly before 1762 the burgesses proposed that the Townhill (the mountain) should be divided into parcels and the parcel's leased 'for long terms … to such burgesses as are willing to take the same'.

Since the 12th century the Townhill had been common land where the burgesses were at liberty to pasture their livestock, cut furze and reap other benefits – but the Townhill belonged to the Duke, though he derived no financial benefits from it. It, therefore, fell to Gabriel to obtain the Duke's consent to the proposal, and once he obtained that he added the coastal strip known as the Burrows (now the Sandfields) to the scheme. He then obtained from Parliament the necessary act, namely the 'Townhill and Burrows Enclosure Act' of 1762. As a result of this act around 80 burgesses had the option of taking out long-term leases on between five and 50 acres, which they were at liberty to enclose with hedges and the like. Initially, Gabriel took out a lease on 50 acres, but in time he increased his share to 177 acres. Others had their share, including the Duke who also retained rights to all minerals beneath the soil and all quarries of stone and slate. The people who derived no benefit at all were the non-burgess.

The Survey of Gower and Kilvey

In September 1760 Gabriel began a survey of the Seignories of Gower and Kilvey, and did so on behalf of Elizabeth, dowager Duchess of Beaufort, who was mother and guardian of the young Henry Somerset (his father, Charles Noel, had died in 1756). The purpose of the survey was to provide a detailed record of all that young Henry would one day own and what would be due to him in the way of rents, etc. It was to be Gower's own Domesday Book and it took a little over four years to complete (November 1764).

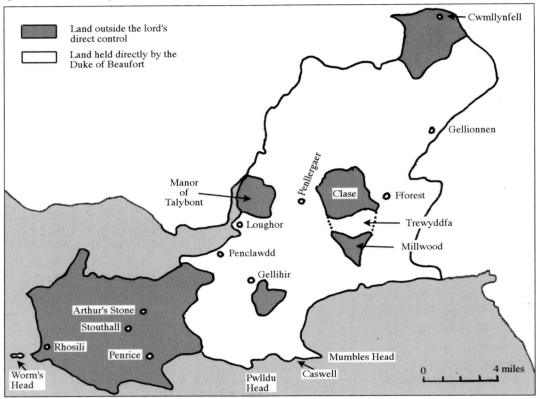

Gower and Kilvey in 1764

Henry Somerset was by far the biggest landowner in the lordship, holding in demesne the manorial boroughs of Swansea and Loughor, the demesne manors of Oystermouth, Bishopston and Pennard (with its subsidiary fees of Kittle, Lunnon and Trewyddfa), and also the Welsh manors of Supraboscus, Subboscus and Kilvey, as well as other districts in east Gower. Henry could in fact claim more than half the lordship as his own personal property, and although much of what he owned was common and waste land, it was nevertheless rich in that it contained two boroughs and most of the coal fields in Gower.

As to the owners of mesne lands, most of which lay in west Gower, by far the largest was Thomas Mansel Talbot of Margam and Penrice, Esquire, who had acquired the huge Mansel estate on the death of the last Lord Mansel in 1750, and did so by right of his mother, Mary Mansel, to whom the estate had devolved. Thomas Mansel Talbot held the manors of Oxwich, Penrice, Horton, Port Eynon, Stembridge, Llynybough (Llwyn y Bwlch), Scurlage, Walterston and Kellibion, Nicholaston, Henllys, Landimore, Rhosili, Llanrhidian, Weobley, Bishopston (that is, the northern part of the parish), Reynoldston and Leaston.

Among the lesser gentry Joseph Price held Gellihir, and continued to do so until his death in 1785, at which point his estate was shared between his two daughters, Mary and Mayzod Elizabeth. Price's neighbour, William Dawkin, was only an infant at the time of the survey; as such he stood to inherit Kilvrough, numerous parcels of land in the manor of Oystermouth and also a half share in the manor of Talybont (the other half belonged to another member of the Price family). William is said to have 'built or enlarged the mansion of Kilvrough as it may now be seen', but what he really did was remodel the house in 1785.

The Castle

During the 100 years that followed the Civil War the New Castle at Swansea had a chequered history. Shortly before 1678 the North East Tower and most of the Hall Block had been used as a glass house for the production of wine bottles; it continued as such until after 1696. By 1741 the North East Tower had become derelict, as evidenced by its ruinous appearance in the Bucks' engraving of that year. At an unrecorded date in the late 18th century the first floor of the tower was rebuilt for use as a debtors' prison, at times accommodating as many as ten inmates, and continued to be used as such until 1869.

In August 1742 Leyson Morgan, a Swansea mercer, took out a lease on that part of the Hall Block 'late in the possession of James Griffith', one-time owner of the Swansea copperworks. Then, in 1750, the 'Churchwardens and Overseers of the Poor' took out a lease on the Hall Block with the intention of converting it into a work-house. One of the churchwardens named was Gabriel himself, evidence perhaps of his desire to have a say in all things relevant to the borough. At the time of the

The North East Tower of the New Castle

survey – or at least its completion in 1764 – Gabriel held not only the stewardship, but he was also the Recorder, the Coroner and the Bailiff of the Liberties; his duties relating to the last-named office being to execute all writs.

As to the Old Castle – or at least the site on which the remains stood – there is an interesting lease recorded in the survey, which states that:

> George Venables Vernon, Esquire, held by lease which expired at Lady Day 1762, and now holds from year to year, all those two gardens called the Castle Gardens, and the summer house thereto belonging, having the back court belonging to the dwelling house in the possession of Sir Edward Mansel and the garden of William Hurst and Calvert Richard Jones, Esquires, on the west, the new Postern on the south, the Strand towards the east and the old Postern on the north.

Over a 100 years earlier, Cromwell's survey recorded that Walter Thomas held 'Two little gardens adjoining to the house of the said Walter called the Old Castle Gardens'. These two gardens cannot be seen on Francis Place's drawing of 1678 because they are hidden by a curtain wall that runs from the North East Tower to a much smaller tower with a pyramid-shaped roof. On the Bucks' engraving of 1741 part of the curtain wall has been removed, revealing a line of trees and a bench, which may have been the location of one garden. Further north part of the wall remains (identified by its crenellation) and terminates at the same small tower with a pyramid-shaped roof. The uncrenellated wall that runs towards Castle Street is probably one that was built to enclose what may have been the second garden. In the Bucks' engraving of 1748 the position of the crenellated wall and the small tower has been distorted to show another crenelated wall that should

The Buck brothers' East View of Swansea Castle as it appeared in 1741.
Points to note are (1) the Townhall can be seen through a breach in the east curtain wall of the New Castle (between the south block and the north-east tower), and (2) the Old Castle curtain wall has been partially demolished since Francis Plate depicted it in 1678 (a row of trees stand in the gap), and (3) the small tower attached to the northern end of the remaining section of the curtain wall is the summer house referred to in the text

really be facing north in the direction of High Street. The small tower is believed to have been an Old Castle tower converted to serve as the summer house mentioned in Vernon's lease. How the gardens and the tower came into the possession of Vernon can be explained by the fact that when Walter Thomas of Swansea died his estate passed to William Thomas of Danygraig who, in 1662, renewed the lease on 'A parcel of land known …[as] the Old Castle, estimated at half an acre'.

When William Thomas died in 1665 his estate was valued at £891, which included his coalworks at Llansamlet. Some authorities maintain that the estate then passed to his brother-in-law, Bussy Mansel of Briton Ferry (d.1699). Other authorities maintain that the estate passed to William's younger brother, Hopkin (who died without issue) and then to Bussy Mansel. Bussy's grandson, Thomas, also died childless, and the combined Briton Ferry – Danygraig estate was bequeathed to a relative, Sir Bussy Mansel of Margam and Penrice (d.1750). Sir Bussy had a daughter, Barbara, and she married George Venables Vernon. As a result of their marriage settlement George and Barbara took up residence at Briton Ferry House, and it is through Barbara that George acquired the lease on 'two gardens called the Castle Gardens'.

Improved Highways
The year that Gabriel completed his survey Parliament passes an act for improving communications in Glamorgan. The main highway from Cardiff to Swansea ran through the Vale, along the coastal strip between Margam and Briton Ferry and from Neath over Coed Ffranc (in the vicinity of Llandarcy) and the Crymlyn Burrows to the River Tawe. The Turnpike Act of 1764 divided the county into five trusts, each with powers to widen the main highways, to repair their surfaces and erect barriers for the collection of tolls.

The Swansea Trust had charge of the highway from Crymlyn Brook, through Swansea to Penlle'r Castell on Gower's remote northern border; it was also responsible for the alternative routes to Carmarthenshire via Loughor and Pontardulais. In 1765 the trust straightened the Strand by removing a forge and a sycamore tree, and placed a toll gate there. What the trustees were powerless to improve was the ferry at the Tawe Estuary, which was obstructed

> for many hours in the day from tides, and the passing and repassing of ships and other vessels in and out of the harbour [and] … by the rapidity of land floods [freshets after heavy rain].

To speed up the ferry crossing a capstan was erected near the Beaufort Arms in 1769, but many continued to make use of a ford further south (near the present-day barrage). In his book *In and Around Swansea* (1896) E.E. Rowse maintained that

> Heavily laden wagons … would constantly ford the river when the tide was out. Cattle and horses, and even litters of pigs crossed the river when the tide was at its lowest.

An alternative route from Neath to Carmarthenshire led to Llansamlet Church, and from there followed a winding course through fields to Robert Popkin's house at Upper

Fforest where an ancient bridge spanned the Tawe. Known as Fforest Bridge, this wooden structure dated back to at least the 16th century, and may even have been used in Medieval times by pilgrims on their way to St. David's. It was approximately 90 metres in length and supported by about 1,000 oak stakes. It soon became recognized that, apart from the delays at the Tawe ferry, the highway from Neath to Swansea was far too circuitous for travellers heading for West Wales. To facilitate the establishment of a direct route from Neath via Llangyfelach Church to Pontardulais and Loughor, an act was passed in 1778 'for building a bridge across the River Tawe at a place called Wych Tree [Morriston] … [and] for making proper avenues or roads to and from the said bridge'.

Because the Lower Tawe Valley was considered 'very populous and full of mines and manufactures' the same act permitted the 'repairing and widening of the road from Pentre Brook, near a place called Aberdyberthi … near Swansea, to the said intended bridge'.

All these new highways were to be no less than 24 feet wide between the hedge-banks – to allow cattle and coaches to pass in opposite directions – and to prevent evasion of tolls the Wych Tree Bridge Trust had permission to 'destroy the Upper Fforest Ford and stop up every avenue or approach thereto on the Llangyfelach side'.

An act of 1785 was intended to transform the 'long lines of barren, desolate, unin-habited tracks' in the Gower Peninsula, which were narrow, deeply rutted and strewn with rocky outcrops. For centuries the main route into the Peninsula from Swansea had commenced at the West Gate and continued along what is now the Kingsway, St. Helen's Road, Brynamor Road and on to Sketty and beyond. Improving this and other roads into the Peninsula would take time, but the main highway through Glamorgan had already been improved to the extent that coaches could run according to a timetable – at least that was the situation in 1788 when the *Bristol Gazette* announced that *The Diligence* would leave the Mackworth Arms, Swansea, at 4 o'clock in the morning every Sunday, Wednesday and Friday to arrive in the evening at the New Passage, where a boat would ferry passengers over the Severn; at 8 o'clock the following morning a coach would take them to Bristol.

Gabriel in his Latter Years

By the time he had completed his survey in 1764, Gabriel was 54 year old. Whether he welcomed the changes that were soon to be implemented by the first Turnpike Act is not known. Whatever his views there was nothing he could do to stop them, but as he got older he found himself obliged to defend the old order against men who called for changes that, in his opinion, would lead to

the manifest destruction of the Corporation's most valuable rights and privileges.

The call for change came from industrialists who wanted improvements to be carried out to harbour. There were also those who wanted to bring the town in line with what was expected of a fashionable resort. The demands for change had to be thwarted, and Gabriel was the man to do just that.

CHAPTER XIII
Gabriel Powell (2)

While Gabriel and his fellow burgesses continued to exercise their ancient privileges within Swansea – and by doing so maintain the Medieval character of the town with all its attendant filth – industrialists were changing the face of the Lower Tawe Valley beyond all recognition. On the west bank the Morris family still reigned supreme. When Robert Morris died in 1768 he was not succeeded in business by his eldest son, Robert, but by his younger son, John (1745-1819), later to become Sir John Morris. John's business ventures are beyond the scope of this work, but to impart some idea of how he left his mark locally it is worth quoting the following:

> Sir John Morris, Bart., of Clasemont … seems to have been the most extensive individual builder of comfortable habitation for the labouring class. He first erected a kind of castellated, lofty mansion … containing dwellings for 40 families, all colliers, excepting one tailor, and one shoemaker, who were considered as useful appendages to the fraternity … about the year 1768, he laid the foundation of Morriston, so called from the founder's surname; where dwellings have been erected for colliers and manufactures, in well formed and spacious streets: with a church [St. John's, built in 1789], containing an organ for such of his workmen as prefer the established religion … Being somewhat of a latitudinarian he erected also a chapel for non-conformists [Libanus].
>
> The founder of Morriston's plan was to grant leases on plots of land, about a square rood each, for three lives, or 50 years, at 7s. 6d. a year each plot. The lessees were to build according to prescribed plans. He moreover encouraged some of the more steady labourers … with a quantity of land each, sufficient to keep a cow. Only two or three thatched hovels once occupied where this neat little town, containing a population of about 1,000, now stands … Mr Fox, in the year 1796, says that in the year 1780, there was not a single house where Morriston now stands: that in 1796 there was 141 houses inhabited by 619 persons; so that in the last 16 years the population has nearly doubled.

Sir John built his Georgian-style mansion of Clasemont in c. 1775 on the site of the present-day DVLC. Between 1768 and 1775 he built Morris Castle, one of the first blocks of flats ever built in this country for the working-class; it contained accommodation for

Morris Castle, a block of flats built c.1775 to house 24 colliery workers and their families

24 families, not 40. On a smaller scale, cottage rows had sprung up all over the Lower Swansea Valley, all of them in close proximity to collieries and other places of work. In 1722, for example, the then Lord Mansel of Briton Ferry had built 75 cottages for his colliers at Llansamlet. On the heights of Trewyddfa, workers had encroached on the common on either side of the road, where they built their hastily-erected one-night cottages, using whatever materials were at hand. They had then built more substantial homes at a later date and enclosed the same with gardens, a practice permitted provided they paid rent.

On the east side of the Tawe a new coal owner had risen to prominence. In 1750 the last of the Briton Ferry Mansels had died and his collieries at Llansamlet had been acquired on lease by a London financier, Chauncey Townsend. During the ten years that followed, Chauncey had transformed the Great Coal Road – from Llansamlet to Foxhole – into a wagon-way, the tracks made of wood, the wagons pulled by oxen. In 1755 he had established the Middle Bank works at Foxhole; two years later the Upper Bank works were established close by. Both works were initially producing lead (the latter zinc as well), but they were eventually converted to smelting copper.

Chauncey's wagon-way may have been the first to appear in the Swansea Valley; other coal owners were quick to follow his example. Another possible first occurred in 1772-4 when John Morris built a masonry quay at Landore (which survives to this day). John then followed this up in 1776 by ordering the first consignment of 'cast iron plates for wheeling coal in' his collieries. Twelve years later he had 'about 240 tons of cast iron tram plates underground in [his] Landore colliery', which suggest $3\frac{3}{4}$ miles of underground iron tramways. Other colliery owners soon followed John's example. All these innovations helped to convey coal quickly and in quantity to works and river-side quays – and there was the rub: the river was becoming unnavigable.

The Harbour

In his *Letters*, published in 1804, the Rev. J. Evans stated that the navigable part of the river with all its quays and docks (including Fabian's Bay) constituted the 'Harbour of Swansea'. At a public meeting held in 1768 it was recorded that:

> the bar [accumulations of soil and sand] below the ferry was evidently increasing, and consequently the navigation of vessels of burden rendered more difficult except on the top of high tides.

Below the ferry the river flowed into Fabian's Bay. In the western half of this bay lay a tract of sand, soil and stones, which at ebb tide had the appearance of an island and caused the river to divide into two channels. The western channel appears to have been the more important of the two, but navigation in this channel – as in the eastern one – could be seriously effected by a bar, in part the result of debris scoured from the river bed after heavy rain, and in part by sand brought in by the tide. The bar might increase or decrease due to the action of river floods (freshets) or rough sea. At its worst the bar formed a barrier to ships requiring a deep draught; such ships could be left stranded for days until an exceptionally high tide carried them off.

To make matters worse there were several accumulations (paddocks) of sand, gravel and industrial waste in the river as far inland as Foxhole. Clearly, something had to be done to prevent the harbour becoming unnavigable. The first attempt to tackle the problem occurred in 1768 when a number of unnamed men – some of them undoubtedly industrialists and ship owners – attended a public meeting in Swansea. There is no reference to this meeting in the Common Hall Book, but what happened when the meeting convened was recorded by Dr. Charles Collins, Surgeon, a burgess keen to have the harbour improved; he wrote:

> Mr. Gruffydd Price was put into the chair, and the meeting all agreed upon the utility of the measure, but Mr. Gabriel Powell, who said that the Corporation was against, and would oppose it. Upon which I addressed the Chairman and declared to my knowledge the burgesses were unanimously for it, but that as a Corporate Body they knew nothing about it, it never having been brought before them, and consequently Mr. Powell had no authority to make the declaration he did … had things gone on then I should have been obliged to appear before the House of Commons.

What Charles Collins meant in respect of 'the House of Commons' was that he would petition Parliament for an act to be passed for the improvement of the harbour; that, Gabriel did not want. The harbour was a valuable source of income for the Corporation in the way of leases and tolls, whereas an act of Parliament would result in outsiders – non-burgesses – having a say in how the harbour should be administered; worse, the money derived from the harbour would be transferred to a body of trustees, many of them non-burgesses. Three years were to pass before the issue was raised again. At a Common Hall in October 1771 it was stated that:

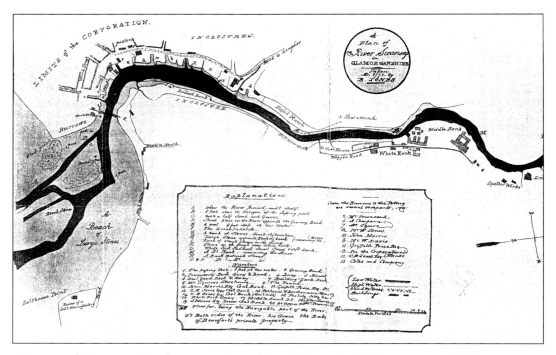

A map of Swansea Harbour produced by B. Jones in 1771, presumably in connection with proposed harbour improvements. Note how the Tawe divided into severl channels when it reached Fabian's Bay at low tide

> Whereas we have this day been informed that there had been lately a meeting of several coal masters, masters of ships and others to take into consideration the clearing of the bar … and whereas we are greatly interested in the trade and navigation of the said harbour and think it our duty … to preserve … promote and encourage the trade thereof in all its branches … we do agree and order that a committee be appointed.

The Committee comprised mostly of burgesses who were opposed to petitioning Parliament, which was Gabriel's way of ensuring that Collins and his supporters were in the minority, and that the Corporation would, therefore, have the final word on any decision made. Three months later – nothing having been resolved – a letter was read out at a Common Hall that a meeting would be held at the Falcon Inn where the attendance of the Corporation was desired. Evidently the non-burgesses wanted a meeting held at a venue of their choosing. It did them no good apparently, because the Corporation resolved that:

> upon considering the same we think that if any act be passed in Parliament to carry the said resolution into law it will or may be very prejudicial to this town and borough, and tend to the manifest destruction of many of our most valuable rights

and privileges. We therefore think it our duty to oppose the passing of such act into a law, and for that purpose we do hereby ... direct and impower the Portreeve and Recorder [Gabriel] to borrow any sums of money not exceeding ... two hundred pounds

for use in opposing any attempt by the opposition to petition Parliament. However, under pressure from the opposition, Gabriel and his supporters changed their stance to one of compromise, for at a Common Hall in June 1772 it was decided that 'a subscription should be opened' and used to remove some of the paddocks in the river. For its part the Corporation subscribed £50 in the hope that that it would no longer be troubled by the opposition. Then, three years later, the sea demonstrated its power, for the Common Hall Book records;

the high tide attended by a violent storm on Tuesday night last has destroyed the sea banks in such a manner as to endanger the lower end of the town and the navigation of the river.

Rather than deal with the problem the Corporation called a meeting for

all the proprietors of lands and houses within the said town, and of all other persons [in] any ways concerned in the trade and navigation of the river.

In the absence of records it can be assumed that the object of the meeting was to get the townspeople and others to foot the bill with regard to the damage incurred. As to the harbour, the issue appears to have been ignored for a further 12 years. In the meantime, public-spirited townspeople were beginning to voice their discontent about an inconvenience that could be found right outside Gabriel's front door.

Call for a Paving Act

The court leet, which met twice a year, was the only body concerned with issues that today are dealt with by the City Council. In 1772 the leet jury had complained that all the streets in Swansea were badly in need of repair, and proposed that an act of Parliament should be obtained as a means of rectifying the situation. Nothing was done, however, and two years later the leet jury described the streets as in 'a ruinous condition', again to no avail. Part of the problem was that, as Steward, Gabriel presided over the court leet and he would have nothing to do with repairs; nor would he agree to a paving act that would allow strangers to meddle in the borough's administrative affairs. Gabriel simply ignored the proposal of leet jury and the matter lay dormant for 15 years. In the meantime, the Corporation got itself involved in another long-standing dispute, with the town traders.

The Castle Market

Throughout the first 60 years of Gabriel's lifetime the population of Gower and Kilvey had been on the increase, and this was to accelerate from *c.*1770 onwards. Industrialization had encouraged large numbers of Welshmen to settle in the Lower Swansea Valley, their presence there contributing to the survival of the Welsh language into the 20th century. Swansea also had its immigrants, most of them English-speaking. Some came from the Gower Peninsula in search of work, some were seamen and some were entrepreneurs desiring to set up a new enterprise in a thriving town. Consequently, the Welsh language had become marginalized in Swansea, so much so that in 1875 the vestry abolished Welsh services at St. Mary's.

An expanding population had to be fed and many families, both within and from outside the town, bought their provisions from the Swansea market, which resulted in congestion in the surrounding streets. The Cromwellian Market still occupied its place at the top end of what is now Wind Street where, according to Lewis W. Dillwyn (1840) the stallholders sold 'corn and vegetables'. A little to the south stood Island House, the most northerly of several buildings situated in the middle of upper Wind Street. The ground floor of Island House was surrounded on three sides by a verandah with pillars and a copper roof, beneath which butchers and local farmers sold their produce. To the west – in the narrow space between Island House and St. Mary Street – was the Fish Market, which became congested on Saturdays, but the greatest congestion of all was in Butter Street (or rather St. Mary Street) where, according to Lewis W. Dillwyn:

> A row of shambles [meat stalls] on each side of Butter Street was chiefly used for the sale of butchers' meat, so as to prevent any other than pedestrians from passing through the street on Saturdays.

The Market Place was in one sense a shambles in that its original meaning was 'butchers' stools or stalls', but in today's terminology it was also a place of complete disorder on Saturdays. Something had to be done, so the Corporation obtained an Act of Parliament early in 1774

> for fixing and regulating a public market and shambles for the sale of meat within the Town and Borough of Swansea.

That the Corporation obtained an act on this occasion is unsurprising because, as custodians of the market, the Corporate Body had no fear of 'manifest destruction of its most valuable rights and privileges'. The site chosen for the proposed shambles was the New Castle courtyard, for which a lease was obtained from the Duke, undoubtedly at Gabriel's request. The lease confined the site to:

> All that … close of land … within the walls of the castle … and also that part of the new postern opposite to the north [curtain] wall of the said castle … save … the

ancient footway leading from Castle Bailey Street to the Strand and also … a way … to pass and repass to and from the Gardens now in the possession of the Honourable George Venables Vernon, Esquire.

The southern half of the new Shambles of 1774, its location in the New Castle courtyard. The tall building on the far right is the Townhall

Work started in May 1774; it entailed taking down a surviving section of curtain wall near the Townhall steps, most of the surviving north curtain wall, 'together with the lean-to houses and the smith's forge built against the same' and also a cottage and a workshop that were situated in the New Postern. Part of the new meat market opened in September that year, the remaining work being finished the following year. The new Shambles should have eased congestion in the old Market Place, but there was a problem. A clause had been added to the act whereby the butchers – most of whom, if not all, were non-burgesses – were to be compensated for their loss of earnings ('more than £100 per annum', it was claimed), but the Corporation refused to pay. Although the records are silent about Gabriel's part in all this, there can be little doubt that he, being the most influential member of the Corporation, would have been behind the refusal. The outcome of the dispute was that Parliament supported the butchers desire to stay put. As to the new Shambles, it was reported by Lewis W. Dillwyn in 1840 that:

> Though this market-place at different times was used on a Wednesday for provisions of all sorts, or more generally as a butter market on Saturdays, yet it proved on the whole to be a failure … [whereas] the old market for corn and vegetables, and Butter Street for butchers' meat, continued to be chiefly resorted to.

Dillwyn also pointed out that 'the Fish Market – which was kept in the narrow space between Island House and St. Mary Street – was moved to a more commodious situation within the new Shambles in about the year 1825, after which the narrow space became known as Potato Street'.

The First Theatre

In 1775 a band of actors had successfully performed at Neath and wished to perform in Swansea, but knowing Gabriel would oppose them they approached an industrial magnet, Sir Herbert Mackworth of the Gnoll, to speak on their behalf. Sir Herbert wrote to Gabriel, informing him of how he and his family had enjoyed several performances by the actors, and assured him that, contrary to the prevailing opinion that theatricals lured working-class men from their work, the lower orders had no desire to spend their hard-earned money on any such entertainment. Gabriel would not be swayed. Theatres were for the idle; moreover, they were, as the Methodists maintained, the haunts of the devil. Gabriel wrote in reply:

> the principal inhabitants [of Swansea] disapproved of their coming to the town, and I have told them more than once that I would not consent to it.

When the theatrical manager's son came to Swansea to find out if what Gabriel had said about the 'principal inhabitants' was true, he discovered that:

> every person waited upon seemed anxiously desirous of our coming, [all except the Portreeve] who said he gave his word to Mr Powell not to let them in [and warned the son to tell his] father if he attempted to come into town … danger would be near him.

Ten years later a company of actors from Bath opened a theatre in Wind Street, next door to the Custom House. It comprised of the first floor of a house where 'overhead there's a Catholic Chapel – under foot there's a blacksmith's shop'. The Wind Street venue continued in use until 1807 when the Swansea Tontine Society opened the Theatre Royal in Goat Street, on a site formerly occupied by part of the Outer Bailey ditch, by which time Gabriel was long dead. The theatre was referred to locally as the Temple (of Thespis), and in c.1800, when The Plas gatehouse and outbuildings were pulled down to make way for the creation of a new thoroughfare, that thoroughfare became known as Temple Street (now a walkway between what was once David Evans' Stores and Castle Gardens).

The Powell Family

Gabriel may have had problems with the disaffected in the 1770s, but the decade proved to be one of repeated celebrations for the Powell family. Gabriel's younger brother, William, had been elected Portreeve in 1768 and, over the succeeding years, several family members were sworn in as burgesses, among them Gabriel's sons, Gabriel the Younger in 1774 and Thomas in 1776, and also Thomas Harcourt Powell (son of Gabriel's elder brother, John, by his second wife, Amy Harcourt) in 1777. Both sons were elected Portreeve during the same decade, Gabriel the Younger in 1776 and Thomas in 1778. In fact, it is hardly surprising that during Gabriel's stewardship all four relatives held the portreeveship at least once, William on three occasions.

In 1778 Gabriel the Younger (later to become Sir Gabriel) married Mary, daughter and co-heiress of Joseph Price of Gellihir, Esquire, a descendant of John Price of the Civil War period. For two years the couple resided at Gellihir where a long, straight, oak-lined avenue led to the Prices' ancestral mansion. Then, in c.1780, Gabriel the Younger had a new house built only 100 yards from Mary's old home. It was during that two-year period that young Gabriel's mother Mary died, aged 58. She was buried in St. Mary's Church.

Development

Coal, metal works, seaborne trade and visitors all contributed to Swansea's growing prosperity, in response to which the Bank of England opened a branch in the town. The following year a branch of the Glamorganshire Bank was established in Wind Street. Prosperity manifested itself in other areas too. In the Gower Peninsula 'all the modern improvements in agriculture' had made it possible for Thomas Mansel Talbot of Margam and Penrice to build what one visitor described as an 'elegant modern mansion [Penrice Castle] surrounded by diversified woodland walks', which, in the opinion of the visitor, 'contrasted with the asperities of the surrounding scenery'. This mansion was built between 1773 and 1777, and a later commentator mentioned that the old Medieval castle on higher ground had been 'converted into an aviary'.

Several other stately homes in Gower were either built or improved upon during this period. Stouthall, for example, was built for John Lucas in 1788-90, apparently on similar lines to Gellihir. Kilvrough, on the other hand, was completely remodelled in 1785 for the benefit of William Dawkin, and his daughter, Mary, was the last of the Kilvrough Dawkins.

Kilvrough Manor, once the ancestral home of the Dawkin family

From *c.*1770 onwards new buildings began to appear in Swansea, too, both within and without the area that had once been enclosed by town walls. One site ripe for development was the waste land on the east side of Goat Street, which had formerly been the site of the Outer Bailey ditch. Excavation in 1975 revealed that, from the Restoration of Charles Stuart onwards, this ditch had been used as a rubbish dump, as evidenced by the 17th and 18th-century pottery shards that were found in the infill. In 1765 the new owner of The Plas, Calvert Richard Jones of Gloucester, demolished the 'new stables' and deposited the debris on the Goat Street waste land. He then tried to encroach on the said land. Gabriel soon put a stop to Calvert's designs, and from 1773 onwards new, Corporation-approved buildings were erected on the east side of Goat Street.

Similar development took place on the infilled waste land on both the north (West Street) and south (Caer Street) side of what had been the Outer Bailey area, but more extensive development took place on the Burrows – or rather the Little Burrows – to the south of Wind Street. In 1776 the Corporation granted permission for the erection of 15 terraced houses that became known as Somerset Place (which no longer exists, but stood opposite what is now the Dylan Thomas Centre). This impressive, Georgian-style development can be seen in several drawing dated to the 1790s, being depicted as a long, three-storied, whitish building with a gabled centre block.

Swansea – a Fashionable Resort

Improved roads made it easier for the well-to-do of Swansea and Gower to travel by coach to sophisticated places such as Bath and Bristol, where they witnessed what public-spirited citizens had done to improve their towns. When they returned to Swansea these same travellers wanted better things for their own town, but there was also another consideration. From the mid-18th century onwards, doctors had been encouraging people to drink and bathe in sea water, believing it to be beneficial to health. Swansea was well situated to meet such a requirement, and by 1786 it was also providing the additional amenities that were expected of a fashionable resort – indeed, that same year it was announced in the *Gloucester Journal* that:

> *Swansea, in point of spirit, fashion and politeness, has now become the Brighton of Wales.*

Undoubtedly the best inn in town was the Mackworth Arms Hotel in Wind Street (on the south-west corner of what is now Green Dragon Lane). By January 1786 the Mackworth was providing all the amenities that were to be found in the Assembly Rooms of a later date – music, dancing, cards, public breakfasts, etc. It was here that coaches arrived from, and departed for Bristol in 1788. That same year the proprietor, James Lake, advertised in the *Bristol Journal* that this hotel was 'a house of truly comfortable accommodation', even for the nobility. Lake also advertised the fact that his establishment provided a bathing machine for guests.

The Mackworth Arms in Wind Street

The Bush Inn in High Street was another well known establishment, one of many that provided accommodation for visitors. However, it is likely that visitors who could afford to spend a month, or even a whole season in Swansea would have preferred to stay at a lodging house, or in rented accommodation. There are no figures for Gabriel's time, but in 1802 there were 36 lodging houses in the town, about a third of them located on the Burrows or in Somerset Place.

What Gabriel made of all this fuss over visitors can only be surmised. Perhaps he took the view that as long as visitors did not cost the Corporation anything they were to be tolerated. The Duke of Beaufort, Henry Somerset, did not subscribe to such a view, however, for in 1785 he obtained permission from the Corporation to construct, at his expense, a 'walk' over the Burrows, one that permitted walkers to enjoy all-round views – of the harbour, of the sea with the hills of Devon and Somerset in the distance, of Mumbles Head and of Townhill, the slopes of which where probably still wooded at the time.

Second Attempt at a Paving Act

In 1787 those who wished to improve the town petitioned Parliament to pass a local paving act. On 19th May that year a House of Commons Committee examined witnesses for and against the bill, Gabriel being one of the witnesses. In his speech Gabriel tried to deceive the Parliamentary Committee into believing that Swansea was of no consequence and, therefore, unworthy of a paving act. Someone, possibly Moses Harris, summed up Gabriel's deceit in a cartoon, which depicts him standing in Wind Street near a well, the street strewn with rubbish on which pigs feed. Behind him is a theatre, which only a town of consequence would have had. The accompanying caption reads:

> Swansea is a poor town mostly inhabited by copper men and colliers; but as well paved as most country towns are. I know of no theatre there, I may have heard of one; I never was at it.

Such was his determination to prevent a paving act being passed, Gabriel launched his own paving scheme, using Corporation funds, which proved to be only 'partial and incomplete'. Consequently, the opposition never had their paving act and no more is heard of the matter until long after Gabriel's death.

Challenged in Court

The opposition had no sooner failed to procure a paving act than Robert Morris II challenged Gabriel personally over his right to hold court barons without a jury, something that Gabriel had been doing for at least 20 years. Robert, a barrister who had long been involved in radical politics, took exception to feudal rights and had a personal dislike for the Duke's disagreeable Steward. One day Robert turned up at a court baron in Swansea with a large folio book tucked under his arm and, without interrupting proceedings, made a show of reading from the folio. He was soon joined by two other men, one of them Moses Harris, who both made a show of reading from their own folios. Gabriel was aghast. He wrote to the Duke, complaining that his:

Gabriel Powell in Wind Street as depicted by a cartoonist in 1787

Grace's rights and privileges [had been] openly attacked by Mr. Robert Morris in such a manner as I never knew before or ever heard of.

At a subsequent court baron Robert opened a large book and proceeded to question Gabriel's right to hold a court baron without a jury. Gabriel accused Robert of disrupting proceedings, but Robert countered that as a freeholder he had every right to take his place as a juror, and that Gabriel had no right to preside over a manorial court without jurors. Robert then made it plain that he would disrupt all future court barons and challenged Gabriel to do something about it. Gabriel was flummoxed. He wrote to the Duke for guidance, only to be told that Robert Morris was right: as a juror it was his place to judge; Gabriel could only preside.

A Fracas at the Townhall

On 10th October 1787 a general meeting took place 'for the improving of the navigation of the Port of Swansea' at the Mackworth Arms Hotel in Wind Street. Nothing is known of what actually took place at the meeting other than 'several resolutions were very precipitately entered into'. The Corporation obviously had intelligence of what had been discussed because, at a Common Hall held at the Townhall on 2nd November, it was recorded in the minutes that

> on considering the same [resolutions] we think that if any act be passed … it would be prejudicial to this town … and may tend to the manifest destruction of many of our valuable rights and privileges.

which is exactly what the Corporation said in 1772; moreover, if it proved necessary, the Corporation would borrow up to £500 for use in opposing any harbour or paving acts. What the minutes do not record is the fracas that disrupted the proceedings. One of the burgess present, Moses Harris, mercer, depicted what happened in a cartoon, the caption of which reads:

THE WELSH CORPORATION MEETING

The Corporation of Swansea met at their Guildhall, November 2 1787, when Gabriel Powell, Recorder, Steward to the Duke of Beaufort [who was] brought up to be an attorney, etc., aged 77, snatched out of the hands of Mr Padley a paper which he was reading that contained a proposition made by Gabriel Powell to mortgage the Corporation estates for £500 to oppose an act for new paving the town and improving the harbour; his son, Thomas Powell, a clergyman and alderman afterwards knocked down Mr Charles Collins, an eminent surgeon, another burgess who insisted on reading the paper before he was called to for his vote, and while on the ground most malignantly and cowardly kicked him in the breast. The father seized Mr Collin's wig. Robert Morris, Esquire, burst into the room, restores the wig, and puts an end to the affray. The disgraceful proposal was afterwards carried 10 to 5.

The Welsh Corporation Meeting

Gabriel is identified in the cartoon as the man holding a wig. His son, the Revd. Thomas Powell, is the tall, extremely thin man directing a kick at Charles Collins, a burgess who had stood up to Gabriel way back in 1768 and no doubt on numerous occasions after that date. Although rector of Cantreff in Brecon, the Revd. Thomas must have had a reputation for aggression because, in a cartoon dated the following year, he is depicted at the head of a procession, his fists raised as if he were about to engage in fisticuffs. Robert Morris (II) is the man restraining Gabriel. As a non-burgess, Robert must have been waiting outside the room prior to rushing in to restore calm. It would appear that both William Padly and Collins left the Townhall shortly after the incident as their names are absent from a list of those who voted, the vote being carried ten to five in Gabriel's favour.

The Destruction of Gellihir

The mansion that Gabriel's eldest son had built at Gellihir had been standing less than eight years when, in January 1788, *The Gentleman's Magazine* reported that:

> Last Sunday morning about three o'clock, a fire broke out at Gellihir, the mansion-house of Gabriel Powell, Esq. Junior, near Swansea; the house was all in flames before it was discovered and they were so rapid that nothing could be saved, the whole fabric being entirely burnt down by six o'clock. Mr Powell was the first who escaped in his

[night-]shirt and some of the servants were forced to jump out of the garret windows to save their lives. Mrs Powell [née Mary Price] was at her mother's house at Swansea confined by illness. The house had lately been enlarged and improved at considerable expense: the loss is computed at £3,000 and nothing insured.

Gabriel – if not Mary – took up residence at Fairwood Lodge (now a hospital in Upper Killay) and some time after December 1788, when he inherited a share in his father's estate, he commissioned a local architect, William Jernegan, to design a new house for him on the slopes of Mount Pleasant. The house, which became known both as Heathfield and Heathfield Lodge, was completed in 1792. Whether Mary lived there is not known. She died without issue in 1793, and her estate passed to her niece in accordance with the terms of her will.

*Heathfield Lodge, Mount Pleasant, home of (Sir) Gabriel Powell,
eldest son of Gabriel Powell the Steward*

Stately Homes

In building Heathfield Lodge (which no longer exists) Gabriel the Younger was one of the first to start a new trend in housing – at least for those who could afford the luxury. There had been mansions built on the open ground east of the town in his father's day – St Helen's (near the present-day Guildhall; built on the site of a nunnery), the Rhyddings (which still occupies a knoll in Brynmill) and Brynymor (built *c.* 1780 and survives as Stella Maris). There had been stately homes to the north of Swansea as well, such as John Morris's Clasemont (on the site of the DVLC) and Gwernllwynchwyth in Llansamlet, home of the industrious Townsend/Smith dynasty. But the trend started by Gabriel the Younger and others was to get away from the congested town with all its attendant filth and build on the lower slopes of Mount Pleasant, thereby reaping the benefits of fresh air and fine views over Swansea Bay. Housing of this sort gradually spread westwards to the Uplands and beyond. Many of these fine houses have long gone – Rhianfa, Ffynone House and Glanmor to name but a few. Others have survived, among them Windsor Lodge (near the foot of Mount Pleasant Hill), Brooklands (the Lord Mayor's Mansion) and Mirador (now Sancta Maria).

Gabriel's Passing

In the Gower Society's *Survey, 1764* it states that Gabriel

> appears to have held court for the last time early in 1788 but his signature endorsed the accounts of the overseers of the poor on the 4th August in that year.

Gabriel died on 29th December 1788, aged 78. In his will, which was proved on 22nd May 1789, the beneficiaries were his sons, Gabriel of Gellihir and Thomas, rector of Cantreff; his daughter, Elizabeth Maria Campbell (she had married Alexander Campbell, an army officer); his grandson, Gabriel, son of Thomas Powell; his grand-daughter, Mary, daughter of Thomas Powell; his younger brother, William; his nephews, Thomas Edwards and Thomas Harcourt Powell (son of his elder brother, John (d.1769). His executors, Thomas Edwards and Thomas Harcourt Powell, were directed to build a room over the vault where his wife, Mary, had been interred; that is, over the west end of St. Mary's Church. His executors were then to convert the vault into a vestry room (later to become the west porch) in which they were to erect an inscription to Mary and himself. The inscription read:

> IN A VAULT
>
> Underneath, lie the remains of Gabriel Powell of Swansea, Esquire, and Mary, his wife, who was the second daughter of …

On the 5th January 1789 the *Hereford Journal* stated in Gabriel's obituary that

> He was commonly called 'King of Swansea', a nominal dignity arising from an old custom.

It has been said that the reference to 'a nominal dignity' is absurd; that it was more likely to be a sly dig at his dictatorial manner and his dogged persistence to have all his own way. There is certainly no reference to the title 'King of Swansea' in any earlier documents relating to Swansea and Gower. That, then, should have been the end of the story of a man who had a direct influence on the history of Swansea in that he obstructed the town's development for twenty years at least – but there is more.

The £1,000 Loan

On 6th January, eight days after Gabriel's demise, a Common Hall was held:

> to enquire about the Corporation papers and records which some years before had been carried in [a] chest to the house of the late Gabriel Powell, and had since been in his sole custody.

Over a period of years, Gabriel had loaned the Corporation several sums of money amounting to £1,000, of which £500 related to opposing a paving bill. Gabriel had, of course, the Corporation bonds, but to make sure that they settled their debt with his executors he had taken away 'the Corporation papers and records'. With the object of getting the chest returned the Corporation twice sent four of their number to Gabriel's executors – his nephews, Thomas Edward and Thomas Harcourt Powell – but they were not prepared to part with the chest until the Corporation paid 'the £1,000 and interest due'.

This put the Corporation in a fix, as it did not have that kind of money in its coffers – but someone else did. The Duke had appointed Thomas Morgan of Penderry, Esquire, barrister-at-law, as his new Steward of Gower and Kilvey, and on 17th January Thomas Morgan tendered an offer of the Duke to lend the money required. This the Corporation declined to accept, presumably because it would have given the Duke an even greater say in their affairs. Instead, the Corporation borrowed the required sum from six local men, all of them obviously wealthy.

The Corporation

At the time of Gabriel's death there had been only 35 burgesses. There can be no doubt that by restricting their number Gabriel had been better able to control the Corporation, to say nothing of keeping strangers and trouble-makers out. Numbers rose slowly but steadily during the decades that followed until, in 1831, there were 104 burgesses. More significant still is that the Corporation had met on average between one and four times a year, presumably because Gabriel had no trouble manipulating an aldermanic council made up of men chosen by himself. The year following his death the Corporation convened on no less than 23 occasions.

The Bathing House

Even with Gabriel out of the way the Corporation did not consent to a paving act until 1809. That is not say it had no wish to promote the amenities associated with a fashionable resort. In the autumn of 1789 the Corporation borrowed £100 to purchase an existing bathing house on the Burrows (situated at the western end of what is now County Hall) and did so

> in order to render the bathing at this place as commodious as possible for the public convenience.

The Bathing House that once stood where County Hall now stands.
The large house on the right is Heathfield Lodge, which should be
a litle higher up the slopes of Mount Pleasant.
Near the water's edge are three bathing machines

The following year a Corporation Committee engaged a local architect to improve and extend the Bathing House for use 'as an inn and lodging house' in which one large room would be set aside for public breakfasts, dinners and balls. Although, early in 1791, the Committee leased the premises to a Mrs Landeg, widow, work on the building was not completed until three years later, by which time several builders had tried their hand and the cost had soared. The Committee was also responsible for providing a bathing machine modelled on those used at Weymouth.

A local wheelwright soon provided the town with a machine that cost 14 guineas. It probably consisted 'of a carriage similar to that of a coach'. Bathers might enter the machine via a platform at the front. Inside there would be a bench on either side, where the bathers undressed before descending into the water via a flight of steps at the rear. 'A large umbrella of canvas stretched on hoops' was often used to conceal bathers from prying eyes, especially when the bathers were ladies. By 1798 there were three such machines in use.

The Bathing House was leased to several people in succession, but ultimately it proved a dismal failure because (1) it was half a mile from the town, (2) descent to the water's edge meant negotiating 'a ridge of loose limestone pebbles, thrown up like a wall, which ladies' found 'formidable', and (3) by 1804 there were too many machines available for hire close to the town. By 1815 the Bathing House had been converted for use as a school. Two years later part of the building became a workhouse, and part of it an infirmary.

A Change in the Town's Appearance

How Swansea's appearance changed after Gabriel's demise is made evident by what several visitors had to say over a period of 30 years. In 1774, for example, H.P. Wyndham maintained that

> a large part of this trading town actually consists of more miserable hovels than are to be found in the most indigent villages in England.

The year before Gabriel's demise, J. Byng described Swansea as

> a nasty town and our inn, the M—- A—-, very dirty and very dear … [and complained of] much bad pavement to our inn in the High Street.

Conditions had apparently improved by 1798 because H. Skrine praised

> Swansea, both in extent, the width of its streets and the aspect of its buildings [in that it] far exceeds all other towns in South Wales; it has of late been greatly improved.

That same year the Revd. Richard Warner wrote

> The town is large and well built … the houses chiefly modern, handsome and commodious.

Thomas Morgan – the Last Steward

The Duke's new Steward, Thomas Morgan of Penderry, in the parish of Llangyfelach, was apparently a forceful man, short and stocky, loyal to the Duke, but not obstructive like his predecessor. During his lengthy stewardship he actively participated in bringing about a tremendous amount of change, both to the town and the harbour, but most of all he is remembered for two things; the first is that in October 1790 he acquired a lease from the Duke on

> All that ground being part of the [Old] Castle Gardens late in the occupation of George Venables Vernon, having the New Market on the south, the footpath to the Strand … on

the east, that part of the Old Postern then on lease to the late Morgan Bevan on the north, and the new street or way [now Worcester Place] … on the west.

Half way along 'the new street or way' (Worcester Place) Thomas Morgan erected for himself a large, two-storied house with an equally large bow window on the east, overlooking the Strand. Thomas named his new home Worcester Place House in honour of the Duke, Henry Somerset, who still held the title of Earl of Worcester. Eventually the house gave its name to 'the new street' – Worcester Place. To the north of Worcester Place House two groups of three houses were also built on the leased land. The whole development was well on the way to completion by 1792, as all three buildings can be seen on Thomas Rothwell's *North-East View of the Town of Swansea*, published that same year. What is significant about this development is that it entailed the destruction of the old walls and ruins of the Old Castle, a symbol of almost 600 years of Marcher and Seigniorial rule. The removal of the ruins heralded the end of that rule. By a series of acts in the early 1830s the dukes of Beaufort lost their controlling influence over the boroughs of Swansea and Loughor; they became no more than absentee landlords. Consequently – and this is the second thing that he is remembered for – Thomas Morgan was to be the last Steward of Gower and Kilvey.

CONCLUSION

Before considering the reasons why in 1835 the then Duke of Beaufort and his Steward, Thomas Morgan, lost their controlling influence in the boroughs of Swansea and Loughor – and consequently in Gower and Kilvey as well – it is necessary to consider first the changes that took place in the years leading up to 1835.

Communications – the Harbour and Related Acts

Following Gabriel's demise the Swansea Corporation did a complete U-turn, supporting the industrialist in their call for a harbour act. The 'Act for enlarging and preserving the Harbour of Swansea' came into force in June 1791. It gave trustees – the majority of them burgesses – authority to widen, deepen and straighten the

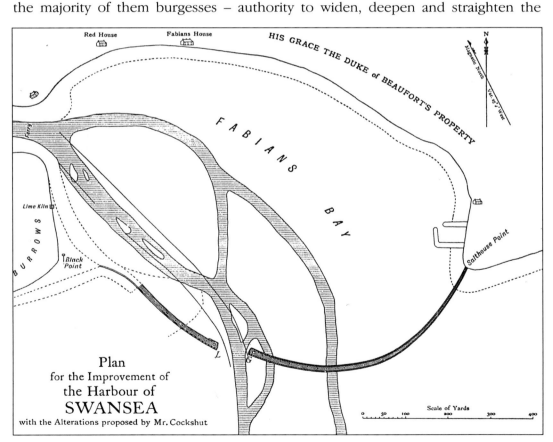

Plan
for the Improvement of
the Harbour of
SWANSEA
with the Alterations proposed by Mr. Cockshut

Mumbles lighthouse

western channel in Fabian's Bay, to construct a pier from the ferry to Black Point (later to be extended further out into Swansea Bay) and to remove all paddocks in the river above the ferry. The work took many years to complete due to the enormity of the task in an age when earth-moving equipment consisted of wheelbarrows and carts. There were delays, too, due to a shortage of money and to serious setbacks such as the one that occurred in 1803 when, as a result of an unusually high tide, 'a boat was … left by the tide opposite the Custom-house in Wind Street'.

The act resulted in the infilling of the eastern channel of the river – thereby increasing the depth of water in the western channel – and to the enclosure of Fabian's Bay by an eastern pier, which reached out from Salt-house Point. The act also empowered the trustees to erect a lighthouse on Mumbles Head. Initially, light was provided by two coal braziers, one positioned six metres above the other. Work commenced in the summer of 1792, but within a few short months part of the tower collapsed; what remained had to be dismantled. Work was resumed in 1793, and it took until the following summer to complete. Five years later the braziers were replaced by oil lights and reflectors. Further changes came as a result of the Common Hall that convened on 18th March 1793

> for the purpose of taking into consideration the propriety of having a canal made up the Vale of Swansea River, and into Breconshire as far as may be beneficial.

What was to become the Swansea Canal was not the first man-made waterway for conveying bulk commodities such as coal from inland sites to the harbour. When Chauncey Townsend died in 1770 his business interests passed to his son-in-law, John Smith of London. In 1783-5 John constructed a three-mile-long waterway from his collieries in Llansamlet to Foxhole, which became known as the Smith's Canal. At a slightly later date a three-mile-long waterway, the Clawdd y Saison (finished in 1790), was constructed from a colliery on the north-east side of Kilvey Hill to the River Neath, no easy feat as it entailed cutting through 'the soft spongy' morass of Cymlyn Bog.

The earliest canal of all, however, was the one-mile-long excavation between Landore and the Fforest Copper Works, Morriston, which had been cut sometime after 1754 by a consortium of coal owners, John Morris being one of them. It appears that when traffic on this waterway ceased in c.1794 it was taken over by the Duke and – as the Trewyddfa Canal – later incorporated into the Swansea Canal. It took four years to construct the Swansea Canal (1794-8) and in 1802 the Revd. Oldisworth described it as extending

> from the pottery [on the Strand] by Landore, Morriston, Clydach, Ynispenllwch and Yniscedwyn to Hen-noyadd in Breconshire. On the line of this canal [numerous] collieries are worked ... There are no less than 36 locks in the space of 16 miles ... and several aqueducts. Adjoining are large smelting copper-works, the iron forge, brass and tin-works, a fine copper rolling-mill, iron furnaces and foundry.

On 29th June 1804 Parliament passed an act for

> the making ... of a Railway or Tramroad for the passage of wagons and other carriages to communicate with the Swansea Canal near a certain place called the Brewery Bank ... to, or near to, a certain field called Castle Hill in ... Oystermouth ... and also ... a branch ... from a certain place near the Mount ... to, or nearly to, the Pier ... [and also] another branch ... from a certain place near Black Pill, to ... a certain place called Ynys [in Clyne Valley].

Mumbles Railway as painted by J. Ashford in 1819

John Morris, the principal promoter of the scheme, was eager to establish communications between his coal mines in Clyne Valley and the harbour at Swansea, whereas other promoters wanted to convey limestone and iron from Oystermouth. The first horse-drawn wagon left Swansea in the spring of 1806. On 25th March the following year the first passenger carriage set off, making the venture the earliest (and for a long time the oldest) passenger railway in the world. In 1808 a visiting novelist, Miss Elizabeth Spence, wrote in a letter about

> exploring the romantic scenery of Oystermouth. I was conveyed there in a carriage of a singular construction, built for the convenience of parties, who go hence to Oystermouth to spend the day. This car contains twelve persons and is constructed chiefly of iron, its four wheels run on an iron railway by the aid of one horse.

As to locomotives, there is a suggestion that a Blenkinsop rack locomotive was in use at Landore as early as *c*.1814. On a more positive note, in 1817-9 John Scott of London built a tramroad from Scott's Pit, Birchgrove, to shipping facilities at White Rock. For a short while a locomotive of the George Stephenson type operated on this tramroad. According to one source a

> Mr Maddison came from Newcastle with the engine to be its driver … It appears that this loco. came into Wales about the year 1820-1.

Another locomotive is known to have run on this tramroad in 1833, after the line had passed into the possession of C.H. Smith. Within a decade or so several locomotives were operating within the Lordship of Gower and Kilvey.

The Revd. J. Evans

All the above acts led to improved communications, which enabled industrialists to convey their wares to the harbour more efficiently. In turn this led to a tremendous increase in trade. Increased trade brought prosperity, which in turn attracted more workers and entrepreneurs to the town and its environs. Consequently, according to the first census ever taken in England and Wales the population of the Lordship of Gower and Kilvey in 1801 stood at 22,135, of which 6,099 resided in the Town and Franchise of Swansea, which made the borough almost as populous as Merthyr Tydful with its 7,705 inhabitants, whereas Cardiff had a population of only 1,870.

Increased trade and prosperity must also have had a knock-on effect on Swansea's potential as a fashionable resort. Prior to 1835 there was no serious conflict of interest between industrialists and those who wished to promote Swansea as a bathing place. This is made evident in the works of two turn-of-the-century writers. One of them, the Revd. John Evans, described Swansea and Gower from a visitor's point of view. In his *Letters written during a Tour through South Wales, in the year 1803*, he wrote:

> The sea being out, we proceeded over the sands under Kilvey Hill, and ferrying over the Tawe, entered the town of Swansea … In the street our attention was called by a shrill voice … Hastening to the spot, we found it was the crier of the town, a female, announcing to the public the arrival of a cargo of goods, which were then selling on the quay for ready money.

*Swansea Harbour in 1792. Ten years later Revd. Evans used the ferry (A)
to cross the Tawe, from where he would have observed
the Beaufort Arms (B), Somerset Place (C) and the Mount (D)*

The Revd. Evans described Swansea Bay as:

most charming … a most delightful object whether you view it towards the sea, or take
your station in a boat … It has been compared to the Bay of Naples … [moreover,
there were] traces that the present bay was once a wood, numbers of stools of large
trees being yet visible.

As to Swansea he considered it:

well built, and has an increasing population of more than seven thousand people; and
from the spaciousness of its streets, the appearance of the buildings, and the beauty
of its situation, may be considered as the first town in South Wales … [even though it

could] boast of few public or elegant buildings; [and] the old ruinous [Cromwellian] market-house in the centre of one of its principal streets is a disgrace.

He spoke of The Plas as:

the ruins of an abbey ... [the gatehouse of which had] been taken down to open a communication between Goat-street and Castle Bailey ... These [ruins] were now fitted up by some emigrant French priest as a Catholic chapel.

The west / Goat Street front of The Plas, 1826

With regard to trade:

within the last twenty years it has increased ... with almost unexampled rapidity ... The number of vessels that cleared out in 1768 was 694 ... and in 1800 the supposed number was 3,000 ... The trade is principally with London, the coasts of Devon and Cornwall, Bristol, Ireland and the Baltic ... The imports consist of tallow, hides, cattle, bacon, etc. from Ireland; tin, clay and copper ore from Cornwall; grocery, bale goods and utensils from Bristol; its exports of coal, culm, lime, iron, copper, rotten stone [a form of limestone used as an abrasive] and earthen ware.

Visitors were often given a guided tour of industrial sites. On one such tour the Revd. Evans discovered that:

The largest pit is at Pentre [a little north of Brynhyfryd Square], the property of Mr Morris of Clasemont. The whole hill is full of coal, and is obtained by what miners term open adits, i.e. horizontal shafts driven into the hill, which form ... ways for delivery of the coal... One of these adits, which we traced about a mile in length, admits low wagons ... running on an iron railway, one horse with ease delivers [the coal] to the quay.

Industry fascinated him almost as much as the bay, causing him to write:

The smoke from the different manufactories, which at night appears so many distinct scenes of smoke and flame, give you an idea of the solfateras in the vicinity of Vesuvius ... [however] The volumes of smoke ... contribute to make Swansea, if not an unwholesome, a very disagreeable place of residence.

In many respects the Revd. Evans wrote favourably about the town and its industrial surroundings, but he evidently frowned on being told that:

it is the wish of the inhabitants, that Swansea should be viewed in the light of a fashionable resort, rather than a trading town; and a bathing place, rather than a sea-port.

He conceded that:

Numerous houses are fitted up as lodgings ... and some in the Burrows are neat and pleasant [but there is] not a single accommodation proper for the convalescent, or desirable for the robust.

In fact he gave a long 'list of negatives', which in his opinion made Swansea inferior to 'a place like Weymouth', one being that:

A great objection against this place for bathing is the flatness of the shore, tendering it very inconvenient to bathe ... [and to reach the bathing machines one had] to descend ... over a ridge of loose limestone pebbles.

In proceeding westwards he and his company passed:

the pleasant rural residence of Marino, Upper and Lower Sketty. etc. till we came to the small village of Oystermouth ... principally inhabited by fishermen ... [as] the sea here abounds with [all kinds of fish] crabs, lobsters, prawns, limpets, shrimps and other shell fish. [He noted] the castle with its ivy-mantled walls, is a fine ruin. [After passing] the village of Newton [he came to] a small bay called Caswell, famed for the number and beauty of its shells ... [which he] considered an epitome of Lulworth Cove.

Further west the Revd. Evans and his company arrived at:

Penrice Castle, the seat of Mr Talbot. The ruin stands in the background of an elegant modern mansion, surrounded by diversified wooded walks ... but the effect [is] totally destroyed by the standing comparison of the smooth lawn ... and the asperities of the surrounding scenery ... and the entrance through an artificial ruin [on the corner of the main road leading to Oxwich] but ill accords with the venerable walls of ... [Penrice Castle].

Four miles north of Penrice ... [they found] the principal object of ... [their] pursuit ... King Arthur's stone; and beneath, a circumstance seldom observed, is a spring ebbing and flowing with the tide, celebrated as a Ffynnon Vair, or my lady's well, and resorted to for the cure of various disorders.

The Revd. Evans does not appear to have proceeded further west. Had he reached Rhosili, one wonders what he would have said about Worm's Head.

The Revd. J. Oldisworth

The second writer, the Revd. John Oldisworth, master of the Free Grammar School founded by Bishop Gore, wrote *The Swansea Guide* in 1802 for the benefit of the 'inquisitive traveller', providing them (and historians) with factual information that would otherwise have been unavailable – for example, he records the town's population as 6,831, of which 1,312 persons were 'chiefly employed in trade, manufacture or handicrafts', and a further 163 'in agriculture'. A total of 1,318 houses in the borough were occupied by 1,652 families, and 21 houses were uninhabited. As a local man the Revd. Oldisworth's intention was to promote the town and its environs in the best possible light – for example, the Beaufort Arms (demolished in 1947) at the ferry-side

The Beaufort Arms c.*1880*

is ... where good entertainment will be found seasoned with civility, and which is fitted up to accommodate a few lodgers during the season.

Wind Street is handsome and well paved ... The Mackworth Arms ... a good house, admirably adapted for the accommodation of the stylish traveller.

High Street or Upper-town; this is fine street, nearly a mile in length, in which are many excellent houses. The Bush Inn ... is well accommodated for travellers, containing a good ball-room, and is pleasantly situated ... And far up is the almost dilapidated Church of St. John [now St. Matthew's].

The 'almost dilapidated Church of St. John' was rebuilt in 1824, and continued to function as a parish church until 1880 when it was transferred to the Hafod district. Six years later a newly-built church on the High Street site opened its doors; it was dedicated to St. Matthew.

There were 36 lodging houses in the town, 12 of which were located on the Burrows. Other entries point out that there were two physicians in the town – one in High Street and one in Fisher Street – two chemists and six apothecaries (sellers of medicine) and surgeons, one of them Charles Collins (whose wig Gabriel Powell snatched in 1787). There were two circulating libraries – 'Mrs Oakley & Daughter's' and 'Evans & Son's', both of them in Wind Street – where, for periodic fees, one could borrow books. Other entries inform of:

A good Ball-court & Billiard-table at the George in Wind Street.
Billiard-tables at the Fountain and Red Lion on the Strand.

Meeting houses were to be found at:

Greenhill – Independent Methodists
Upper-town – Quakers, Baptists, Presbyterians
Back Lane – Baptists
Goat Street – Followers of Mr Wesley
Burrows – Followers of Lady Huntingdon
Wind Street – Jew's Synagogue
The Plas – Roman Catholics

For those who wish to send, or expect to receive a letter:

The Mail-coach, with a guard, arrives at the Mackworth Arms, from London through Bristol, every morning about five o'clock; and from Milford it arrives at the same place about eight o'clock every evening, from whence it sets out immediately for London. Letters must be in the [post] office, in Wind Street, before seven in the evening, and are delivered out at eight in the morning.

Swansea in c.1792 as depicted by Paul Padley. Left of centre (A) is where St. John's the Cambrian Pottery complex (B). On the far right is the north-ea

Alternatively:

A Packet [a ship carrying mail] commodiously fitted up, sails twice and occasionally three times a week to and from Ilfracombe; fare for passengers ten shillings and sixpence.

For those who preferred to keep their feet on *terra firma*, then:

The Cambrian pottery, on Mr Wedgewood's plan, cannot fail to be an agreeable morning's amusement to those acquainted with this kind of manufacture. This concern has long been carried on by Mr Haynes, to whose public spirit the town ... is much indebted. The clay made use of is brought from various parts of England.

The Cambrian Pottery occupied the site of the former copper works immediately below what is now High Street Station. Production commenced at this river-side location soon after William Coles of Cadoxton took out a lease in 1764 for 'a stone-ware manufactory'. George Haynes of Warwickshire joined the company in c.1786, and four

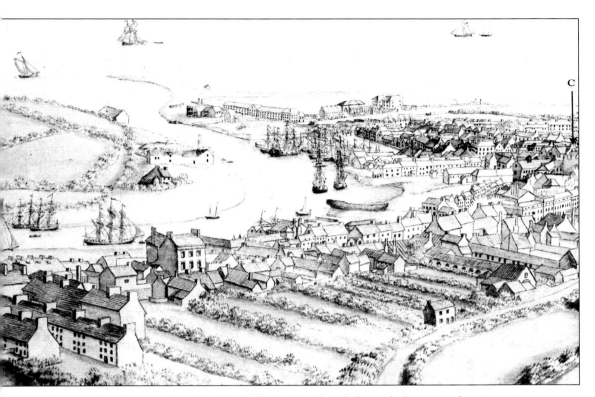

*h (now St. Matthew's opposite the Tax Office). Further left and closer to the river is
er of the castle (C) – a rather vague shape with three crenellations*

years later he became manager, being responsible for the production of quality earthenware comparable to 'Mr Wedgewood's plan'. In 1801 William Dillwyn purchased a controlling interest in the firm on behalf of his son, Lewis Weston Dillwyn. In time the pottery became famous for producing earthenware on a par with Staffordshire Ware, and later still for 'Dillwyn's Etruscan Ware'. During times of peak production the Cambrian Pottery employed some 400 persons. Its close proximity to the Swansea Canal provided visitors with yet another diversion, for

> By the side of this canal the walk is very pleasant, affording many objects worth observation … [including] White Rock, a barren hill [below Kilvey Hill] rendered so by the sulphurous influence of the neighbouring copper works [which was one way of turning a negative into a positive].

There were also excursions westwards, and what the Revd. Oldisworth wrote of the Gower Peninsula reads like a modern guide book. He refers to all places of interest from Sketty to Oystermouth Castle and the 'much admired and frequently visited' lighthouse on Mumbles Head. The village of Oystermouth must have been situated south of All Saints Church, on the steep part of the hillside below Thistleboon, for he says:

> The village of Oystermouth is singular for loosing all sight of the sun for upwards of three months in the year. There are several small houses for the accommodation of travellers, particularly the Old and New Mermaids.

From 'the beautiful Bay of Caswell' the excursion led to Worm's Head

> so called because the sailors used to think it resembled a worm creeping with its head erect.

From Rhosili the Revd. directs travellers to Llangennith and along the north Gower coast to 'the copper and coal works' at Penclawdd (though he makes no mention of the docks that were there) and on to the 'poor village' of Loughor (though it was still a borough at the time) where there were 'considerable copper and coal works'. Coal had been mined in the vicinity of both Penclawdd and Loughor since before the Civil War, and copper works had existed at both places for some time. John Vivian of Truro was a partner in the Penclawdd Copper Works (1800-11) before he established the Hafod Copper Works in 1810.

One of the Revd. Oldisworth's last entries relating to Gower was a brief reference to 'Penllergaer, the seat of John Llewelyn, Esq.' When Gruffydd, the last of the Prices of Penllergaer, died childless in 1787, he bequeathed his estate to a distant cousin, John Llewelyn of Ynysgerwn, near Neath. Both the Ynysgerwn and Penllergaer estates devolved on John Llewelyn's son, Colonel John Llewelyn, and then on the Colonel's illegitimate daughter, Mary, and she married Lewis Weston Dillwyn. As a result of this marriage Lewis Weston Dillwyn held the two estates in trust until his eldest son, John Dillwyn, became of age in 1831. According to the terms of his maternal grandfather's will, whereby he stood to inherit both estates, John Dillwyn added Llewelyn to his name. In 1834-5 John Dillwyn Llewelyn rebuilt the house at Penllergaer; its neglected shell was demolished in 1961 and the site later became the Lliw Valley Council offices. The parkland adjoining the house has also been subjected to neglect and development, but some of it still haunts the wooded Llan Valley to the east, and the horse-carriage driveway can still be traced all the way down past The Lake to the surviving lodge house at Cadle Mill.

Jews and Catholics

The Revd. Oldisworth referred to a Jewish synagogue in Wind Street. The first Jews to settle in Swansea did so at least 70 years earlier, as a Solomon Lyons is known to have established a business in the town in 1731. Thirty-seven years later a David Michael took out a lease on a plot of ground at North Hill for use as a burial ground. According to the terms of the lease, David had to

> enclose the same [plot] with a good and sufficient stone wall with good lime and mortar at least 8 foot high and 20 inches thick.

The remains of this burial ground can still be seen today. The Wind Street synagogue was at the back of David Michael's sitting room. Sometime after 1802 the 'Jews worshiped God with their hats on' in a room on the Strand. This last synagogue was translocated in 1818 to premises in Waterloo Street (now White Walls), which had 55 seats. In 1847 the Jewish community in Swansea consisted of 133 individuals. Among the notable members of this community were David Michael's sons, Levi and Jacob, who traded as silversmiths, jewellers, milliners and general furnishers. One of the sons, Michael John Michael, became an alderman in 1836 and was elected Mayor 12 years later.

Equally enlightening are the references by both Oldisworth and Evans to a Catholic chapel in The Plas, which presumably superseded the Wind Street chapel above the theatre. The community associated with these chapels was not as old as the Jewish one, the reason being that, from the mid-16th century onwards, Catholics throughout the realm had been persecuted more than any other sect – in Wales almost to extinction. In Glamorgan a few diehard (recusant or Papist) families had managed to hold out in the Vale, but there is no record of any recusants in Gower. The situation was such that a report of 1773 stated there were only 750 Catholics in the whole of Wales, and many of these were unlikely to have been Welsh-born.

The 'emigrant French priest' referred to by the Revd. Evans was Abbé Séjan, one time confessor to King Louis XVI (guillotined in 1793) and, therefore, a refugee of the French Revolution. Sometime after 1802 the chapel appears to have been translocated to the New Castle because, in his *Topographical Description of Wales, 1810*, Thomas Evans stated that The Plas

> is now converted into a warehouse and stables [and the castle] is now used for a gaol, workhouse, Catholic chapel and market place.

Presumably Father Séjan officiated at the castle; he was certainly the parish priest when a new purpose-built chapel was established in Nelson Place in 1812. His congregation was probably quite small, but numbers rose until, in 1838, there were some 400 Catholics in Swansea, or at lease the Swansea parish, which included Aberafon, Neath and Llanelli. Few of the 400 would have been converts, so where did these Catholics come from? According to Fr. Robert Plowden – a Jesuit who had taken out the original lease on a room in The Plas in *c*.1797 – Swansea was:

> a large trading town and much frequented by the Irish … [so much] so as to … [warrant] a permanent mission.

The Irish settled in Swansea in increasing numbers from about 1780 onwards. Some came in search of seasonal employment; others to earn their fare to America. Those who settled in the town did so wherever they found lodgings, but as time went by increasing numbers settled in the Greenhill district, which eventually became known as Little Ireland.

Smuggling and Strife

The works of both Evans and Oldisworth portray an idyllic picture of tranquility in the Lordship of Gower and Kilvey. Nothing could be further from the truth. There was no efficient law-enforcement agency, and when law-breakers were caught their sentences were brutal, ranging from flogging, hard labour, transportation and death, even for the most trivial offences.

Press gangs were still active in the Swansea Bay area, perhaps more so while the country was at war with France (1793 – 1802 and 1803-15). Not that war curbed the smuggling activities of either the French or the Gowerians. Smuggling involved almost everyone in the Peninsula from the gentry who provided the cash to the farm labourers and quarrymen who, to supplement their meagre wages and bring colour into their otherwise drab lives, carried contraband from coves to secure hideouts inland and who were prepared to deal harshly with any customs officer who tried to stop them, as happened when William Webb and Thomas Seward surprised smugglers at Rhosili in 1805. Both officers were set upon with the result that Seward sustained serious injury and Webb ended up imprisoned in a cellar at Middleton. That same year, when customs officer George Beynon and a company of Sea Fencibles (militia) swooped down on Rhosili beach, the smugglers fled, abandoning their horses and leaving hundreds of casks littering the sandy foreshore. A success such as the last was rare, however, as most smuggled goods were landed without detection. This is borne out by a report submitted to the customs office in Wind Street in 1795, which stated that:

> at least 5,000 kegs of liquor had been landed from the [Loughor] river to the Mumbles Point within six months, and all the vessels from Ireland that come for coals to the said river bring soap or salt in great quantities.

Nor was there peace in the industrialized areas. An ever-expanding workforce had to be fed, as did the workers' families, and local farmers could not meet the demand. Food had, therefore, to be imported, which made it costly, and in the event of a poor harvest the cost soared. A poor harvest in 1792 made people desperate, so much so that in January the following year hundreds of townspeople gathered on several occasions to demand corn and distribute pamphlets. On the first market day in February a huge crowd gathered to intimidate farmers, merchants and malsters. Two days later several hundred copper workers and colliers left Morriston to march on Swansea to protest about the high price of grain, cheese, butter and other commodities. During their march they raided farms for corn; they stopped at several works, calling upon other workers to join them. When they entered Swansea they continued their search for corn and threatened to demolish the house of one malster if he did not agree to sell his corn in the market. At the Townhall they expressed their grievances to the portreeve and the magistrates. Powerless and in a state of panic, the magistrates sent for military assistance, with the result that a detachment of dragoons were dispatched to restore order.

In April 1801 women and children were in the forefront of another corn riot that took place in Swansea. The women marched through the streets, demanding corn, and broke into a warehouse. The militia was called in, the Riot Act read and two ring-leaders were taken into custody, but later allowed to escape. Sporadic disturbances continued until late in the evening, by which time the authorities, fearing the arrival of colliers, had sent a message to Cardiff for military assistance. The military arrived the following day to find order had already been restored.

As they were no match for armed troops and militia, workers soon realized that, rather than challenge the authorities for a reduction in the price of food, it was less risky to pressurize their employers for wage increases. Consequently, workers formed themselves into secret societies that later became trade unions.

The Cambrian Newspaper

On 28 January 1804 *The Cambrian* – Wales' first weekly newspaper – was launched from offices in Wind Street. In time *The Cambrian* was to circulate all over Wales and as far afield as Birmingham and Bristol. One of the most notable articles to appear in this newspaper during the first year relates to horse racing on the Crymlyn Burrows (where Fords once stood). This is the first refer-ence to such an event, though it must have been well established by 1804. Race Week took place in July or August and according to later editions of *The Cambrian* it

The Assembly Rooms, Cambrian Place, where the well-to-do socialized in what was, in the early 19th century, the most fasionable part of town

attracted a large and brilliant assemblage, not only from the town and neighbourhood, but also from distant places [and] thronged with female beauty and elegance.

One visitor, Elizabeth Spence, wrote about the

beautiful scenery … enlivened by the addition of carriages, horsemen, foot passengers and booths scattered in all directions.

In July 1804 *The Cambrian* announced that plans were afoot to build Assembly Rooms on the Burrows. Unfortunately work did not commence until 1811, after which it was sporadic due to lack of funds. Although a 'sumptuous dinner', ending with a splendid display of fireworks, was laid on for 135 Freemasons in 1821, the Assembly Rooms were not completed until the following year. *The Cambrian* described them as:

> spacious, [comprising of] a Commercial Room, Library and Reading Rooms, Ball Room, Supper Room, Card Room and Billiard Room; Bar, Kitchen, Pantries, etc.

The New Guildhall

The Corporation obviously had money to spare on improving the town's image, for in 1825 work commenced on a new Guildhall on the Burrows (on the site of the present-day Dylan Thomas Centre). When completed four years later this Guildhall – like the old one near the castle – served both as a townhall and law court. It must have been an impressive building with its Doric columns and its twin curving stairways. Unfortunately, it remained in use for only 19 years because the administrative and judicial requirements of a rapidly expanding town necessitated something more spacious. Consequently, it was altered and enlarged in 1848 to become the building that can be seen today. Had the new Guildhall survived in its original form, it would have been Swansea's architectural gem.

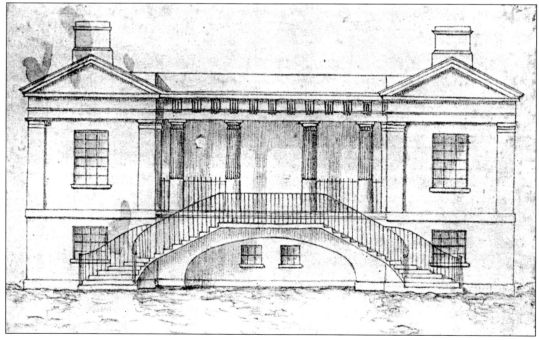

Elevation of the new Guildhall, built in 1825-9 in Somerset Place.
The site is now occupied by the Dylan Thomas Centre

The 240-year-old Townhall adjoining the castle was later made use of by the police, the first floor serving as a police court, and two store rooms on the ground floor were converted into a police station; its use as such continued until 1845.

Oxford Street Market

Between 1821 and 1831 the population of the Town and Franchise of Swansea rose from 10,007 to 13,256. This rising population – to say nothing of those who came from outside the borough – had to be fed and shopping excursions must, therefore, have

caused unprecedented congestion on Market days, especially at the top end of Wind Street, if not in the castle precinct as well. The old Cromwellian Market appears to have been demolished in 1822-4, but Market Place and its adjacent streets were still obstructed by stalls. Something had to be done and in 1828 a prominent burgess came up with a solution. The burgess was Calvert Richard Jones (II) – son and namesake of the Calvert Richard Jones who had inherited the Herbert estate in Swansea and Gower, including the

First Oxford Street Market built 1828-30

ruined Plas. Calvert (II) proposed making a gift of the Ropewalk Field to the Corporation for the express purpose of erecting a new market.

The Ropewalk Field was ideally situated, lying just beyond the built-up area of the town. On the east the field was bounded by Waterloo Street (part of which survives as White Walls), which had been built over the foundations of the old town walls. On the south side of the Ropewalk Field lay the relatively new houses of Orange Street (which no longer exists). In May 1828 the Corporation obtained an act of Parliament for the erection of

> a new Market for corn, cattle, horses, sheep, butchers' meat, poultry and all other marketable commodities [at a] place … called the Rope-walk Field.

Completed at a cost of £20,000, the new Oxford Street Market opened on 25th September 1830. Its internal layout was as follows:

> The butchers' stalls, or shambles, surrounded the square on three sides, and on all four sides after the transfer of the Cattle Market, with a covered walk before them. Within what was left of the ample market square area there stood several roofed parts,

the greatest of which was found at the east or upper end. Underneath the latter area were sold butter, eggs, poultry, toys, hardware, baskets, and in particular china, with flannel and cloth stalls by the market tower.

Between 1828-30 Oxford Street was formed by creating a gap in Goat Street – directly in line with Temple Street – and by erecting three-storied Georgian houses on the north side of Oxford Street, as far as present-day Union Street. Pretty soon these houses were converted into shops; thus began Swansea's commercial and residential expansion westwards.

The Town's Northern Slums

From what has so far been said it would appear that Swansea could rightly claim to be 'the Brighton of Wales', but those who proclaimed it as such simply ignored the dark side of the town's development. In Paul Padley's view of Swansea from the north-west (c.1792), housing in High Street 'above the gates' extended no further than St. John's Church (later St. Matthew's, opposite the Tax Office). Development beyond this church can be measured by studying three maps dated 1803, 1813 and 1823. They show development had been slight between 1803 and 1813, but became more intensive in the period 1813-23. The houses in this northern suburb were for the working class. They were to be found on both sides of High Street and in the adjoining side streets, such as Pottery Street (which existed between High Street Station and Powell Street).

The houses in Pottery Street survived until 1954-5. They were of a type that dominated the town's northern suburb. They were small, the majority consisting of two rooms, one up, one down, with a staircase opposite the front door. Each room (including the space occupied by the staircase) measured a little over four metres square. In the front wall were two sash windows, one on each floor, and a door. At the back there were no windows, only a door behind the staircase, leading to a small garden. Some of the houses in Pottery Street were slightly larger in that the rear roofs extended downwards to cover two additional rooms that were unbelievably small.

There was no running water in any of these ill-ventilated houses, nor in the much larger houses of the well-to-do. Water, for both rich and poor, was obtained from wells and streams, or from water-vendors who obtained their supply from the same wells and streams. Everyone used privies (soak-aways) in which unmentionable sewage was 'allowed to soak into the adjacent soil' and contaminate the wells. The only real difference between the privies of the rich and poor was that the rich had their own,

KEY TO PLAN OPPOSITE

A. Carmarthen Road
B. St. John's Church
C. Back Lane
D. Orchard Field
E. Orchard Street
F. Waterloo Street
G. St. Mary's Church
H. Huntingdon Chapel
I. Somerset Place
J. Brewery
K. Cambrian Pottery
L. Pottery Street
M. Swansea Canal
N. Neath Road
O. West Pier

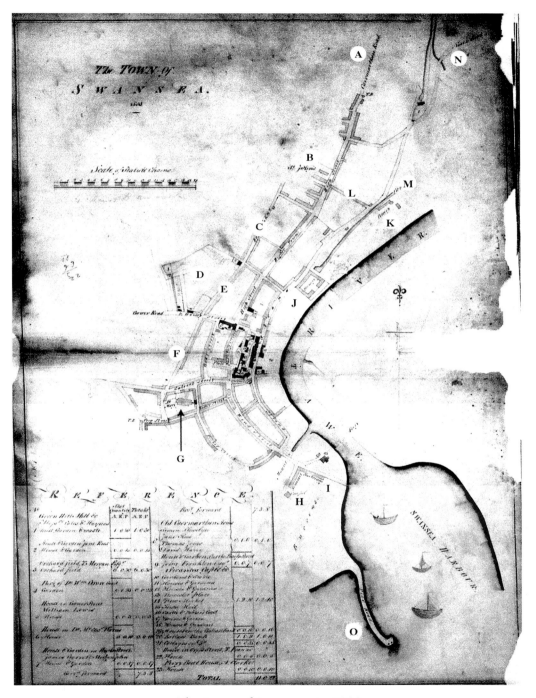

The town of Swansea in 1803

whereas those of the poor were shared by up to seven households, each of which consisted of six or seven persons on average. All ash and household rubbish was simply dumped in the streets.

A second thoroughfare ran northwards from St. Mary's Church along Waterloo Street and Orchard Street (which at the time extended no further north than its junction with King's Street). From the King's Street junction the thoroughfare continued as 'Back Street' with all 'its lanes and alleys' as far as Ebenezer Street. The houses around Back Street were much the same as those in Pottery Street. When new, they may have been a delight to the families that first occupied them, but they soon developed into damp, dingy hovels, surrounded by rat-infested filth and the stench of privies and cesspools. Condition were exacerbated by the fact that many families in the northern suburb kept one or more animals, be they

> pigs, horses, cows, asses, poultry, etc, in or immediately contiguous to their houses, in the small ... gardens, from which, instead of nature's odious perfume, arise ever nauseous and sickening smells.

If conditions were bad in the streets and alleys, they were far worse in the courts. Any waste ground between the two northern thoroughfares and their connection side-streets were infilled with courts: two rows of terraced houses, separated by alleyways and connected with the main thoroughfares by passageways similar to the existing Salubrious Passage in Wind Street. In these muddy courts, where stagnant water could not escape, conditions, it seems, could never be worse – but they most certainly were in the 'beggar hotels' where, in the 1840s, it was reported that up to 16 persons slept in the same room.

Although it is known that there were severe outbreaks of typhus and cholera in Swansea during the first half of the 19th century, details of these epidemics are not available until 1845 and later. The 1845 report on the health of the town makes grim reading. It states that one third of all 'labourers and artisans' died as a result of epidemics of one sort or another; that the average age of death for the same was 22, which compares badly with the 39 years of male gentry. The worse affected areas then were in Greenhill, the top of High Street and the Strand. Another area to suffer badly from fever epidemics due to damp, overcrowded housing, stagnant sewage and filthy water was Morriston.

A Rich Man's Paradise

In contrast to Swansea's developing slums, Sketty was seen as an idyllic haven for those who could afford to live there; it lay outside the borough's western boundary, between the Brynmill and Clyne streams. *The Swansea Guide* of 1823 refers to several noteworthy residences in Sketty: Marino (now part of Singleton Abbey), Verandah (part dismantled in 1853), Parc-wern (later to become Park Beck Nurses' Quarters), Sketty Hall (magnificently refurbished in 1994), Lower Sketty (later to be incorporated into The Bible College of Wales) and Sketty Park (demolished 1975).

Sketty Hall, its southern front in 2005

Sketty Hall (also known as New House in the 18th century) is believed to have been built originally by Rawleigh Mansel in *c.*1720, but it could have been built some 20 years earlier, which makes it the oldest surviving mansion-house in Swansea. About 1780 John Morris of Clasemont altered Sketty Hall's southern front by installing two bay windows and a balcony; this is how the house appeared in a sketch of 1783. John Morris had bought the property in 1771, and for the next fifty years the house was for the most part let to well-to-do tenants. Notes relating to an advertisement to let during the 1770s describe the property as

> well known [for its] beautiful situation. It consists of three parlours on the ground floor, and a kitchen, servants' hall, larders, and two small cellars underground. On the first floor three bed chambers, overhead four garrets ... Out of doors, a brew house with space for washing, stable for six horses, with hay loft and coach-house for two carriages, cold bath in the garden close to the house, and pig-sties at a convenient distance ... Twenty acres of pasture land surround the house [all of which is] in order for producing hay ... rent ... twenty guineas a year.

The notes give insight into how the gentry and their well-to-do tenants lived. It is also apparent from an engraving of 1792 that the above description refers to what later became the east/domestic wing, as the engraving shows an extension on the west that is larger than the house built by Rawleigh Mansel. Sketty Hall not only changed hands many times throughout its long existence, but it was altered and enlarged several times – in 1822, 1834 and 1881. While it was undergoing refurbishment in 1994, it was discovered that beneath the wallplaster the walls built by Rawleigh Mansel were still there, for the most part intact, incorporated into the alterations and enlargements of 1822. Today Sketty Hall stands magnificently restored to its former late 19th century glory, complete with ornamental gardens. It serves a useful function as a high-class restaurant and the College Conference and Catering School of Swansea (Ty-coch) College.

At the turn of the century the Lower Swansea Valley had become a magnet for those in search of work or investment opportunities, which is unsurprising as Swansea was then the third largest coal port in the kingdom; moreover, two-thirds of the copper smelted in the UK came from the Swansea Bay area. At the time, the Morris and Townsend/Smith dynasties still dominated their respective sides of the Tawe, but from 1810 onwards a new industrial dynasty was to make its presence known, one that would tower above all others and make Swansea the copper metropolis of the world. This new phase of industrialization started in 1810 when a rich Cornish copper mine owner, John Vivian of Truro, took out a lease on a riverside site in the Lower Swansea Valley, where he built the Hafod Copper Works, the ruins of which can be seen today from the Park & Ride compound near Morfa Stadium. New accommodation for his workers, which sprang up in the vicinity of the works, soon took on the name of Trevivian, meaning Vivian's Town, and in time the industrial empire created by John's descendants made the name Vivian known throughout the world.

The rural beauty of Sketty was not lost to the industrial families mentioned above. According to a tradition, John Morris had Clasemont

> taken down and then removed in one night to Sketty Park, where it was re-erected about the year 1805.

It is also claimed that John had moved in anticipation of becoming Sir John Morris, Baronet – a title he received the following year – knowing that residing in Sketty would be socially advantageous for a man of his standing. Whether or not the claims are true, Sir John's Sketty Park residence was but a poor imitation of Clasemont; it was demolished in 1975.

When the industrialist, Charles Henry Smith of Gwernllwynchwyth, Llansamlet, moved to Sketty he named his new residence Derwen Fawr after a huge oak that stood adjacent to what is now Derwen Fawr Road. In the early 20th century the property became incorporated into The Bible College of Wales.

The first of the Vivians to settle in Sketty was John Henry Vivian, eldest son of John Vivian of Truro. In 1817 John Henry purchased Marino – a curious octagonal villa built by Edward King sometime after 1784 – which he enlarged between 1818 and 1821 by adding two wings and a conservatory. John Henry, however, was never a man to be satisfied, and between 1827 and 1836 he enlarged Marino again to become the Gothic-styled Singleton Abbey that can be seen today. This greatly enlarged Mansion he re-named Singleton, taking the name from the ancient Singleton Farm, which, under the name of Home Farm, still occupies a site immediately north of Singleton Hospital.

Singleton Abbey, its southern front in 2002

In the decades following 1817, J.H. Vivian bought up to 15 neighbouring farms (including Ty Gwyn) and miscellaneous properties to create an estate that is occupied today by Singleton Park, Singleton Hospital, the University and the playing fields on the west side of Sketty Lane. Around the periphery of these acquisitions there were more than ten lodges and cottages for his estate workers, as well as Home Farm with its stylish buildings (built in the 1840s). Among the lodges and cottages that have survived are Verandah Lodge (at the top entrance to Singleton Park), Brynmill Lodge (at the Park's Mumbles Road entrance), Ty Harry (near the Boating Lake) and Swiss Cottage (built in 1826).

On the north side of the estate stood the mansion known as Verandah, built by John Morris in *c*.1800 on a small escarpment, now occupied by the Botanic Gardens in Singleton Park. J.H. Vivian bought Verandah in 1847. Six years later his eldest son dismantled the mansion, but some of the outbuildings, which, at one time provided accommodation for gardeners, still exist on the west side of the Botanic Gardens, along with a stone-built, water-storage tower. Parc-wern (later to be known as Park Beck) was added to the estate in 1853, and Sketty Hall with its adjacent land in 1898. At the time of its sale to the Council in 1920, the Singleton Estate consisted of some 250 acres, a small reflection of the Vivian family's remarkable rise to wealth and influence.

The Paving Act of 1809
Swansea finally had its paving act in 1809. By this act improvement commissioners were made responsible

> for the better repairing, cleansing, lighting and watching the several streets and other public passages and places within the town … and for the removing and preventing annoyances and obstructions therein.

One of the first measures taken by the commissioners was to ban the use of thatch on all new buildings within half a mile of the town limits, thereby reducing a potential fire hazard. Work relating to repairing and lighting the streets proved immeasurably slow, but in 1821 *The Cambrian* reported that

> both the horse-road and the foot paths were completely and substantially new-laid. In Wind Street the pavement was in like manner new-laid, and the flagging on each side … [which was] filled up with pebbles, between it and the houses, was carried close to the walls … and the street, for its general breadth and the peculiar width of its flagging, is now, we believe, the handsomest in Wales … small paths, a little elevated above the ordinary level of the pavement, have been formed at the principal crossings of the streets, to the very great comfort of foot passengers in dirty weather.

That same year *The Cambrian* reported that on St. David's Day 120 public gas lamps lit up the more important streets in the town, the gas coming from works at Dyfatty. Recorded events such as these suggest progress, but in reality all improvements were limited in extent, the improvement commissioners being so desperately short of money. With regard to cleansing the streets, a variety of schemes – including the use of unpaid pauper labour – were adopted to little effect, for even as late as 1845 there were only eight men and four carts employed to scavenge some five miles of filthy streets. That same year it was reported that there were only six principal sewers in the town, five of them discharging into the Tawe River. These sewers were woefully inadequate and so badly constructed that, during high tides, they were flooded. There was certainly no water to flush them – other than rain water – as the town's first reservoir (constructed in 1837 and now a lake in Brynmill Park) did not have the capacity to provide such a service. As to 'watching the several streets' – or rather policing them – the improvement commissioners' efforts in this area were again woefully inadequate.

The earliest reference to a law-enforcement officer is to be found in a document dated 1400. The document refers to a Thomas Somora as catchpole and gaoler at the castle. The Common Hall Book relating to 1553 refers to both sergeants-at-mace and constables. The former were officers of the manorial courts and had, therefore, little to do with enforcing the king's peace. Constables, on the other hand, were burgesses appointed to the task of maintaining the peace for one whole year; it was an appointment no burgess liked and many were prepared to be disfranchised rather than fulfil their duties. By Gabriel Powell's time the appointed burgesses were paying untrustworthy watchmen to do the job for them.

In 1821 John Luce became Swansea's first paid constable. Four years later the improvement commissioners appointed seven watchmen to patrol the streets at night, providing each of them with a coat and a rattle. At roughly the same time three paid constables were appointed to patrol the streets by day. In 1833 the unreliable watchmen were replaced by three full-time constables. Two years later an anonymous satirist expressed amazement at how law-abiding the people of Swansea were, requiring only three constables to police the streets by day and night.

The truth, however, was that most crimes went unreported, one reason for this being that victims of petty crime could end up out of pocket after paying constables for their services as well as legal expenses – in short, victims preferred to settle matters themselves. Another reason for not reporting petty theft was that punishment invariably outweighed the crime – even children could be sentenced to transportation for ludicrously minor offences. In an attempt to bring petty criminals to book, the local Society for the Apprehension and Prosecution of Thieves appointed 13 special constables in 1829. The situation relating to crime and policing, however, remained chaotic for many decades to come.

The Call for Change

Although there were burgesses among the improvement commissioners, the Corporation and the Paving Commissioner were two separate bodies. The latter existed to fulfil the requirements of the Paving Act, whereas the prime concern of the former was to administer the borough estate. This estate brought in revenue, some of which came from tolls such as quayage, wharfage, keelage, assize of ale and market dues. Non-burgesses hated these tolls because they – not the burgesses – paid them, and because the revenue went into the portreeve's pocket to cover his expenses, so it was claimed, which in 1833 alone amounted to around £750. This caused so much resentment that in 1830 the town's tradesmen banded together to oppose payment. In response the Corporation resolved to defend its privileges to the utmost, but four years later the portreeve had to surrender his claim to all tolls in favour of a relatively small salary.

Tolls and the privileges of burgesses were only two aspects of the growing discontent with the established order. Throughout the early decades of the 19th century the growth of an assertive middle-class had become a force to be reckoned with. The people within this class – in both England and Wales – made their money from industry, commerce and the professions. What these people wanted was the right to vote so that they, and not only landowners and burgesses, might have a say in how the country should be run. Under pressure the government passed the Reform Act of 1832.

Prior to the implementation of this act, Glamorgan had sent two MPs to Parliament, one to represent the county and one to represent the burgesses of Cardiff and its seven contributory boroughs. From 1832 onwards, Glamorgan sent five MPs to Parliament, two to represent the county, one to represent Cardiff and its contributory boroughs of Llantrisant and Cowbridge, one to represent Merthyr Tydful and one to represent Swansea and its contributory boroughs of Loughor, Neath, Aberavon and Kenfig, which together constituted the Parliamenary Borough of Swansea and District. With regard to Swansea, voting was no longer restricted to burgesses, but extended to all middle-class men of means within the enlarged voting area of the Parliamentary

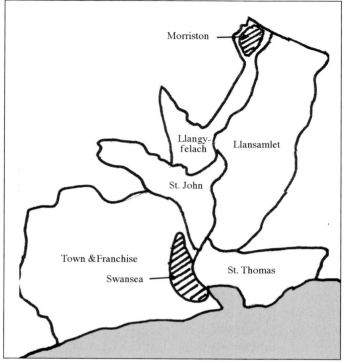

Borough of Swansea, which included the hamlet of St. Thomas, the parish of St. John, and parts of the parishes of Llangyfelach and Llansamlet. The first man to represent the Swansea and District constituency was the industrialist, John Henry Vivian, and he held the seat as a Liberal until his death in 1855.

Voting in national elections, however, was not enough for middle-class men of means; they wanted a say in the administration of their boroughs as well. In 1833 Municipal Corporation Commissioners were sent to Swansea and other boroughs throughout the realm to examine borough administration. In the case of Swansea the commissioners reported that the Corporation was wholly under the control of the lord and his steward, Thomas Morgan. This set-up

The Parliamentary Borough of Swansea, created in 1832 by adding neighbouring districts to the old Town and Franchise. Three years later the boundaries of the Parliamentary Borough became synonymous with those of the new Municipal Borough of Swansea

was to change when the Municipal Corporation Act of 1835 came into effect in November that year.

The act repealed all existing acts, charters and customs so that, instead of a Corporation comprising of a privileged group of burgesses (there were 104 of them in 1831), Swansea could claim to be, as a Municipal Borough, administered by a Council elected by male ratepayers of three years' standing. The reality, however, was quite different, for although the borough had increased in size – from 1,918 acres (the Town and Franchise) to 5,400 acres (the Parliamentary Borough) – the jurisdiction of the 24 elected councillors (six of them aldermen) extended only to those parts of the town that lay within 80 metres of a public lamp. Beyond these limits large areas of the Municipal Borough continued to be administered by parish authorities.

The last Portreeve, Calvert Richard Jones, was re-elected at Michaelmas 1835. On the 9th November that same year he stood down to allow Swansea's first elected

Mayor, Nathaniel Cameron, to take up office, the principal function of which was to preside as Chairman at council meetings. Interestingly – at least from the point of continuity – Nathaniel had married Laetitia Price Cuny, only child of Mayzod, second daughter of Joseph Price (d.1785) of Gellihir. When Mayzod's elder sister, Mary (née Price) Powell, had died in 1793 the Gellihir estate had passed intact to Mayzod's daughter, Laetitia, and by marriage to Laetitia's husband, Nathaniel Cameron. The Camerons also owned Danygraig House – which they purchased in *c.*1829 – as well as several houses in London.

The new Council proved no more effective in dealing with the requirements of an expanding town than a corporation consisting exclusively of burgesses. This is unsurprising: the Council was something new. It was made up of burgesses and improvement commissioners whose first concern continued to be administering the Corporation estate because that was the Council's principal source of revenue. The Council also took responsibility for the market and the police, which in 1836 consisted of one inspector and six constables. All other public services continued to be the responsibility of the improvement commissioners, who were themselves hampered by insufficient funds. This woefully inadequate system of municipal government persisted for some 15 years before Parliament began giving guidelines and powers to councils that enabled them to function more effectively.

The Municipal Corporation Act of 1835 may not have brought about significant improvement to the way Swansea was administered, but two very important aspect of borough administration did change. Firstly, the town was no longer administered by an oligarchy of burgesses and, secondly, the lord of the manor no longer had overall control through his steward and the manorial courts over which the steward presided. Indeed, the lord's influence in the lordship as a whole had truly diminished to that of an absentee landlord, whereas the status of his steward was reduced to that of a land agent. Henceforth no lord or his steward would be able to use and abuse their positions in authority to the extent that they could become Gower Rogues.

Further Reading

Boorman, David, *The Brighton of Wales*

Child, Jeff., *Colonel Philip Jones (1618-74). A Note on his Birthplace and Antecedents.*

Clarke, G.T., *Limbus Patrum Morganiae et Glamorganiae*

Davies, J.D., *History of West Gower.* (contains information on the affray at Oxwich, 1557)

Dillwyn, L.W., *Contributions towards a History of Swansea* (1840)

Draisey, Derek, *A History of Gower*

Draisey, Derek, *The People of Gower*

Evans, Revd. John, *Letters written during a Tour through South Wales, 1803.*

Francis, G.G., *Charters granted to the Chief Borough of Swansea* (1867)

Francis, G.G. & Baker, C., *The Lordhip of Gower in the Marches of Wales*

Gibbs, Michael & Morris, Bernard, *Thomas Rothwell Views of Swansea in the 1790s*

Griffith, H., *The New Swansea Guide, 1823*

Griffith, Ralph, *The City of Swansea, Challenges and Change*

Havard, D.G., *The Lordship of the de Braose Family in the Marches of Wales*

Hughes, Stephen, *Industrial Archaeology of the Swansea Region*

Jones, Ifano, 'Sir Matthew Cradock and some of his contemporaries', *Arch. Camb.,* 1919

Jones, I.H., 'Gellihir', *Gower* 19

Jones, Thomas, *Brut y Tywsogion/ The Chronicle of the Princes, Peniarth ms 20 version*

Jones, Thomas, *Brut y Tywsogion/ The Chronicle of the Princes, The Red Book of Hergist Version.*

Jones, W.H., *History of Swansea and the Lordship of Gower, Vols 1 (1920) and 2.*

Jones, W.H., *History of the Port of Swansea.* (1922)

Lloyd, Thomas, 'The Destruction of Gellihir', *Gower* 37

Marr, L., *Swansea Hebrew Congregation*

Morgan, W.Ll., *An Antiquarian Survey of East Gower.* (1899)

Morgan, W.Ll., *The Town and Manor of Swansea.* (1924)

Morris, Bernard, 'The Earliest View of Swansea', *1678, Gower* 1982

Morris, Bernard, *The House of Singleton.* (1995)

Morris, Bernard, (Ed.), *Gabriel Powell's Survey of Gower, 1764.* (A Gower Society Pub.)

Morris, Bernard, *Swansea Castle* (sponsored by the Education Service at Swansea Museum)

Morris, Bernard, 'Swansea Houses – Working Class Houses 1800-1850', *Gower* 26

Oldisworth, Revd. John, *The Swansea Guide, 1802*

Price, Michael, *The Account Book of the Borough 1640-60*

Price, R.T., *Little Ireland*

Rees, David, *Gower Anthology*

Ridd, T., 'Gabriel Powell: The Uncrowned King of Swansea', in *Glamorgan Historian*, 5

Ridd, Tom, *Victorian Swansea - in* Gower 13.

Roberts, G., *The Municipal Development of the Borough of Swansea*. (1940)

Robinson, W.R.B., 'Sir George Herbert of Swansea', *B.B.C.S.* XXVII, ii

Rogers, W.C., *A Pictorial History of Swansea*

Rogers, W.C., 'Swansea and Glamorgan Calendar' – unpublished ms. compiled in 1943

Thomas, N.L., *The Story of Swansea's Markets*

Thomas, W.S.K., *The History of Swansea from Rover Settlement to the Restoration*

Traherne, John Montgomery, *Historical notices of Sir Matthew Cradock, Knight, of Swansea: In the reign of Henry VII and Henry VIII*

Veysey, A.G., '*Colonel Philip Jones 1618-74*', *Trans Cymm.*, 1966

Warren, W.L., *King John*

Williams, Glanmor, *Swansea: an Illustrated History*

Williams, Glanmor, 'The Herberts of Swansea', *Glamorgan Historian*, 12

Pugh, T.B., (ed.), *Glamorgan County History, Vol III*

Williams, Glanmor, (ed.), *Glamorgan County History, Vol IV*

John A.H., (ed.), *Glamorgan County History, Vol V*

Morgan, Prys, (ed.), *Glamorgan County History, Vol VI*

RCAHM(W), Part I: Non Defensive